"This valuable clinical guide expands our understanding and ways to cultivate resilience in therapy with clients who face injustice, hardship, and adversity. Chapters center marginalized peoples and their social context, sensitively attuned to their lived experience, beliefs, and aspirations. In our increasingly complex world, this systemic approach attends to the interconnection of individual, relational, family, community, cultural, and spiritual influences in overcoming adversity and flourishing in life. Highly recommended to inform and inspire both beginning and seasoned practitioners!"

Froma Walsh, *PhD, Professor Emerita, University of Chicago, Co-Founder & Co-Director, Chicago Center for Family Health, Author*, Strengthening Family Resilience (3rd Ed.)

"Having served as a clinical director for many years, I know my students would enjoy and benefit from this text. The book presents theories of resilience in a manner that is easy to understand and apply in diverse settings."

Martha Morgan Gobert, *PhD, Associate Professor, University of Massachusetts Global*

"Dr. Christie Eppler has assembled a diverse and experienced group of authors who have written about the important topic of cultivating systemic resilience in families, relationships, and individuals. As a resilience researcher, I am impressed by the depth and scope of this work and the wide range of populations and identities to which it applies. I found each chapter to be practical, and a resource for all systemic therapists."

Adrian Blow, *PhD, Professor of Couple and Family Therapy, Michigan State University*

CULTIVATING SYSTEMIC RESILIENCE IN THERAPY

Therapists intuitively know that the families, partnerships, and individuals they treat have strengths but may not know how to identify or utilize them. This edited collection aims to help therapists understand and apply concepts of systemic resilience in clinical practice, supporting them in conceptualizing cases, treatment planning, and developing supportive therapeutic relationships.

Christie Eppler, PhD, brings together a collection of voices to provide comprehensive guidance on what systemic resilience is and how therapists can enhance the lives and relationships of their clients. Based on contemporary training standards, this text emphasizes practice-based applications and focuses on diversity, equity, and inclusion. Chapters address how to foster resilience in clinical treatment with individual and relational clients, supervisees, and in the therapist's own life. With case studies, clinical activities, interventions, and reflective questions throughout, this approachable text will help therapists empower their clients. This book demonstrates to practicing and established therapists how connections, community involvement, shared visions and a sense of purpose, and healthy relationships can promote growth, healing, and transformation.

This is essential reading for students and professionals in counseling, clinical social work, and marriage and family therapy.

Christie Eppler, PhD, LMFT is a program director and professor of Seattle University's Master of Arts in Couples and Family Therapy. She is an American Association of Marriage and Family Therapy (AAMFT) approved supervisor. The focus of her clinical practice, teaching, and research is systemic resilience, justice, and narrative therapy.

CULTIVATING SYSTEMIC RESILIENCE IN THERAPY

Applications and Interventions for
Families, Relationships, and Individuals

Edited by
Christie Eppler

Routledge
Taylor & Francis Group

NEW YORK AND LONDON

Designed cover image: Delmaine Donson © Getty Images

First published 2025
by Routledge
605 Third Avenue, New York, NY 10158

and by Routledge
4 Park Square, Milton Park, Abingdon, Oxon, OX14 4RN

Routledge is an imprint of the Taylor & Francis Group, an informa business

Library of Congress Cataloging-in-Publication Data
Names: Eppler, Christie, editor. | Martin, Raquel (Psychologist), editor.
Title: Cultivating systemic resilience in therapy : applications and
    interventions for families, relationships, and individuals / edited
    by Christie Eppler and Raquel Martin.
Description: New York, NY : Routledge, [2025] | Includes bibliographical
    references and index.
Identifiers: LCCN 2024001219 (print) | LCCN 2024001220 (ebook) |
    ISBN 9781032447056 (hardback) | ISBN 9781032447070 (paperback) |
    ISBN 9781003373513 (ebook)
Subjects: LCSH: Resilience (Personality trait) | Adjustment (Psychology) |
    Psychotherapy. | Counseling.
Classification: LCC BF698.35.R47 C85 2025 (print) | LCC BF698.35.R47 (ebook) |
    DDC 155.2/4—dc23/eng/20240221
LC record available at https://lccn.loc.gov/2024001219
LC ebook record available at https://lccn.loc.gov/2024001220

ISBN: 978-1-032-44705-6 (hbk)
ISBN: 978-1-032-44707-0 (pbk)
ISBN: 978-1-003-37351-3 (ebk)

DOI: 10.4324/9781003373513

Typeset in Times New Roman
by Apex CoVantage, LLC

I express my deep appreciation to my family: my mom, Laurie, John, Luke, and Mossy; and my kinship group—all of whom inspire me to laugh and find glimpses of resilience in all places. I am grateful to Seattle University for granting me a sabbatical to work on this project.

Thank you to the chapter authors for sharing their experiences and ideas. For their advice and guidance, I acknowledge our ancestors, mentors, colleagues, and the teams at Routledge and Heartful Editor.

I would like to thank you, the reader. As you read these chapters, may you generate intentional and sustainable ways of caring for yourself, those in your clinical practice, people in your communities, and beyond.

CONTENTS

1

INTRODUCTION TO CULTIVATING SYSTEMIC RESILIENCE IN THERAPY

Applications and Interventions for Families, Relationships, and Individuals

Christie Eppler

Christie Eppler, PhD, LMFT (she/her) is a program director and professor in Couples and Family Therapy at Seattle University. She is a Euro-American, middle class, spiritual, heterosexual, cisgender woman. Her qualitative research areas include systemic resilience, justice, and narrative therapy. Dr. Eppler is an AAMFT-Approved Supervisor and a Licensed Marriage and Family Therapist (LMFT; Washington). She enjoys helping new interns mitigate their anxieties while utilizing systems theories and common factors to conceptualize clients. She is a certified yoga instructor and marathoner who loves hiking with her Golden Retriever, Mossy.

Zandashé L'orelia Brown (2021) tweeted that she imagined not being referred to as resilient again. For her, being strong was exhausting. Instead of trite congratulations for taking hit after hit, she longed for support, ease, and connection with others. Brown's words speak for many who have become disillusioned with the common misconception that to be resilient, one must embody stoic individualism and unwavering

DOI: 10.4324/9781003373513-1

endurance in the face of injustice and suffering. Popular culture has redefined the concept of resilience from its roots as strength-based functioning and relational support to toughness, solo endurance, and a pick-yourself-up attitude. Taking a bubble bath or connecting with nature, according to social narratives, nurtures resilience. A person's and community's strengths and care habits can be useful, but resilience is influenced by other factors as well.

In an increasingly complex and interconnected world, systemic resilience has emerged as a crucial paradigm that recognizes the importance of collective adaptive capabilities in the face of adversity (Ungar, 2011, 2021; Walsh, 2016, 2023). There is no one definition of systemic resilience. Cultivating systemic resilience is a lifelong process of healing, sustaining, transforming, growing, and thriving that involves a combination of cognitive, emotional, behavioral, and social skills (Ungar, 2021; Walsh, 2016, 2023). When it comes to bolstering systemic resilience, the goal is not to ascribe one right way, but rather to support people—individually and relationally—to navigate everyday life and to cope with and overcome obstacles, setbacks, and hardships.

Systemic resilience and systemic family theory have several constructs in common. Becvar and Becvar (1998) defined the basic concepts of systems theory as focusing on the whole, asking about the what instead of the why, observing patterns, and being attuned to relationships and context. Instead of asking why suffering happens, systemic resilience observes what is happening and what needs to be done to thrive or survive. A systems orientation acknowledges that what happens in one sphere often ripples out to other dynamics (e.g., what is happening in the community influences family dynamics). To thrive, systems must be adaptable, cohesive, clear and flexible in their rules and boundaries, and equitable. Resilience involves both the content (i.e., traits or specific criteria) and process (i.e., the interactions and patterns related to building psychological and relational strengths; Becvar, 2013; Ungar, 2021; Walsh, 2021, 2023). To take a systemic perspective on resilience is to acknowledge there are many solutions to simple and complex problems and to wonder (a) how the whole is more than the sum of the parts; (b) how behaviors often make sense when we better understand the context; and (c) how reciprocity affects feelings, thoughts, and behaviors.

Resilience may be strengthened or weakened at different times in life, during different periods, and even in certain environments (Ungar, 2021; Walsh, 2016, 2023). Resilience can be developed and strengthened through various practices and experiences, such as building strong relationships, cultivating a growth mindset, practicing self and community care, and seeking social support (Becvar, 2013; Ungar, 2021; Walsh, 2016, 2021, 2023). Augmenting systemic resilience is an important aspect of well-being and can help clients, therapists, and communities lead fulfilling and productive lives, even in the face of adversity (Wicks, 2007, 2010).

Importance of Relationships

Becvar's (2013), Walsh's (2016, 2023), and Ungar's (2021) writings contained consistent themes of systemic resilience. Systemic resilience is ignited and maintained by creating life-giving relationships with ourselves, significant others, community members, and higher powers. It entails conflict resolution and collaborative decision-making. Resilience can look like exercising sensitivity, asking for help, practicing active listening, taking accountability, and accepting or ignoring criticism. Perhaps above all, resilience is justice—to be systemically resilient is to be humble, aware, equitable, and a voice for peace.

Initial resilience models emphasized the importance of at least one significant and supportive relationship (Carver, 2010; Fraser, 1997; Kaplan, 1999; Masten & Garmezy, 1985; Masten & Reed, 2002; Werner, 2000). Early studies examined what was beneficial for children growing up in at-risk situations (Werner, 1993, 1994). Schools, families, and communities could implement creative interventions (Henderson et al., 1999). Benson's (1999) developmental asset model expanded resilience research to people who were not at risk. This research queried what people need to thrive throughout their lives. For those at risk (e.g., those having experienced adverse events) and for those who have experienced a more typical developmental trajectory, becoming resilient entails building protective factors to avoid future risk and cultivate the ability to recover from challenges, stressors, and disruptions. Milestones such as birth, grief and loss, and everyday stressors and events (e.g., economic downturns, natural disasters, cybersecurity threats, or other unexpected events) can threaten the stability and wellness of those affected (Ungar, 2021; Walsh, 2016). Still, through their interconnections and resources, humans can adapt and recover from difficult situations.

Models of Resilience

There exist myriad theories and models about what promotes resilience; for example, Mitchell et al. (1999) studied people who made successful career transitions and found curiosity, persistence, flexibility, options, and risk taking were critical parts of navigating difficult transitions. Themes of this research included having life-giving connections, leveraging community strengths, and coping with and overcoming adversity across multiple contexts. Systemic resilience involves being adaptable with self and others, sharing visions for growth, having connections with supportive others, and finding purpose even when suffering occurs (Becvar, 2013; Ungar, 2021; Walsh, 2016, 2021). Being resilient is not equivalent to having no problems or minimizing problems; rather, it is the ability to thrive in all situations. A few of the models with brief explanations are provided next.

Walsh (2016, 2021) centered three aspects of family resilience:

- Belief systems: meaning making, positive outlook/hope, transcendence/spirituality.
- Organizational processes: flexibility, connectedness, social and community resources.
- Communication processes: clear information, emotional sharing, problem solving/prevention.

Brendtro et al.'s (2019) circle of courage model was developed by (US) Indigenous and White clinicians for youth in foster care. Brendtro et al. believed four domains must live in harmony:

- Mastery: a deeply rooted sense of being able to cope and succeed, developed not by competition but by a sense of competence gained from overcoming challenges overseen by a skilled mentor.
- Belonging: participating in powerful social bonds.

- Generosity: altruism and being concerned for others' well-being; participating in prosocial activities throughout one's life.
- Independence: autonomy over one's decisions, bolstered through giving thoughtful feedback, exercising agency to make decisions, taking responsibility, and exerting self-control.

Benson (1999) and the Search Institute studied 40 developmental assets that prevented risky adolescent behaviors, such as drug and alcohol abuse, early pregnancy, and school dropout. Both internal (i.e., personal) protective factors and community strengths were included in these assets. Positive identities, learning values, and social skills were key indicators of student success. By setting clear boundaries and expectations, empowering youth, providing support, and helping adolescents use their time constructively, parents, schools, and neighbors helped young people reduce the risks associated with early development.

Resilient social systems validate distressed emotions, make meaning from adversity, demonstrate reliability and flexibility, provide the benefit of the doubt, and are proactive (Becvar, 2013). Resilient systems prioritize congruent communication, which includes addressing problems, using non-blaming language, collaborating to solve problems, and expressing feelings openly (Walsh, 2016). Resilient relationships are fostered by mutual investment and cooperation, continuity, connectedness, and repair when needed.

Therapy and Systemic Resilience

At some level, successful therapy cultivates resilience; however, therapists can intentionally bolster resilience in general practice and when treating specific presenting issues. Building systemic resilience requires a holistic understanding of the system and its components, along with the relationships and dependencies between them. To integrate systemic resilience into clinical practice, therapists must assess how clients deal with situations and problems, their coping mechanisms, and their support networks (Bowman, 2013; Maltby et al., 2019). As clinicians foster systemic resilience, they help clients cope with difficulties, solve problems, decrease symptoms associated with presenting problems, and affirm clients' identities. Cultivating resilience promotes hope, belonging, and healing (Walsh, 2016, 2023).

Current relational resilience literature has focused largely on what families need to be resilient (Walsh, 2016) or on the traits and processes of systemic resilience (Becvar, 2013; Ungar, 2011, 2021; Walsh, 2023). Additional resources are needed to enhance understanding of how therapists can help build resilient clients, supervisees, and communities. It is essential to understand how systemic resilience can be applied to clinical practice. Those who foster resilience assist others and themselves in resolving their problems and thriving in life. Therapists may be able to conceptualize cases better, plan treatment, and develop supportive therapeutic relationships by understanding and applying systemic resilience.

Vision for This Book

The following chapters present embodied experiences of cultivating resilience from a variety of clinical contexts. The chapters include stories from practitioners across social locations and professional identities that amplify, cultivate, and illustrate systemic resilience. Each chapter begins with authors locating themselves socially and professionally. The goal was to promote justice-informed practices that support clinicians in building resilience in the therapy room, with themselves, and in professional relationships (e.g., supervision). Resilience is tied to liberation. Liberation psychology, with its foundational focus on the social, political, and cultural forces affecting individual and collective well-being, offers a robust framework to understand resilience as an individual trait and as a collective endeavor rooted in community and contextual experiences. By critiquing dominant ideologies that perpetuate oppression and emphasizing the importance of critical consciousness, liberation psychology provides a roadmap for communities to cultivate systemic resilience against external threats and internal vulnerabilities. It also gives voice to the strengths and freedoms embedded within clinical work that cultivates resilience.

I desired for this book to edify and be a practical resource to guide resilient clinicians who promote systemic resilience with those who attend clinical sessions (e.g., authors use various nomenclatures, such as clients or patients and therapists or clinicians). As such, I sent out a call to authors for submissions focused on fostering systemic resilience in clinical practice (e.g., promoting relational hope, healing, adaptability, communal resource use, and shared meaning). I encouraged the authors to write about a topic, intervention, or idea highlighting their lived experiences and asked them to consider equity, justice, and inclusion in doing so. My purpose was to assist clinical students, counselor educators, new therapists, and seasoned clinicians in identifying and augmenting systemic strengths. I hope these stories are meaningful to you in that they inspire you to shift perspectives, increase your creativity, and amplify resilience in multiple facets of clinical practice, self-care, community care, and relationships with colleagues, supervisors, instructors, and significant others.

References

Becvar, D. S. (Ed.). (2013). *Handbook of family resilience.* Springer. https://doi.org/10.1007/978-1-4614-3917-2

Becvar, D. S., & Becvar, R. J. (1998). *Family therapy: Systemic integration* (3rd ed.). Allyn and Bacon.

Benson, P. L. (1999). *All kids are our kids: What communities must do to raise caring and responsible children and adolescents.* Jossey-Bass.

Bowman, P. J. (2013). A strengths-based social psychological approach to resiliency: Cultural diversity, ecological, and life span issues. In S. Prince-Embury & D. H. Saklofske (Eds.), *Resilience in children, adolescents, and adults: Translating research into practice* (pp. 299–324). Springer Science + Business Media. https://doi.org/10.1007/978-1-4614-4939-3_21

Brendtro, L., Brokenleg, M., & Van Bockern, S. (2019). *Reclaiming youth at risk: Futures of promise* (3rd ed.). Solution Tree.

Brown, Z. A. [@zandashe]. (2021, May 21). *I dream of never being called resilient again in my life. I'm exhausted by strength. I want support. I want* [Tweet]. X. https://twitter.com/zandashe/status/1394805726825099279?lang=en

Carver, C. S. (2010). Resilience and thriving: Issues, models, and linkages. *Journal of Social Issues, 54*(2), 245–266. https://doi.org/10.1111/j.1540-4560.1998.tb01217.x

Fraser, M. W. (Ed.). (1997). *Risk and resilience in childhood: An ecological perspective* (1st ed.). National Association of Social Workers Press.

Henderson, N., Benard, B., & Sharp-Light, N. (Eds.). (1999). *Resiliency in action: Practical ideas for overcoming risks and building strengths in youth, families, & communities.* Resiliency in Action.

Kaplan, H. B. (1999). Toward an understanding of resilience: A critical review of definitions and models. In M. D. Glantz & J. L. Johnson (Eds.), *Resilience and development: Positive life adaptations* (pp. 17–83). Kluwer Academic/Plenum.

Maltby, J., Day, L., Hall, S. S., & Chivers, S. (2019). The measurement and role of ecological resilience systems theory across domain-specific outcomes: The domain-specific resilient systems scales. *Assessment, 26*(8), 1444–1461. https://doi.org/10.1177/1073191117738045

Masten, A. S., & Garmezy, N. (1985). Risk vulnerability and protective factors in developmental psychopathology. In B. B. Lahey & A. E. Kazidin (Eds.), *Advances in clinical child psychology* Vol. 8, pp. 1–52). Plenum. https://doi.org/10.1007/978-1-4613-9820-2_1

Masten, A. S., & Reed, M.-G. J. (2002). Resilience in development. In C. R. Snyder & S. J. Lopez (Eds.), *Handbook of positive psychology* (pp. 74–88). Oxford University Press.

Mitchell, K. E., Levin, A. S., & Krumboltz, J. D. (1999). Planned happenstance: Constructing unexpected career opportunities. *Journal of Counseling & Development, 77*(2), 115–124. https://doi.org/10.1002/j.1556-6676.1999.tb02431.x

Ungar, M. (2011). *The social ecology of resilience: A handbook of theory and practice.* Springer. https://doi.org/10.1007/978-1-4614-0586-3_2

Ungar, M. (2021). *Multisystemic resilience.* Oxford University Press.

Walsh, F. (2016). Family resilience: A development systems framework. *European Journal of Developmental Psychology, 13*(3), 1–12. http://doi.org/10.1080/17405629.2016.1154035

Walsh, F. (2021). Family resilience: A dynamic systemic framework. In M. Ungar (Ed.), *Multisystemic resilience* (pp. 255–270). Oxford University Press.

Walsh, F. (2023). *Complex and traumatic loss: Fostering healing and resilience.* Guildford Press.

Werner, E. E. (1993). Risk, resilience, and recovery: Perspectives from the Kauai longitudinal study. *Development and Psychopathology, 5,* 503–515. https://doi.org/10.1017/s095457940000612x

Werner, E. E. (1994). Overcoming the odds. *Journal of Developmental and Behavioral Pediatrics, 15,* 131–136. https://journals.lww.com/jrnldbp/citation/1994/04000/overcoming_the_odds.12.aspx

Werner, E. E. (2000). Protective factors and individual resilience. In J. P. Shonkoff & S. J. Meisels (Eds.), *Handbook of early childhood intervention* (pp. 118–132). Cambridge University Press.

Wicks, R. J. (2007). *The resilient clinician: Secondary stress, mindfulness, positive psychology, and enhancing the self-care protocol of the psychotherapist, counselor, and social worker.* Oxford University Press.

Wicks, R. J. (2010). *Bounce: Living the resilient life.* Oxford University Press.

2

EMPOWERING COMMUNITIES THROUGH SYSTEMIC RESILIENCE

A Fusion of Liberation Psychology and Adaptive Coping Strategies

Raquel Martin

A 34-year-old cisgender, heterosexual Black woman, wife, and mother born and residing in the United States, Dr. Raquel Martin has dedicated her professional journey to the specialty of Black mental health and connects deeply with liberation psychology. Throughout her career as a professor, scientist, and licensed clinical psychologist, Dr. Martin has passionately advocated for herself and her community. Her endeavors aim to challenge and reshape systems that perpetuate harm to marginalized and oppressed groups. She works toward creating spaces where Black voices resonate with authenticity and power. Beyond her professional commitments, Dr. Martin is devoted to sculpting a safer world for her children, family, and community, anchoring her advocacy in the pursuit of well-being and equitable representation in all spheres of life.

Liberation is a concept intertwined with healing, evolution, and resilience. When an individual makes a decision to approach an issue or work on oneself, there is something from which that individual wishes to

DOI: 10.4324/9781003373513-2

be liberated. This effort could include liberation from constant negative thoughts, pain of trauma, or even internal resistance to opening oneself up to a new way of communicating with others. Pursuing resilience is to dedicate oneself to freeing oneself from limits and repeatedly emancipating oneself from one's pain. As a Black licensed clinical psychologist specializing in Black mental health and using liberation psychology, I believe no conversation about resilience is complete without including the conversation of oppression, particularly for patients of African descent. To appropriately serve these individuals and assist them with many aspects of resilience—from cognitive to social—the clinician must understand liberation psychology.

Liberation Psychology: A Primer

Dr. Ignacio Martín-Baró (1994), a licensed clinical psychologist, developed liberation psychology. Martín-Baró was from Latin America and developed liberation psychology to emphasize the role of social, political, and cultural contexts as a method of understanding individuals' experiences and behaviors. When it comes to marginalized and oppressed groups, Martín-Baró specified that one could learn about the system in which individuals have been socialized and, as a result, serve them better by observing and understanding their standard of living, how their free time is spent, and where they seek enjoyment. Some key principles of liberation psychology include conscientization, contextual understanding, critique of traditional psychology, challenging the status quo, and praxis.

- *Conscientization* is the overarching principle for the entirety of liberation psychology, which Paulo Freire (2022) introduced. This concept refers to cultivating an understanding and keen awareness of societal frameworks that sustain disparities and subjugation. Such understanding can occur through external agents of change who work (e.g., intellectuals, activists, and professionals) alongside internal agents of change (e.g., those belonging to oppressed and marginalized communities; Freire, 2022).
- *Contextual understanding* underscores the significance of viewing individuals through the lens of their sociopolitical and historical

backgrounds. In contextual understanding, numerous psychological challenges stem from broader systems of inequality and unfairness (Comas-Díaz & Rivera, 2020).

- *Critique of traditional psychology* refers to Martín-Baró (1994) consistently challenging prevailing views in mainstream psychology. According to Martín-Baró, mainstream psychology's supposed neutrality or apolitical stance at the time perpetuated existing power dynamics. When faced with oppression and injustice, a neutral position reflects an alignment with the oppressor via complicity.
- *Challenging the status quo* is important for understanding the world because (a) it impacts those who have been marginalized, oppressed, and historically excluded, and (b) it works to change existing systems of oppression (Martín-Baró, 1994).
- *Praxis* involves meaningful and informed change. Liberation psychology emphasizes the intersection of theory, reflection, and action. After seeking education and reflecting on the issues from a historical and current context, the next step involves praxis; however, this cycle is continuous between learning, reflection, and action and promotes collaboration within the community or the study participants (Martín-Baró, 1994).

These liberation psychology concepts require a shift in thinking from abstract to applied principles. Next, I share examples for integrating each theme of liberation psychology to target patients of African descent.

- Conscientization: As a clinician, introduce colleagues to literature that delves into the systems of oppression in the United States. As a professor, incorporate this same level of information into the curriculum and take it a step further by not simply teaching an introduction to psychology but by incorporating a decolonizing perspective and integrating intersectional research methods into courses. As a supervisor or mentor to the next generation of clinicians, challenge those involved to critically examine and discuss the structural racism embedded in various institutions, from education to the criminal justice system.
- Contextual understanding: Use previous education that centers the experiences of individuals of African descent to incorporate

assessment techniques, treatment methods, and paradigms that have been researched primarily with patients of African descent (Anderson & Stevenson, 2019; Metzger et al., 2021). Incorporate societal factors such as dehumanization, racism, and oppression into the case conceptualization and treatment planning. Use resources and strategies known to improve these unique factors of the Black experience, such as racial socialization and Black identity development.

- Critique of traditional psychology and challenging the status quo: Acknowledge the disparity between traditional psychological treatment orientations that center European Americans' narratives and their effectiveness with individuals of African descent. Investigate how being educated in the former perspective—which fails to honor the unique experiences, cultural values, and challenges faced by individuals of African descent—can contribute to harm (i.e., intentional or intentional) against patients, students, and trainees. Take the time to identify areas of practice, education, or mentorship that combat these challenges.

- Praxis: Take the time to learn the history of individuals of African descent and that this history does not begin with enslavement. Use myriad resources (e.g., workshops, research studies, podcasts, documentaries) that focus on stressors such as racism, oppression, and dehumanization and strength-based narratives such as empowerment, Black identity development, and community cultivation. Use the information garnered to engage with those within the community—personal and professional—to advocate for policy changes in government and professional practice. Identify policies within the clinic, hospital, or university that disproportionately impact oppressed individuals and work to change them.

In each of these instances, the crucial element is recognizing and tackling the distinct challenges faced by individuals of African descent in the United States to foster empowerment, comprehension, and proactive change. When working with clients in clinical environments, identifying the presence and type of oppression will guide treatment planning and case conceptualization to collaborate and identify how systemic resilience can improve their lives.

Oppression and Clinical Treatment

The connections between liberation, oppression, and systemic resilience are seamless. There are multiple levels of oppression, including cultural, systemic, injected, and interpersonal (David et al., 2019; Kelly & Varghese, 2018; Schiele, 2005). Ultimately, the underlying narrative or ideology of oppression is people's belief that one group or groups are smarter, better than, more evolved, and so on, than another group; as a result, that group(s) should have the right to decide what access they have to education, income, and freedoms. Exposure to oppression can have a significant psychological impact, including traumatization (Williams et al., 2023). This form of racism and oppression-related stress has also been referred to as racial battle fatigue. Symptoms of racial battle fatigue include powerlessness, hopelessness, loss of identity, difficulty trusting others, traumatic stress, lowered self-esteem, and isolation (Okello et al., 2020; Quaye et al., 2019; Smith et al., 2020). When investigating the aspect of oppression, it is important to look at multiple aspects of identity. There are realms where I feel oppression as a Black person, a Black woman, and a Black mother; however, these experiences do not always occur in the same environment.

In therapy, assessments provide information required for diagnosis, understanding the client, goal setting, treatment planning, building a therapeutic alliance, and identifying potential barriers. Formal and informal assessments will take place throughout the therapeutic process. However, the most formidable way to begin the assessment process is with a thorough initial intake (e.g., taking time to engage with the patient, noticing silence and spoken words). A clinician may lose the salience of their words when they limit themselves to checklists and surveys. Black people have been consistently and historically invalidated and dehumanized by silencing their speech and narratives; therefore, taking time to listen is an act of liberation (Toliver, 2021). Next, I include starter questions, grouped by symptoms of racial battle fatigue, that may be helpful to ask when working to understand the patient and help them as a result.

- Powerlessness.
  - Do you feel as though things are out of your control? Can you provide me with an example of when you felt this way?

- Do you feel heard and understood in your relationships?
- Do you ever feel pressure due to societal expectations or norms? If so, what do you feel is the impact of this pressure on your sense of agency?
- Do you feel you have the resources and support needed to make a change in your life?
- Do medical or health concerns cause you to feel out of control?
- Hopelessness.
  - How do you feel about the future?
  - When was the last time that you felt hopeful about the future? What was happening during that time? What has changed since then?
  - How do you feel about your ability to manage, change, or improve current health concerns?
  - What do you feel is your purpose or meaning in life? Do you feel as though your life lacks meaning? Do you have values or beliefs that support your well-being?
- Loss of identity.
  - Do you have a sense of belonging to the Black community?
  - How would you describe yourself? Make note if your patient only identifies themselves in relationship to others such as partner, father, daughter, or employee.
  - Identify strengths, capabilities, and/or skills you are proud of.
  - Do you have access to communities, environments, or people where you do not feel the need to code switch or mask? How often can you spend time in these communities, environments, or with these people?
  - How much time per day do you spend engaging in tasks and activities solely for the purpose of your enjoyment? What pockets of joy do you have throughout the day? Do you have any hobbies or interests outside of work, school, and parenting?
  - Do you ever feel the need to hide or dampen aspects of your identity to feel accepted or avoid potential harm?
- Difficulty trusting others.
  - On a scale of 1 to 10, how would you rate your ability to trust others?

- Do you have a pattern in emotional or behavioral responses when you feel your trust has been broken?
- Can you identify individuals within your life who are difficult to trust? If so, why?
- Are there scenarios, situations, or environments where your distrust or trust is heightened? Where do you feel safest, and where do you feel the most unsafe?
- Tell me about your relationships with your caregivers and significant figures in your life.
- Can you imagine a scenario where you would feel more comfortable trusting others? What does that look like regarding your relationship with yourself and others?
- Traumatic stress.
  - Have you experienced incidents where you felt treated unfairly or harmed because of your cultural background?
  - How does your body respond during and after a racism-based incident? What are you feeling in your body, what thoughts arise, and what emotions become present?
  - How often do you experience feeling that you need to be on guard about your surroundings because of your culture?
  - How safe do you feel in your community, workplace, and school?
  - What are your typical coping methods when faced with racism and oppression?
  - Do you experience any recurring symptoms such as nightmares, flashbacks, or out-of-body experiences following racism-based encounters that you have witnessed or directly experienced?
  - Do you have any concerns about facing racism and oppression in the future? What are they? How do these fears impact your life and decisions?
- Lowered self-esteem.
  - Have experiences of discrimination, racism, and oppression made you doubt your abilities?
  - Do you feel connected to your cultural community? If so, what does that connection feel like? Do certain activities make you feel a greater or lesser connection?

- How do you feel about the way the media has portrayed Black people? Do these portrayals impact the way you feel about yourself?
- Can you identify internalized messages or beliefs that manifest in your daily life regarding any of your social identities?
- Isolation.
  - Do you feel disconnected, distanced, or separated from family, friends, or communities due to your ethnic background?
  - Do you avoid certain spaces, events, individuals, or communities due to concerns about racism, oppression, or discrimination?
  - Do you feel as though there are people in your life who understand and validate your values, beliefs, and experiences?
  - Do you feel a sense of isolation within your community?
  - Are you hesitant to form new relationships or connections due to fear of prejudice or discrimination?
  - Can you identify any barriers to discussing your feelings of isolation?

Each of these areas will have differences, as will the distinct types of oppression, to reveal what resources or plans come next. I focus on four types of oppression during therapy: cultural, injected, which transitions to internalized, systemic, and interpersonal.

- *Cultural oppression* consists of beliefs, values, and ideals imposed on people of the global majority by the dominant group, severing them from their individual culture (Schiele, 2005).
- *Injected internalized oppression* involves negative messages and attitudes that become part of one's nature due to oppression reflected institutionally and interpersonally (David et al., 2019).
- *Systemic or institutional oppression* is embedded in the education system, public policy, media, and laws (Esquierdo-Leal & Houmanfar, 2021).
- *Interpersonal oppression* includes individual attacks including bullying, beatings, threats, and harassment (Holmes et al., 2016) from peers, colleagues, etc. (Nadal et al., 2021).

Based on the different levels of oppression present, I might provide the following recommendations to a patient.

- Cultural: To address this level, a therapist may:
  - Suggest their patients increase activities where they are able to express their culture and be around individuals where they do not need to code-switch or mask.
- Injected internalized: To address this level, a therapist may:
  - Incorporate ethnic identity development models while addressing socialization methods that contributed to the oppression (e.g., stereotypes, media, and relationships).
- Systemic or institutional: To address this level, a therapist may:
  - Advocate for policy change within their work environment and for changes in laws and standards worldwide.
- Interpersonal: To address this level, a therapist may:
  - Incorporate education regarding the root of the stereotypes and the lack of truth within the statements.
  - Address ways for the patient to advocate for themselves when faced with this form of oppression.
  - Collaborate to devise an exit strategy for the environment, such as work, if it is not a sustainable environment in which to reside.

One aspect many clinicians miss, which plays into the role of misdiagnosis, is the impact of cultural display rules on the symptom presentation.

Cultural Display Rules

Cultural display rules are informal standards set by a social group or culture that dictate how individuals should express themselves. They are rules ingrained in people from a young age through interactions and social experiences within their communities (Matsumoto et al., 2008). Cultural display rules must also be viewed through the lens of oppression and racism. Researchers have indicated that mothers of young Black men find it less appropriate for children to display negative emotions (e.g., anger, fear, sadness, and crying) in public and private settings than European American parents due to significant social consequences (Brown et al., 2015; Nelson et al., 2012). As a result, Black children and eventually adults might be less inclined to show cognitive mental health symptoms because these indicate emotional expression, as opposed to somatic symptoms, which seem more medically grounded and safer to express. When people are shown through media, literature, and even through direct statements that their emotions are not safe, they learn to sublimate and deny their existence.

As a result, patients of African descent may have a tendency to report somatic symptoms rather than what may be deemed as typical emotional symptoms; for example, anxiety may take the form of a stomachache, or back pain may be the result of consistent muscle tension in a stressful environment. Therefore, taking special care when doing intake assessments and using pencil and paper assessments is important. A clinician must not assume that because something is not elevated, it is not relevant to the patient's treatment plan; rather, they should take the time to go through relevant questions, scales, and subscales. By using the previously mentioned concepts, clinicians can collaborate with their clients to identify skills that will help them, which can occur by identifying coping skills in a collective and individualistic concept.

Redefining Coping Skills in a Collective Context

When working with individuals of African descent, certain aspects will come into play in addition to liberation and oppression—strong sense of community and collective identity. As such, coping skills within a collective context are paramount. Clinicians can work firsthand with patients through a strength-based perspective. Too often, within the psychological field, focus is placed on inadequacies, problems, and what is lacking within individuals and, by extension, their communities (del Rio-Gonzalez et al., 2021; Harris et al., 2020). However, this form of deficit-based treatment orientation contributes to the maintenance of stereotypes that mental health professionals should be rallying against. Instead, mental health professionals must espouse a strength-based approach to assist patients in rewriting their own narratives, identify ways to challenge harmful biases within themselves and their surroundings, and embolden themselves to be active participants in their well-being journeys. Focuses on the inherent strengths of patients can occur in many ways:

- Power of the narrative: For many people of African descent, their stories are often untold, hidden, or negated, perpetuating a subconscious view that holds their stories as less than. Throughout history, Black culture has been a source of strength and resilience through a rich tapestry of cultural practices, stories, and traditions. Therefore, the use of racial socialization is a key factor in treatment progress. Racial socialization and African-centered therapy have been found to improve treatment outcomes for patients (Lateef, 2021; Turner et al., 2022; Winchester et al., 2022). Clinicians must embolden their patients to identify ways to live as the main characters of their stories and use this as a strength.

- Self-recognition: Collaborate with patients to recognize their abilities and resources to improve their self-esteem and self-concept. Ask questions about things they enjoy and feel a sense of accomplishment after, and collaborate to identify ways to incorporate more opportunities that help them feel this type of accomplishment. Due to pay inequities, disparities in job access, and the expectation to work twice as hard to get half as far, individuals of African descent may not have the time to take a step back and affirm themselves. Too concerned with being perceived as egotistical, these individuals may miss out on an important aspect of well-being, which is the recognition of one's self-worth as a way of creating a proactive approach to well-being rather than a reactive approach (Valadez et al., 2021).
- Autonomy in session: Ensure patients understand their position as autonomous participants in the session. Though clinicians are the mental health experts in the room, the patient will always be the expert when it comes to themselves. Many times, individuals have misconceived notions of what therapy entails, such as expecting to be told what to do instead of realizing the session is a collaboration. This can also be a result of certain cultures' tendency to engage in a hierarchical manner with medical professionals. To truly foster resilience in your patients, ensure they understand they will do the heavy lifting. The clinician is a member of their support team, but they are why change will occur and be sustained.
- Community engagement: Recognize the strengths present in patients' communities.
- Integration of multiple identities: When working with patients, clinicians must discuss and amplify the multiple aspects of their identity. Some communities affirm me as a Black woman, others affirm me as a Black mother, and others affirm me as a Black person in general. Sometimes, patients may feel as though something is missing. They may be unable to identify what is missing, but they do not feel fulfilled.

Cultivating Coping Skills in an Individualistic Context

During patients' healing journeys, it can be helpful for many to think of coping skills in different ways for them to be long-term tools. Individual coping skills are as important as collective coping skills for identifying sustainable practices; however, it can be difficult to identify a framework that resonates with patients to identify coping skills. I find it more helpful to identify a framework instead of choosing specific skills for the patient because doing so can guide them to identify additional skills. I often use the following frameworks in sessions.

Filling the Gap

Characteristics that serve clinicians in one environment may not serve them in others. For example, during my journey to my current career, I often had to have what I call "big boss energy." I found I was challenged more, critiqued more, and praised less than my European American peers. To make matters more stressful, few people work with me who look like me and advocate for people who look like me. In addition to being isolated in my experiences, I have often felt the need to advocate for those who look like me, often alone. Still, I cannot maintain that energy all the time. This dynamic must have an off switch because, although it has served me in my career, it is antithetical to who I am around my friends and family, where I get to take a step back. With my friends and family, I do not need to be the leader, and I do not need to have big boss energy; that environment allows me the ability to rest and let other people take the lead.

When working with patients in this framework, it can be helpful to start with value identification and specific traits they feel as though they contribute to their success. Clinicians should walk patients through scenarios where there has been unhealthy conflict resolution or miscommunication of some sort and pay attention to themes that may arise. Such a process may lead patients to realize the fact other characteristics may serve them in one environment that do not serve them in another.

To become one of the 5% of psychologists who are Black (American Psychological Association, n.d.), I had to begin the PhD process with the end in mind. I could not celebrate my accomplishments because I had to move to the next step; however, that personality does not serve me when it comes to my family, when it comes to my children, and when it comes to enjoying life outside of work. The point was to complete each step and each goal without time to celebrate an accomplishment because I had to move on to the next one. When with my family, I need to sit down and resonate with my blessings. When I spend time with others and have a silent moment, I do not need to think about what I need to do next. I may need to enjoy this silence, and I need to read a book.

I often find it difficult for my patients of African descent to rest without feeling they are wasting time. Many of us are reared to think that we must do twice as much to get half as far; as a result, we miss out on opportunities often allotted to our European American counterparts, such as the freedom to grow and enjoy the journey. This framework is great for those who may be suffering from racism-related stress or struggling with loss of identity because it provides the opportunity to identify roots, values, and characteristics that will guide all future behaviors. A helpful prompt for clinicians to patients may be:

> I want you to think about things and characteristics that really help you to succeed in one environment. Think about whether they are serving you in another. It does not mean get rid of that characteristic altogether. That just means let it take a step back.

MODES

It is important to have many different coping skills because, at one point in time, one skill may work and another skill may not work—especially when dealing with more stress. An exercise I created to use with my patients is reviewing their MODES (i.e., mindfulness, opposite action, distractors, emotion identification, and support system). It is helpful to separate these skills into different categories so that patients can organize their options as well as research other skills that fit into the category. For example, if a patient realizes that emotion identification techniques work better than mindfulness, they will have the vocabulary to look up other options outside of therapy.

Mindfulness includes yoga, meditation, and grounding exercises.

Opposite action. This strategy means I would like the individual to do the exact opposite of what they feel like during times of stress. For example, if someone is depressed and wants to crawl into bed, they instead get out of bed, walk out the door, and move around.

Distractors. Distractors tend to be the easiest skills to identify with patients because they often incorporate these tasks into their daily lives. Distractor tasks can include coloring, exercising, going for walks, listening to music, and singing.

Emotion identification. This strategy includes expressing feelings through talking or journaling. During this time, it can be helpful for the patient to identify the feeling and what precedes the feeling; after they are out of the thick of it with emotion, it is important to consider what contributed to the symptom reduction.

Support system. This strategy can include contacting a friend, family member, colleague, or anyone the patient feels can help with coping in a healthy manner.

It is incredibly helpful to have a wealth of exercises in a mental health toolbox because something may not work, and that does not mean you are going to stop and go back into that negative mood. That means you want to rotate and try another skill.

Coping Kit

This coping skill is incredibly helpful for my patients who have panic attacks and intrusive symptoms, such as flashbacks, because it is customizable and will work anywhere. Most of the time, my patient and I collaborate to create the kit according to their unique skills and their unique presenting symptoms. I find a helpful way to build this kit is according to the five senses.

My patient will bring a little bag (e.g., a makeup bag) to the session. Note: I find when I create these bags with my younger patients, they enjoy customizing them, so purchasing small canvas bags can also be helpful. Then, we work together to identify skills that can help the patient according to each sense that resonates with them:

- Smell (e.g., room sprays, candles, aromatherapy necklace, fragrant lotion). Patients identify scents that help to decrease their stress, and we identify the best method of administration.

- Sight (e.g., funny images or images that make them happy or remind them of a happier time). Patients bring images and print them, and I laminate* them or the patient puts them in their coping kit.
  * Note: I think a laminator is a must-have tool for mental health professionals. Please be aware a laminator with hot and cold lamination settings is best to avoid laminating an image using the hot setting.
- Sound (e.g., specific playlists with sounds or songs the patient enjoys). Appealing to this sense may involve an enjoyable podcast—although I recommend they stay away from true crime podcasts—therapeutic sounds, such as rain, or anything else that suits them. After we identify what works for them, we create a playlist and bookmark it on their phone if they have it with them.
- Taste (e.g., sour candy, as the sour taste brings focus to the current moment; gum; chocolate). Patients can reroute their brain's attention from the stressor to the present moment by focusing on their sense of taste.
- Touch (e.g., crochet yarn, squeeze balls, pets). I have taught individuals to crochet because I realized they would appreciate the tactile aspect of feeling some nice, chunky yarn and doing knots. If the knot was messed up, they just took it out. The yarn and needle were items that patients could carry around with them all the time. Using squeeze balls or caring for a pet can also be grounding. There is a reason a pet's presence is soothing—it is not just their joyful personalities, but it is also soothing to pet them.

Once we have created the coping kit, I suggest patients place it somewhere easily accessible, such as their car or purse. Sometimes, patients make extras and leave them with close friends and family members as a backup.

Conclusion

The intricate dynamics of our interwoven global community necessitate a deeper understanding of resilience that goes beyond individual capacities, reaching into the fabric of our collective experience. This chapter emphasizes the indispensability of merging systemic resilience with liberation psychology and advocating for a community-based approach grounded in cultural understanding and critical awareness.

Liberation psychology, rich in its grasp of sociopolitical influences on well-being, equips clinicians with a lens to view resilience as a shared endeavor rooted deeply in community experiences and reactions against oppressive forces. Furthermore, the chapter enriches the understanding of coping—not merely as individual tactics but as community-driven, culturally rooted practices that bolster collective strength and adaptation. By intertwining theoretical insights with real-world applications, clinicians can pave the way for a reimagined framework where resilience, empowerment, and coping are holistically approached, reflecting the intricacies of community dynamics and the broader systems in which they exist. The collective call to action is clear: to shift the individualistic, westernized counseling paradigm, recognizing the transformative power of a community's adaptive capacity in navigating, confronting, and ultimately reshaping oppressive systems.

Further Reading

Comas-Díaz, L., & Torres Rivera, E. (Eds.). (2020). *Liberation psychology: Theory, method, practice, and social justice (Cultural, racial, and ethnic psychology series)*. American Psychological Association.

Evans, S. Y., Bell, K., & Burton, N. K. (2017). *Black women's mental health: Balancing strength and vulnerability*. Suny Press.

Freire, P. (2020). Pedagogy of the oppressed. In J. Beck, C. Jenks, N. Keddie, & M. F. D. Young (Eds.), *Toward a sociology of education* (pp. 374–386). Routledge.

Martín-Baró, I. (1996). *Writings for a liberation psychology*. Harvard University Press.

Turner, E. (2019). *Mental health among African Americans: Innovations in research and practice*. Rowman & Littlefield.

Walker, R. (2020). *The unapologetic guide to Black mental health: Navigate an unequal system, learn tools for emotional wellness, and get the help you deserve*. New Harbinger Publications.

References

American Psychological Association. (n.d.). *Demographics of U.S. psychology workforce* [Interactive data tool]. Retrieved September 9, 2023, from www.apa.org/workforce/data-tools/demographics

Anderson, R. E., & Stevenson, H. C. (2019). RECASTing racial stress and trauma: Theorizing the healing potential of racial socialization in families. *American Psychologist*, *74*(1), 63. https://doi.org/10.1037/amp0000392

Brown, G. L., Craig, A. B., & Halberstadt, A. G. (2015). Parent gender differences in emotion socialization behaviors vary by ethnicity and child gender. *Parenting*, *15*(3), 135–157. https://doi.org/10.1080/15295192.2015.1053312

Comas-Díaz, L. E., & Rivera, T. (2020). *Liberation psychology: Theory, method, practice, and social justice*. American Psychological Association.

David, E. J. R., Schroeder, T. M., & Fernandez, J. (2019). Internalized racism: A systematic review of the psychological literature on racism's most insidious consequence. *Journal of Social Issues*, *75*(4), 1057–1086. https://doi.org/10.1111/josi.12350

del Rio-Gonzalez, A. M., Holt, S. L., & Bowleg, L. (2021). Powering and structuring intersectionality: Beyond main and interactive associations. *Research on Child and Adolescent Psychopathology*, *49*(1), 33–37. https://doi.org/10.1007/s10802-020-00720-w

Esquierdo-Leal, J. L., & Houmanfar, R. A. (2021). Creating inclusive and equitable cultural practices by linking leadership to systemic change. *Behavior Analysis in Practice*, *14*, 499–512. https://doi.org/10.1007/s40617-020-00519-7

Freire, P. (2022). *Pedagogy of the oppressed: Reliving pedagogy of the oppressed*. Bloomsbury Publishing.

Harris, J. R. A., Crumb, L., Crowe, A., & McKinney, J. G. (2020). African Americans' perceptions of mental illness and preferences for treatment. *Journal of Counselor Practice*, *11*(1), 1–33. https://doi.org/10.22229/afa1112020

Holmes, S. C., Facemire, V. C., & DaFonseca, A. M. (2016). Expanding criterion a for posttraumatic stress disorder: Considering the deleterious impact of oppression. *Traumatology*, *22*(4), 314. https://doi.org/10.1037/trm0000104

Kelly, D. C., & Varghese, R. (2018). Four contexts of institutional oppression: Examining the experiences of Blacks in education, criminal justice and child welfare. *Journal of Human Behavior in the Social Environment*, *28*(7), 874–888. https://doi.org/10.1080/10911359.2018.1466751

Lateef, H. (2021). African-centered frameworks of youth development: Nuanced implications for guiding social work practice with Black youth. *Child and Adolescent Social Work Journal*, *38*(6), 671–678. https://doi.org/10.1007/s10560-020-00703-2

Martín-Baró, I. (1994). *Writings for a liberation psychology*. Harvard University Press.

Matsumoto, D., Yoo, S. H., & Fontaine, J. (2008). Mapping expressive differences around the world: The relationship between emotional display rules and individualism versus collectivism. *Journal of Cross-Cultural Psychology, 39*(1), 55–74. https://doi.org/10.1177/0022022107311854

Metzger, I. W., Anderson, R. E., Are, F., & Ritchwood, T. (2021). Healing interpersonal and racial trauma: Integrating racial socialization into trauma-focused cognitive behavioral therapy for African American youth. *Child Maltreatment, 26*(1), 17–27. https://doi.org/10.1177/1077559520921457

Nadal, K. L., King, R., Sissoko, D. G., Floyd, N., & Hines, D. (2021). The legacies of systemic and internalized oppression: Experiences of microaggressions, imposter phenomenon, and stereotype threat on historically marginalized groups. *New Ideas in Psychology, 63*, Article 100895. https://doi.org/10.1016/j.newideapsych.2021.100895

Nelson, J. A., Leerkes, E. M., O'Brien, M., Calkins, S. D., & Marcovitch, S. (2012). African American and European American mothers' beliefs about negative emotions and emotion socialization practices. *Parenting, 12*(1), 22–41. https://doi.org/10.1080/15295192.2012.638871

Okello, W. K., Quaye, S. J., Allen, C., Carter, K. D., & Karikari, S. N. (2020). "We wear the mask": Self-definition as an approach to healing from racial battle fatigue. *Journal of College Student Development, 61*(4), 422–438. https://doi.org/10.1353/csd.2020.0049

Quaye, S. J., Karikari, S. N., Allen, C. R., Okello, W. K., & Carter, K. D. (2019). Strategies for practicing self-care from racial battle fatigue. *Journal Committed to Social Change on Race and Ethnicity, 5*(2), 95–131. https://doi.org/10.15763/issn.2642-2387.2019.5.2.94-131

Schiele, J. H. (2005). Cultural oppression and the high-risk status of African Americans. *Journal of Black Studies, 35*(6), 802–826. https://doi.org/10.1177/0021934704265560

Smith, W. A., David, R., & Stanton, G. S. (2020). Racial battle fatigue: The long-term effects of racial microaggressions on African American boys and men. In R. Majors, K. Carberry, & T. S. Ransaw (Eds.), *The international handbook of black community mental health* (pp. 83–92). Emerald Publishing. https://doi.org/10.1108/978-1-83909-964-920201006

Toliver, S. R. (2021). Recovering Black storytelling in qualitative research: Endarkened storywork. Routledge.

Turner, E. A., Harrell, S. P., & Bryant-Davis, T. (2022). Black love, activism, and community (BLAC): The BLAC model of healing and resilience. *Journal of Black Psychology, 48*(3–4), 547–568. https://doi.org/10.1177/00957984211018364

Valadez, E. A., Troller-Renfree, S. V., Buzzell, G. A., Henderson, H. A., Chronis-Tuscano, A., Pine, D. S., & Fox, N. A. (2021). Behavioral inhibition and dual mechanisms of anxiety risk: Disentangling neural correlates of proactive and reactive control. *JCPP Advances*, *1*(2), Article e12022. https://doi.org/10.1002/jcv2.12022

Williams, M., Osman, M., & Hyon, C. (2023). Understanding the psychological impact of oppression using the trauma symptoms of discrimination scale. *Chronic Stress*, *7*. https://doi.org/10.1177/24705470221149511

Winchester, L. B., Jones, S. C., Allen, K., Hope, E., & Cryer-Coupet, Q. R. (2022). Let's talk: The impact of gendered racial socialization on Black adolescent girls' mental health. *Cultural Diversity and Ethnic Minority Psychology*, *28*(2), Article 171.

3

INTERSECTIONS OF SYSTEMIC RESILIENCE AND SPIRITUALITY IN FIRST NATION NARRATIVES

Arynn Prescott, Christie Eppler, and Jeanette Rodriguez

The first and second authors identify as White; the third author is Mestiza, of Ecuadorian descent. All are cisgender women. The third author worked directly with Condoled Bear Clan Mother Iakoiane Wakerahkats:teh through ethnographic research and interviews. All authors have, in their own way, been impacted by dominant Eurocentric culture, thought, and education system of the United States. This resource's commitment to decolonization is demonstrated by Indigenous source material, diverse authorship, prioritization of clan language and value assumptions, and de-prioritization of dominant cultural narratives of systemic resilience.

Amid suffering and challenge, transformation occurs, which is often at the intersection of spirituality and resilience (Kirmayer et al., 2011; Walsh, 2016). The integration of clients' strengths and spiritual beliefs in clinical treatment can be a powerful tool for building systemic resilience within relationships, families, and communities (Walsh, 2016). However, counselors may hesitate to introduce spirituality despite their

DOI: 10.4324/9781003373513-3

stance of taking a strength-based approach (Griffith & Griffith, 2002). Clinicians have reported feeling unprepared when it comes to discussing spiritual topics in therapy (Johns, 2017; Robertson, 2010), yet, many clients consider spirituality to be essential to healing (Gockel, 2011; Morrison et al., 2009). Clinicians can promote healing and resilience by integrating clients' faith or spirituality into treatment (Walsh, 2016). For this to be possible, therapists must acquire a basic understanding of spiritual literacy across multiple faith traditions.

Currently, there is a linguistic divide between spiritual narratives and how clinicians define functioning or coping. The languages of spirituality and resilience often reflect similar dynamics, but in different terms. Many therapists are not trained to listen to or use spiritual language. It is important for clinicians to hear stories from marginalized peoples who have cultivated their resilience and spirituality in the face of injustice, hardship, and adversity. When these narratives are synthesized with existing and emerging theories of systemic resilience, counselors may gain a deeper understanding of how clients' spirituality can be ethically integrated into clinical practice.

This chapter presents a linguistic chart integrating systemic resilience and First Nation spirituality using two spiritually oriented narratives by Indigenous authors: Rodriguez and Wakerahkats:teh's (2017) *A Clan Mother's Call: Reconstructing Haudenosaunee Cultural Memory* and Kimmerer's (2013) *Braiding Sweetgrass: Indigenous Wisdom, Scientific Knowledge and the Teachings of Plants*. This chapter may be helpful for counselors who have a humanistic approach to finding strengths and solutions but do not yet speak the spiritual languages of their clients. Clinicians can use this information to educate themselves and identify clients' spiritual resources.

First Nation Peoples in Therapy

To respect First Nations' sovereignty and worldviews, we use terminology chosen by the texts' authors, Indigenous or First Nation. Culturally attuned counselors must integrate strength-based cultural perspectives into therapy with First Nation peoples, particularly after trauma from colonization (Brave Heart et al., 2011; Gameon & Skewes, 2020; Kirmayer et al., 2011). Colonization resulted in the suppression of First

Nation cultures and languages, repeated relocations that denied First Nations' sovereignty (Walls & Whitbeck, 2012), and common experiences of loss and spiritual disconnection (Olson, 2003). Historical and contemporary injustices have contributed to First Nation communities' underrepresentation in counseling approaches and limited access to therapy resources (Moorehead et al., 2015).

Decolonizing and re-indigenizing practices have been adopted in counseling theory and practice to address oppression and a lack of resources (Cox et al., 2021; Datta, 2018; Hernández-Wolfe, 2011; Singh et al., 2020; Thambinathan & Kinsella, 2021). As Eurocentric frameworks are decentralized, cultural essentialism is subsequently avoided, and First Nation communities can access more culturally sensitive therapy (Wendt & Gone, 2012). Indigenous cultural values have also been incorporated into evidence-based practices and tools (Dell et al., 2011; Elliott, 2020; Moorehead et al., 2015; Rowan et al., 2015; Schick et al., 2021). However, recent systematic reviews of overall treatment and trauma-specific interventions with Indigenous peoples in North America found trauma interventions remain lacking in quantity and quality (e.g., research has often used small sample sizes; Gameon & Skewes, 2020; Pomerville et al., 2016). There is a need to integrate Indigenous knowledge into counseling practices and to offer more decolonized and strength-based resources.

Spirituality and Systemic Resilience as Resources

Systemic resilience is similar to spiritually integrated and humanistic clinical treatment approaches. Shared constructs include meaning making, sense of purpose, shared values, and connection to others (Walsh, 2009, 2016, 2023). Spirituality and systemic resilience are rooted in what is beneficial, creative, and life-giving (Walsh, 2009, 2016). Both frameworks respond to questions such as, "What does it mean to be human in community?" and "How can we promote strengths and growth?" Spirituality focuses on ultimate mysteries, divine sources of knowing, practices that illuminate or enhance beliefs, and the transformation of suffering to healing (Anderson, 2009; Petry, 2016). Spirituality is about relationships with significant others and higher powers (Aponte, 2002).

Becvar's (2013), Ungar's (2021), and Walsh's (2016) resilience models were authored by therapists and researchers from non-Indigenous social locations. These models highlight three main categories of systemic resilience processes: belief systems, organizational patterns, and communication. Within belief systems, there are three subcategories: (a) making meaning of adversity; (b) positive outlook; and (c) spirituality—the last concept, which includes larger values, purpose, social action, new possibilities, and connection and access to nature (Becvar, 2013; Ungar, 2021). In Walsh's (2016) framework, family organizational patterns that support resilience are flexible and connected. Walsh's (2016) and Ungar's (2021) models point to the ability to mobilize social and economic resources (e.g., kin networks and accessible mentors) as resilience processes. Lastly, resilient communication, specifically as it relates to problem solving, includes (a) clear, consistent messages; (b) open emotional expression that involves a full range, from humor to pain to empathy; and (c) a collaborative and proactive approach to problem solving (Walsh, 2016). To illustrate resilient communication and family structure, Ungar (2021) emphasized parental support, indicating 71% of youth participants reported that trusting their parents and feeling comfortable discussing challenges with them was important to their resilience.

The circle of courage, a resilience model developed with input from Indigenous and European-American clinicians who worked with youth in foster care, incorporates four principles: mastery, belonging, generosity, and independence (Brendtro et al., 2019). Mastery is marked by a deeply rooted sense of being able to cope and succeed. Mastery develops not by competition but by a thriving sense of competence gained from overcoming challenges overseen by a skilled mentor. Independence, or autonomy over one's decisions, is bolstered when adults provide thoughtful feedback to youth while allowing them the agency to make decisions, take responsibility, and exert self-control. Belonging is about forging powerful and resilient social bonds that are felt and known. Belonging fulfills the longing for human attachment with trustworthy people. The principle of generosity is rooted in purpose, specifically altruism and being concerned for others' well-being, which motivates participating in prosocial activities throughout one's life (Brendtro et al., 2019). These elements of resilience must exist in harmony without one domain overshadowing the others. The model expands systemic resilience from family to community and beyond.

Method

To understand the intersections of Indigenous spiritual stories and systemic resilience, we analyzed two narratives by Indigenous authors: Rodriguez and Wakerahkats:teh's (2017) *A Clan Mother's Call: Restructuring Haudenosaunee Cultural Memory* and Kimmerer's (2013) *Braiding Sweetgrass: Indigenous Wisdom, Scientific Knowledge and the Teachings of Plants*. The authors are culture bearers from Kanien'kehá:ka and Potawatomi communities, respectively. Kimmerer, with permission, shared stories of her neighbors, most often of the Onondaga and Haudenosaunee. We illustrate how the authors described traits and processes of systemic resilience that parallel existing literature and add new insights to existing models.

We selected texts that centered cultural and spiritual reflections. Rodriguez and Wakerahkats:teh's (2017) ethnographic research focused on reclaiming ancestral wisdom through rites of passage. The text documented the reclamation of Haudenosaunee cultural memory as told by the Condoled Bear Clan Mother of the Kanien'kehá:ka people, Iakoiane Wakerahkats:teh. Resilience and cultural and spiritual processes were integrated to support the collective process of re-indigenizing (Rodriguez & Wakerahkats:teh, 2017). According to Rodriguez and Wakerahkats:teh (2017), metaphors from older wisdom and faith traditions can provide a deeper understanding of contemporary problems threatening individuals, families, partnerships, and communities. Kimmerer's (2013) memoir, *Braiding Sweetgrass*, was written from the perspective of a Potawatomi citizen and botanist who integrated Indigenous wisdom and scientific insight. Using ancestral, spiritual, and ecological teachings, Kimmerer provided a framework for modern values and social action. She asserted that ancient plant and wisdom-based teachings offer ways to navigate current ecological crises and our relationships with others, including Creation.

After multiple readings of Kimmerer (2013) and Rodriguez and Wakerahkats:teh (2017), we used Eppler and Hutchings's (2020) framework for synthesizing systemic resilience concepts with movie narratives to map the themes in the text with the resilience models discussed (i.e., Becvar, 2013; Brendtro et al., 2019; Ungar, 2021; Walsh, 2016). In the discussion, we examine how the spiritual themes from Indigenous wisdom enhance or deconstruct existing models and suggest practical applications.

Findings

We determined three themes of spiritually integrated resilience in *Braiding Sweetgrass* (Kimmerer, 2013) and *A Clan Mother's Call* (Rodriguez & Wakerahkats:teh, 2017). The themes are (a) guides and their roles, (b) connections through rituals, and (c) purpose and meaning. Within each theme emerged three to four subthemes, as detailed next. Our findings did not include all the stories presented in the texts. Although specific examples used in this analysis do not represent the full diversity of Indigenous Peoples, they highlight North American Haudenosaunee and Potawatomi spiritual language, stories, resilience, living rituals, and meaningful cultural contexts (see Table 3.1).

Theme 1: Guides and Roles

Guides are significant others with specific roles to lead the community, embody cultural memory, and offer rituals. Guides can be spiritual figures, dignified spiritual roles, and ancestral teachers, each a subtheme. Both texts, in their creation narratives, illustrated the role of Sky Woman and Mother Earth (Kimmerer, 2013; Rodriguez & Wakerahkats:teh, 2017). Traditions and identities are passed on through rituals facilitated by these spiritual figures. Guides parallel systemic resilience concepts such as connection, collaboration, shared values, leadership, inter/independence, and belonging.

Spiritual Figures and Dignified Roles

A relationship with and the duty to protect Mother Earth were prominent themes in both texts. The importance of honoring connection with more-than-human beings was also strongly supported. The result is a sense of belonging (Brendtro et al., 2019), along with organizational patterns that

Table 3.1 Integrating Resilience Themes in Texts and Models

Theme	A Clan Mother's Call	Braiding Sweetgrass	Circle of Courage: Brendtro et al.	Systemic Resiliency Frameworks: Walsh, Ungar, Becvar
Guides and Roles				
Spiritual Figures	Grandmother Moon, Mother Earth, Sky Woman	Sky Woman, Mother Earth	Independence, Belonging, Generosity, Mastery	Connection with nature, collaborative problem-solving, spirituality, relational view of resilience, larger shared values and purpose, social action, strong leadership that nurtures, guides, protects, support life dreams
Dignified Roles	Womanhood is dignified by Creation stories and cosmology; Bear Clan Mother's role is to bestow teachings	Motherhood is dignified through parallels to a nurturing Mother Earth	Independence, Mastery, Generosity, Belonging	Strong leadership that nurtures, guides, protects
Ancestral Teachers	Ancestral guidance from ancient ones in sacred dreams and Moon lodge reflections	Teachings of Maples, Fire, Strawberries, Mother Earth and all ancestrally significant teachers from local ecology and the Original Instructions	Belonging, Mastery, Generosity, Independence	Collaborative problem-solving, shared values, connection with nature, social resource of modeling and mentorship, interdependence, proactive stance, mobilize kin as a social resource

(Continued)

Table 3.1 (Continued)

Theme	A Clan Mother's Call	Braiding Sweetgrass	Circle of Courage: Brendtro et al.	Systemic Resiliency Frameworks: Walsh, Ungar, Becvar
Connections and Rituals				
Interdependence and Kinship	Spiritual Right to Belong, Three Sisters, value equals power to communicate and conduct crossover ceremonies	Sweetgrass (wiingaashk), kinship with the more-than-human world, Three Sisters	Belonging, Mastery, Independence	Communal identity, interdependence, collaborative problem-solving, connection with nature, proactive stance, mobilize kin for social action, connectedness, strong leadership that nurtures, guides, and protects, encourage active initiative, shared decision-making, clear and consistent messages, open communication
Language of Connection	Naming ritual signifies community role and connectedness	Reviving Indigenous language restores animacy and interconnection; certain names are sacred and only used for close relationships or ceremonies	Belonging	Connectedness through commitment, shared values, spiritual community, social resources

Ceremony, Practice, and Ritual	Crossover rituals with fasting (*enhontonkehte*); Moon vigils with red yarn; community witnessing of youth development	Black Ash Basket Weaving (*wisgaak gokpenagen*); First Salmon Ceremony at Cascade Head	Mastery, Independence, Belonging, Generosity	Contextualize distress, positive growth from adversity, sense of coherence, master the possible, hope and optimistic bias, new possibilities, dependable organization, connectedness, commitment, connection to nature, shared values, shared spirituality through contemplative practices and a faith community
Meaning Making and Purpose				
Contextualize Suffering	A shattered spirit linked to trauma; depression is "separation from spirit"; collective renewal from oppression through Re-Indigenizing	Ecological restoration as an antidote for despair; inter-species belonging as an antidote to loneliness	Belonging, Mastery	Contextualize distress, sense of coherence, larger/shared values, making meaning from adversity, adapt to new conditions, perseverance, positive growth from adversity
Prophecy and Calling	Clan Mother calls for re-matriation; The Great Law of Peace	Potawatomi elder's prophecy of the Eighth Fire and green path; The Great Law of Peace	Belonging, Mastery, Generosity	Shared larger values, contextualize distress, strong leadership that nurtures, guides, and protects, hope, social action, connectedness through mutual support and commitment, proactive stance
Affirm Identity	Crossover ceremony; Moon lodge gatherings; naming ritual	Haudenosaunee Thanksgiving Address; annual gatherings	Belonging, Mastery	Optimistic bias, spirituality through connection with nature, life dreams, relational view of resilience, shared values, affirmation of community, social and economic resources that offer a structure for thriving, shared values

promote a sense of connectedness and a sense of shared values, evident in dominant-culture systemic-resilience models. Systemic resilience and spiritual strength arise from uniting in purpose and identifying as part of a larger web of beings. Mother Earth is represented differently by each author. In both narratives, mothering is the medium that allows human love to flourish. For the Haudenosaunee, who follow the *uterine* [womb of life] line, all life is precious (Rodriguez & Wakerahkats:teh, 2017). The tone conveyed in *Braiding Sweetgrass* was one of love, protection, and generosity (Kimmerer, 2013). Kimmerer sought to embody the dignified role of mother by using the guidance and teachings of Mother Earth herself.

In both texts, Sky Woman's creation story elevated and dignified the historically oppressed roles of immigrant, mother, and woman (Kimmerer, 2013; Rodriguez & Wakerahkats:teh, 2017). Sky Woman's journey illustrated how suppressed spiritual narratives of First Nations can become key resilience processes once reinvigorated and shared by strong leaders. The narratives comprised systemic processes of mentoring, modeling, and mobilizing kin, which are components of Walsh's (2016) resiliency framework. Those stories highlighted origin, identity, home, partnership, and shared values to allow for a resilient re-indigenizing in these communities. Kimmerer (2013) described the creation story as using elements of circle of courage (Brendtro et al., 2019), where Sky Woman generously bestows gifts to earth for human sustenance and mobilizes her family to build a home (i.e., mastery). A resilient-oriented belief system was illustrated in Sky Woman's journey, which echoed existing systemic resilience frameworks, described overcoming barriers, provided a relational perspective of resilience, established a sense of coherence that makes challenges meaningful, fostered a connection with nature, considered new possibilities, and explained how Turtle Island was a dream that came true for her.

Rodriguez and Wakerahkats:teh (2017) told the story of Sky Woman within the context of her relationship with her lover and the Sky Chief, her village, and the transformation of her daughter's face into the moon. Women, mothers, and the creation of earth are central to these retellings. In this tale, each figure is responsible for their actions, creations, and roles, conveying a sense of belonging to earth and independence—both found in the circle of courage.

Tota (Grandmother) Moon is a spiritual figure who symbolizes the life-giving power of cisgendered women's wombs and parallels their cycles. Tota Moon is part of the renewal ceremony of the 13-moon vigil marked by the full moon and the gathering of Kanien'kehá:ka clan's sisterhood (Rodriguez & Wakerahkats:teh, 2017). Two of Walsh's (2016) systemic resilience processes are included in this practice: (a) a clear spiritual connection with nature and the gathering that allows for wisdom exchange and (b) collaborative problem-solving enhanced by spiritual insight through dreams and intuition. Sisterhood vigils create a sense of belonging as well as a sense of connection with earth's cycles. Similarly, the circle of courage (Brendtro et al., 2019) describes how to foster a sense of mastery through collective ability to cope in community. As part of the women's crossover ceremonies, the process of generosity is also evident in the dedication to one another, the free sharing of social support and wisdom, and the gifts that are later shared.

Resilient systems have leaders who provide guidance and nurturance, which can be achieved by providing safe containers to self-explore and learn. Illustrated in both texts, guiding youth was offered not just through ritual and gathering but also with ample opportunities to build a sense of mastery over tasks and self. Both youth crossover ceremonies that function as rites of passage (Rodriguez & Wakerahkats:teh, 2017) and cultural activities like Black Ash basket weaving (Kimmerer, 2013) are done independently, which asserts the belief that people are inherently capable, even at a young age. Likewise, dominant literature has pointed to having a resilient belief system that frames problems as manageable and coherent, with an emphasis on perseverance (Walsh, 2016) and the circle of courage's independence and mastery.

Ancestral Teachers

Ancestral teachers described in *Braiding Sweetgrass* (Kimmerer, 2013) were Sweetgrass, Cedar, Maples, Pecans, Strawberries, Beans, the Three Sisters, Fire, Black Ash, and many more. Each of these teachings supported a connection with nature, which all resilience models support (Becvar, 2013; Brendtro et al., 2019; Ungar, 2021; Walsh, 2016). Potawatomi culture, spirituality, and language recognize elements of nature as teachers with their own wisdom; for example, strawberries give their fruit to people every summer, teaching ongoing generosity (Brendtro et al., 2019; Kimmerer, 2013). In Kanien'kehá:ka moon lodge gatherings, the Bear Clan Mother invites in the grandmothers who have passed, or "ancient ones," as their ancestral teachers (Rodriguez & Wakerahkats:teh, 2017) who are the sources of wisdom, allowing for resilient contemplative practices (Walsh, 2016) and an increased sense of belonging, knowing they are held in the "womb of community" (Rodriguez & Wakerahkats:teh, 2017, p. 54).

The Original Instructions are part of the eco-centric cosmology of the Potawatomi. The instructions state all knowledge needed to live is in the land. Fire, an ancestral teacher and generative force, offers resilience. Tending fire is a practice passed between generations that offers opportunities for new fire builders to gain competency through elemental challenge, which all support a sense of mastery (Brendtro et al., 2019; Kimmerer, 2013) and promotes the resilient social resource of intergenerational mentorship. Fire building affirms the circle of courage's concept of generosity as the woods provide the resources, and fire itself is seen as a tool used by the Potawatomi to give back a regenerative force to the land. Potawatomi, the People of the Fire, have a name that affirms a spiritual belonging to nature, a resilient belief orientation recognized by Walsh (2016). In *Braiding Sweetgrass*, belonging and generosity are taught by the Maple Nation. Humans and Maples coexist and recognize their citizenship and belonging within nature as they are tied together by "mutual flourishing" (Kimmerer, 2013, p. 173). The Maples are ancestral teachers of generosity (Brendtro et al., 2019); Kimmerer's (2013) commonly asserted eco-centric value of reciprocity means exchanging social and tangible resources to be rooted in interdependence and create mutual benefit. Maples absorb carbon dioxide, exchange carbon freely, and provide syrup for consumption and carbon with the atmosphere and surrounding plants. Protecting these trees as the climate changes promotes systemic resilience by reflecting shared purpose and values, taking a proactive stance, and mobilizing kin (Becvar, 2013; Walsh, 2016).

Theme 2: Connection and Rituals

Kinship can be defined as those who are familial and culturally linked. Being part of a kinship network bolsters interdependence and connection. The texts included descriptions of ecological kinship, clan kinship, and the spiritual right to belong (Kimmerer, 2013; Rodriguez & Wakerahkats:teh, 2017). This definition is affirmed by shared practices, ceremonies, and rituals, including sacred naming. Rituals, often thought of as formalized religious rites—though not limited to these—can take the form of communal practices, sacred gatherings, holidays, rites of passage, or organized exchanges that facilitate integration and connection to tradition and one another (Walsh, 2016). More simply, rituals mark transitions and affirm connection. Examples can include ceremonies to honor Indigenous land rights that maintain interconnection between land and clan. Sacred names also denote connection, as they are only used for close relationships or in ceremonies.

Interdependence and Kinship

Braiding Sweetgrass (Kimmerer, 2013) illustrated interdependence through reciprocal relationships with more-than-human beings. As Kimmerer (2013) taught botany students to see the gifts of the land, she shared these actions are "a beginning of a reweaving of the bond between people and the land" (p. 237). This bond is already inherent to Potawatomi language and culture, which fosters a sense of broader interdependence—a strong aspect of resilient systems. A prominent example of a relationship with more-than-human-beings is sweetgrass. Both elders and scientific inquiry have shown that sweetgrass depends on sustainable human harvesting to flourish. Such knowledge affirms a larger sense of belonging and interdependence with their ecology.

The Three Sisters (i.e., corn, squash, and beans) were spiritually significant teachers of interdependence in both texts (Kimmerer, 2013; Rodriguez & Wakerahkats:teh, 2017). The ancestral teachings of the Three Sisters share that each plant has its own unique qualities and skills that form a cohesive whole. Resiliency is fostered through nurturing independence, which in turn supports the interdependent whole (i.e., circle of courage's concepts of independence and mastery). Likewise, in *A Clan Mother's Call* (Rodriguez & Wakerahkats:teh, 2017), individuals gain knowledge and skills during isolation rituals that involve *enhontonkehte* (fasting) and reflection on their unique gifts. The rituals are preceded by celebrations and community support, and the crossover ceremonies induct them into their community as respected, reflective, and skilled members. According to the family resilience frameworks, resilient systems believe in and respect individual needs and differences, along with guiding and nurturing leaders for youth (Becvar, 2013; Walsh, 2016). These crossover rituals develop independence and self-mastery within their community, which is imperative to a resilient clan (Brendtro et al., 2019).

Language of Connection

A person's worldview is shaped by their language, which affects their spirituality. Indigenous languages teach interdependence and connection with nature—both resilient values. In both texts, language was used to teach and affirm a worldview that acknowledges the sacredness of all living things. Kimmerer (2013) compared the Potawatomi worldview with how one would speak to their grandmother—that is, with respect and love. To highlight interconnection using animate language, Kimmerer (2013) wrote, "[One] treats nature like family, giving it spirit, the ability to be" (p. 60). Restoring their language reconnects their sacred relationship with creation and offers a sense of belonging. Speaking to and accepting guidance from the waters, plants, and other beings is a resilient way to handle challenges. These texts encouraged a broad view of nonhuman guidance and kinship networks. In the process of using animate language and learning the ancestral language of the Potawatomi, Kimmerer noted this cultural renewal gave spiritual significance to the more-than-human beings with whom they interact and learn from. The language is a clear social resource that affirms spiritual community and belonging to all Creation, cultivating resilience. In *A Clan Mother's Call* (Rodriguez & Wakerahkats:teh, 2017), sacred naming rituals tie a person to their role in their clan, their identity, and their gifts, providing a formalized sense of belonging, which is a resilient social resource.

Ceremony, Practice, and Ritual

Walsh (2016) indicated rituals are especially supportive to restabilize after disruption. Contemplative practices can include prayer, meditation, or other mindful activities requiring focused thought and intention (Walsh, 2016). Contemplative practices could be expanded to meditative gatherings or bearing witness, as illustrated in both texts. Likewise, Kimmerer (2013) shared rituals from several Indigenous peoples, including welcoming salmon at Cascade Head. In this West Coast Indigenous ritual, a beacon is burned to welcome salmon home to spawn. During this ceremony, the entire community participates in an intentional and contemplative spiritual practice. The fish are not captured for four days to honor their journey of renewing the people with food. The salmon teach generosity and belonging to the greater landscape of nature and all of Creation (e.g., constructs from Brendtro et al., 2019). This ritual emphasizes the community's commitment, connection to nature, and eco-centric spirituality—all elements of Walsh's (2016) strength-based framework. Belief systems and practices promote resilience to counter discord and isolation. *Braiding Sweetgrass* (Kimmerer, 2013) and *A Clan Mother's Call* (Rodriguez & Wakerahkats:teh, 2017) also explicated that shared practices mobilize the community to support their youth.

In Rodriguez and Wakerahkats:teh's (2017) text, Kanien'kehá:ka clan ceremonies and rituals induct youth into adulthood. In honor and to create a connection with Tota (Grandmother) Moon, women are given moonstone necklaces and baskets containing prayer materials. Among the practices of belonging are the red yarn ceremony to represent uterine and matrilineal lines and chants of the "Daughters of Sky Woman Song" (Rodriguez & Wakerahkats:teh, 2017, p. 69) to affirm one's origins. Crossover ceremonies result in a (a) resilient organizational structure that is dependable and reinforces commitment; (b) connection to others and nature; and (c) a communal, contemplative practice (Becvar, 2013; Ungar, 2021; Walsh, 2016). This ritual includes communal witnessing of youth entering a new life stage, which points to resilient leadership that offers guidance and nurturance for youth development.

As the Bear Clan Mother, Wakerahkats:teh has the responsibility of culturally and spiritually resourcing the clan. It is part of her role to formalize new members of the clan with a naming ceremony. Interdependence, kinship, connectedness, and shared values are solidified through these ceremonies. The naming process itself is complex and highlights the Clan Mother's pivotal role within the clan structure, which is the framework for the nation (Rodriguez & Wakerahkats:teh, 2017). The ritual of ancient naming or finding one's kasenna'on:we signifies one's role within the community and provides a framework for individual growth and independence. The guidance and structure provided by this leadership are sources of resilience.

In *Braiding Sweetgrass* (Kimmerer, 2013), the Potawatomi ritual of basket weaving with Black Ash is a significant cultural practice that offers a framework for mastery. Black Ash bark is exchanged for prayer and tobacco when the tree consents to being used for a basket. Kimmerer (2013) wrote that the baskets "remind us of the gift of other beings" (p. 151). Learning generosity through interactions with Black Ash and other harvested species can contribute to systemic resiliency. Generosity is demonstrated through reciprocity, consent, and responsibility to sustainably interact with these more-than-human beings (Brendtro et al., 2019). The ritual of Black Ash baskets has many meanings. In resilience terms, weaving parallels the resilient journey of First Nation peoples. Kimmerer noted Indigenous peoples, including the Potawatomi and their neighbors, the Kanien'kehá:ka, were brutally separated by oppressive colonial forces. The baskets comprise a ritual that represents renewed healing and wholeness; as the strands become a basket, she noted, "The journey of the basket is also the journey of a people" (Kimmerer, 2013, p. 256). Dominant frameworks (Becvar, 2013; Walsh, 2016) point to the resilience embodied by this ritual, including taking a proactive stance, generating hope, contextualizing distress, and increasing connectedness.

Theme 3: Meaning Making and Purpose

The ability to make meaning out of adversity, suffering, and ongoing hardship is one of the most important components of systemic resilience. In these texts, resilient resources include contextualizing distress, having a prophecy to guide oneself toward shared values, and strengthening one's identity when faced with challenges. Having a shared spiritual context for adversity can offer a shared and normalized view of loss and hardship that allows for a more meaningful and manageable functioning (Walsh, 2016). Prophecies share greater visions and paths forward for their people, whereas callings from important leaders ignite social action to support these visions. Sharing meaning, a calling, and purpose affirm and strengthen Indigenous identity.

Contextualize Adversity

In each text, trauma, grief, and depression became sources of meaning. Contextualizing adversity and suffering are hallmarks of becoming resilient (Becvar, 2013; Ungar, 2021; Walsh, 2016). Rodriguez and Wakerahkats:teh (2017) named depression and mental unease as "separation from spirit" (p. 58), and Kimmerer (2013) explained ecological restoration as an "antidote to despair" (p. 328) that offers a sense of agency, an anchor in grief, and a hopeful orientation. Iakoiane Wakerahkats:teh, the Condoled Bear Clan Mother, called for ecological justice and the revival of her nation's cultural memory. The Potawatomi elders, whom Kimmerer described, offer direction regarding ecological and cultural loss through a prophecy of the Eighth Fire that calls for reciprocity and ecological justice. Through positive outlooks, proactive approaches, and active initiatives, these prophetic contexts support resilience.

Crossover ceremonies are an opportunity to overcome a series of challenges and create positive change. Wakerahkats:teh affirmed that life's obstacles can instruct and offer a sense of cohesiveness and purpose; for example, when she advised youth to "walk with fear" (Rodriguez & Wakerahkats:teh, 2017, p. 60), Wakerahkats:teh invited them to build a relationship with fear rather than be consumed by it. The crossover rituals and accompanying contemplation periods in isolation lead to a deeper understanding of the interdependence of all living creatures because of the challenge of receiving messages from the spirit. During this time apart, participants learn (a) self-control; (b) a remembrance of who they are and to whom they belong; (c) adaptability to new conditions; and (d) mastery over their own fears, which results in discovering their resilience.

Iakoiane Wahkerahkats:teh emphasized that, through the nurtured youth development in crossover rituals, their nation is rebuilt culturally after much trauma and loss. Clan members' gifts are honored—belonging is not just implied but is part of the initiation process. Wakerahkats:teh began her initiations by saying, "We gather here to remind you that you are our children, you belong to us, we claim you" (Rodriguez & Wakerahkats:teh, 2017, p. 54). This description augments Walsh's (2016) one of mobilizing kin as a social resource that promotes resilience.

In both texts, being estranged from Creation was countered with belonging. Kimmerer (2013) highlighted this species' loneliness as a modern phenomenon that Indigenous spirituality and wisdom can transform. Through assisting salamanders in a perilous road crossing, Kimmerer built a bridge between herself and more-than-human beings in distress. The practice promotes connectedness and reduces xenophobia, or fear of otherness. In saving the salamanders, she reinforced her sense of belonging to all Creation. Even as she mourned distant perils of war, salamanders that died, and other happenings in the world she could not control, she could grieve knowing she belonged. In her description of the experience, Kimmerer highlighted three resilience processes associated with spirituality: (a) connection to nature, (b) spiritual inspiration expressed through social action, and (c) proactively mobilizing kin.

Prophecies and Calling

Indigenous leaders and spiritual figures use prophecies and callings to provide cultural guidance to their people. Both the Condoled Bear Clan Mother's calling and the Potawatomi prophecy of the Eighth Fire call for ecological or green paths to avoid destruction of nature (Kimmerer, 2013; Rodriguez & Wakerahkats:teh, 2017). There is a consensus in these teachings that this time in history is critical to collective well-being for humans, the Earth, and more-than-human-beings (e.g., spiritual forces). The texts shared the same values, contexts, and directions during climate distress and the voice of strong leadership that nurtures, guides, and protects. Leaders who guide, nurture, and protect youth development implement a resilience process that the family resiliency model and the circle of courage frameworks address. Walsh's (2016) framework addresses this process directly as an organizational structure that fosters resilience; the circle of courage's concept of mastery relies on mentors to foster competence and skillfulness.

The Great Law of Peace also appeared in both texts, as did the Peacemaker—an important cultural and spiritual figure. As described by Kimmerer (2013) in *Braiding Sweetgrass*, the Great Law of Peace guides current social action for ecological justice and reclaims the polluted land that the Onondaga people used to cultivate. Kimmerer (2013) wrote that the Great Law is a guide to "act on behalf of peace, the natural

world, and future generations" (p. 319). These actions require perseverance, hope, and commitment to their shared spiritual values, which all
display resilience. Their commitment to one another and future generations ties in with the concept of generosity (Brendtro et al., 2019).
A focus on hope, social action, and mutual support are themes that align
with all dominant multisystemic resilience frameworks (Becvar, 2013;
Ungar, 2021; Walsh, 2016).

Cultural practices that bring renewal and intergenerational healing were described in both texts. *A Clan Mother's Call* (Rodriguez &
Wakerahkats:teh, 2017) restored Haudenosaunee cultural memory by
retrieving their creation story and spiritual practices. Wakerahkats:teh's
spiritual tradition and inherent resilience called for imagining new possibilities and initiating social action. Likewise, in *Braiding Sweetgrass*
(Kimmerer, 2013), resilient teachings and inspiration for social action
came from cultural practices, elders in her community, and more-than-
human teachers.

Affirmations of Identity

A declaration of belonging was expressed in the *Braiding Sweetgrass*
(Kimmerer, 2013) Thanksgiving Address, which affirmed "our minds are
one" (p. 107). This address affirmed not only belonging but also a connected orientation to more-than-human-beings and connection to earth
as it is recited by youth to affirm their cultural identity. The Bear Clan
Mother recreated crossover rituals, Moon lodge gatherings, and many
affirmations of belonging. The Condoled Clan Bear Mother said she realized, "Yes, Grandma moon is in me" (Rodriguez & Wakerahkats:teh,
2017, p. 67) to affirm a sense of spiritual and cultural belonging. The
Moon Lodge is described as a place for ceremony, purification, and the
transition to womanhood. The Moon Lodge provides a place for clan
members to address cultural loss and other forms of spiritual separation
through communal healing and sharing. Likewise, during annual gatherings of the Potawatomi people, Kimmerer (2013) highlighted collaborative problem solving and grief. Cultural teachings, such as that of the
pecan, stresses "standing together for the benefit of all" (Kimmerer, 2013,
p. 21). The gatherings in both texts facilitate spiritual rituals, collective
grieving, and problem solving and allow generosity to be practiced.

Kanien'kehá:ka clan naming rituals reflect attributes of belonging, community roles, and connectedness and are consistent with affirmations of identity throughout both texts. Their tradition focuses on complex rituals associated with naming, which establish a child's belonging and role in the community. Many elements are included in the naming process, including family names, dreams, tobacco gifts, and alignment with a certain leadership lineage. By naming, they affirm their shared spiritual and cultural values, use the Clan Mother's guidance, and are connected to both spiritual and cultural communities.

Clinical Implications

Resilience is fostered in community and is fueled by relationships (Walsh, 2016, 2023). Stories, images, and metaphors from these texts call therapists to understand their clients' cultural memories, ceremonies, and traditions—contrasting existing counseling theories that prioritize a Western model of individualism (e.g., assessing cognitions or behaviors without examining context). With individual and relational clients who request that their traditions be integrated into clinical sessions, it is important for therapists to ask about guides, spiritual figures, and rituals. Clinicians should deepen their understanding and use of clients' languages. Existing literature has noted the importance of open communication (Walsh, 2016), and these texts have advocated for a deeper understanding of how language itself can instill spirit and respect into the world and bolster connection and belonging.

Themes from this analysis augment existing spiritually integrated therapy literature. Puchalski and Romer (2000) articulated questions to assess if clients want their faith, religion, or worldview to be discussed in session. Therapists working with First Nation and Indigenous clients must identify client-centered language used to convey culturally attuned sources of resilience; for example, it may be helpful for counselors to inquire about how organized spiritual ceremonies affect their role in the family and how the family supports this transition when discussing organized spiritual ceremonies. These questions can offer unique outcomes or be hidden stories that families can draw upon when confronted with oppressive forces, transition, instability, or loss.

Questions such as "Who do you love?", "Who offers you protection?", and "How do you define generosity?" can increase a culturally attuned dialogue. It is important for clinicians to be curious without expecting clients to educate them about a culture at large. Specific questions that relate to the presenting problem may help guide the conversation. For example, "How would your elders understand your situation. How may it be different from how you understand what is going on?" could be gentle ways to understand the clients' spiritual and cultural contexts.

It is important to remember that words have multiple meetings influenced by social location. Sisters can connote biological relationships or spiritual metaphors (e.g., kinship connections, relationship to the Earth). It is important to clarify language and listen to how clients use terms. Therapists working with First Nation clients must re-envision talking about relationships to include the living, departed ancestors, and the natural world. For many Indigenous clients, asking about their Creation narrative as related to kin, culture, and place may help clients and clinicians gain a better understanding of the client's sense of belonging and identity.

Using rituals and experiential interventions may be significant. Therapists can ask about or cocreate rituals (e.g., incorporating elements of spiritual retreats or visions) when working with First Nation or Indigenous clients. An example from *A Clan Mother's Call* that highlighted a significant overlap between the therapeutic work of counselors and their spiritual practices was the act of witnessing, which occurs in their crossover ceremonies as a significant offering from elders to youth (Rodriguez & Wakerahkats:teh, 2017). If a client has similar lived experiences in their culture, knowing what elements of an elders' witnessing were most powerful for the client could further support rapport. This work should be client-centered, and consultation with elders or clinical supervisors who are embedded within or have cultivated rich relationships with Indigenous clients is important.

Clients in traditional therapy sessions tend to be individuals or select family members (e.g., caregivers and children). These texts highlight the importance of community and how therapy can be done in community settings. These larger settings may afford communities the opportunity to reflect on their needs. If the client system consists of an individual, therapists should not dismiss the importance of community—the family and beyond—even if those members are not in session.

Conclusion

Further theoretical and empirical researchers should consider mapping resilience processes specific to an adverse experience impacting their communities. Linguistic maps may provide nuance into how systemic resilience themes show up based on different identities, such as two-spirit communities. There are additional domains to explore (e.g., rematriation of leadership, expanded notions of belonging to more-than-human networks, and language itself as a means of affirming belonging). Mapping systemic resilience parallels Kimmerer's (2013) process to pursue a holistic and decolonized approach to biology (i.e., though Westernized biology training offered Kimmerer a structure to observe, holistic Indigenous teachings offered resilient resources to deepen reciprocity and relationship to creation). Practitioners can incorporate this model into their work, promoting systemic resilience with clients across social locations.

Many Indigenous frameworks focus on specific presenting problems (Gone, 2022). These models and techniques need to be amplified when working with Indigenous clients and in clinical training programs. The Building the Sacred program evaluation framework was developed specifically for First Nation victim assistance programs (Polansky & Echo-Hawk, 2021). Using principles from Indigenous culture, such as resiliency and self-determination, *Culture Forward* provided a guide for suicide prevention (O'Keefe et al., 2022). There is much work promoting Indigenous-attuned therapy, and there is more work to be done.

In and out of sessions, Indigenous voices must be centered, Indigenous-led dialogues supported, and knowledge systems that reduce Indigenous ways of knowing to less than Eurocentric sources disrupted (Cox et al., 2021; Datta, 2018; Singh et al., 2020). Indigenous stories can help clinicians better understand resilience. In *Braiding Sweetgrass* (Kimmerer, 2013) and *A Clan Mother's Call* (Rodriguez & Wakerahkats:teh, 2017), Indigenous peoples demonstrated a sense of belonging by tuning into nature and connecting to teachers, ancestors, moon cycles, and rituals. Lessons from these stories may assist clinicians in supporting clients as they navigate their lives.

References

Anderson, D. A. (2009). Beauty heals. *Journal of Spirituality in Mental Health*, *11*, 78–87. https://doi.org/10.1080/19349630902864259

Aponte, H. J. (2002). Spirituality: The heart of therapy. *Journal of Family Psychotherapy*, *13*(1–2), 13–27. https://doi.org/10.1300/J085v13n01_02

Becvar, D. S. (2013). *Handbook of family resilience*. Springer. https://doi.org/10.1007/978-1-4614-3917-2

Brave Heart, M. Y. H., Chase, J., Elkins, J., & Altschul, D. B. (2011). Historical trauma among Indigenous Peoples of the Americas: Concepts, research, and clinical considerations. *Journal of Psychoactive Drugs*, *43*(4), 282–290. https://doi.org/10.1080/02791072.2011. 628913

Brendtro, L., Brokenleg, M., & Van Bockern, S. (2019). *Reclaiming youth at risk: Futures of promise* (3rd ed.). Solution Tree.

Cox, G. R., FireMoon, P., Anastario, M. P., Ricker, A., Escarcega-Growing Thunder, R., Baldwin, J. A., & Rink, E. (2021). Indigenous standpoint theory as a theoretical framework for decolonizing social science health research with American Indian communities. *AlterNative: An International Journal of Indigenous Peoples*, *17*(4), 460–468. https://doi.org/10.1177/11771801211042019

Datta, R. (2018). Decolonizing both researcher and research and its effectiveness in Indigenous research. *Research Ethics Review*, *14*(2), 1–24. https://doi.org/10.1177/1747016117733296

Dell, C., Seguin, M., Hopkins, C., Tempier, R., Mehl-Madrona, L., Dell, D., Duncan, R., & Mosier, K. (2011). From Benzos to berries: Treatment offered at an Aboriginal youth solvent abuse treatment centre relays the importance of culture. *Canadian Journal of Psychiatry*, *56*(2), 75–83. https://doi.org/10.1177/070674371105600202

Elliott, N. (2020). Can spiritual ecograms be utilized in mental health services to promote culturally appropriate family and couples therapy with Indigenous people? *First Peoples Child & Family Review*, *7*(1), 118–126. https://doi.org/10.7202/1068869ar

Eppler, C., & Hutchings, J. (2020). The use of cinematherapy to illustrate systemic resilience. *Journal of Clinical Psychology*, *76*(8), 1463–1471. https://doi.org/10.1002/jclp.22998

Gameon, J. A., & Skewes, M. C. (2020). A systematic review of trauma interventions in Native communities. *American Journal of Community Psychology*, *65*(1–2), 223–241. https://doi.org/10.1002/ajcp.12396

Gockel, A. (2011). Client perspectives on spirituality in the therapeutic relationship. *Humanistic Psychologist, 39*(2), 154–168. https://doi.org/10.1080/08873267.2011.564959

Gone, J. P. (2022). Re-imagining mental health services for American Indian communities: Centering Indigenous perspectives. *American Journal of Community Psychology, 69*, 257–268. https://doi.org/10.1002/ajcp.12591

Griffith, J. L., & Griffith, M. E. (2002). *Encountering the sacred in psychotherapy: How to talk with people about their spiritual lives.* Guilford Press.

Hernández-Wolfe, P. (2011). Decolonization and "mental" health: A mestiza's journey in the borderlands. *Women & Therapy, 34*, 293–306. https://doi.org/10.1080/02703149.2011.580687

Johns, R. D. (2017). Stories matter: Narrative themes of counselor educators' religious and spiritual competency. *Counseling and Values, 62*(1), 72–89. https://doi.org/10.1002/cvj.12050

Kimmerer, R. W. (2013). *Braiding sweetgrass: Indigenous wisdom, scientific knowledge and the teachings of plants.* Milkweed Editions.

Kirmayer, L., Dandeneau, S., Marshall, E., Phillips, M. K., & Williamson, K. J. (2011). Rethinking resilience from Indigenous perspectives. *Canadian Journal of Psychiatry, 56*(2), 84–91. https://doi.org/10.1177/070674371105600203

Moorehead, V. D., Gone, J. P., & December, D. (2015). A gathering of Native American healers: Exploring the interface of Indigenous tradition and professional practice. *American Journal of Community Psychology, 56*(3–4), 383–394. https://doi.org/10.1007/s10464-015-9747-6

Morrison, J. Q., Clutter, S. M., Pritchett, E. M., & Demmitt, A. (2009). Perceptions of clients and counseling professionals regarding spirituality in counseling. *Counseling and Values, 53*(3), 183–194. https://doi.org/10.1002/j.2161-007x.2009.tb00124.x

O'Keefe, V. M., Waugh, E., Grubin, F., Cwik, M., Chambers, R., Ivanich, J., Weeks, R., & Barlow, A. (2022). Development of "CULTURE FORWARD: A strengths and culture-based tool to protect our native youth from suicide." *Cultural Diversity and Ethnic Minority Psychology.* Advance online publication. https://doi.org/10.1037/cdp0000546

Olson, M. J. (2003). Counselor understanding of Native American spiritual loss. *Counseling and Values, 47*(2), 109–117. https://doi.org/10.1002/j.2161-007X.2003.tb00228.x

Petry, S. (2016). Spirituality and the family life cycle. In M. McGoldrick, N. G. Preto, & B. Carter (Eds.), *The expanding family life cycle* (5th ed., pp. 156–171). Pearson.

Polansky, L., & Echo-Hawk, A. (2021). *Building the sacred: An Indigenous evaluation framework for programs serving Native survivors of violence.* Urban Indian Health Institute.

Pomerville, A., Burrage, R. L., & Gone, J. P. (2016). Empirical findings from psychotherapy research with Indigenous populations: A systematic review. *Journal of Consulting and Clinical Psychology, 84*(12), 1023–1038. https://doi.org/10.1037/ccp0000150

Puchalski, C., & Romer, A. L. (2000). Taking a spiritual history allows clinicians to understand patients more fully. *Journal of Palliative Medicine, 3*(1), 129–137. https://doi.org/10.1089/jpm.2000.3.129

Robertson, L. A. (2010). The spiritual competency scale. *Counseling and Values, 55*, 6–24. https://doi.org/10.1002/j.2161-007X.2010.tb00019.x

Rodriguez, J., & Wakerahkats:teh, I. (2017). *A clan mother's call: Reconstructing Haudenosaunee cultural memory*. Routledge.

Rowan, M., Poole, N., Shea, B., Mykota, D., Farag, M., Hopkins, C., Hall, L., Mushquash, C., Fornssler, B., & Dell, C. A. (2015). A scoping study of cultural interventions to treat addictions in Indigenous populations: Methods, strategies and insights from a Two-Eyed Seeing approach. *Substance Abuse Treatment, Prevention and Policy, 10*(1), 26–26. https://doi.org/10.1186/s13011-015-0021-6

Schick, M. R., Kirk-Provencher, K. T., Goldstein, S. C., Nalven, T., & Spillane, N. S. (2021). A framework for the adaptation of positive psychological interventions to North American Indigenous populations. *Prevention Science, 22*(7), 913–922. https://doi.org/10.1007/s11121-021-01282-z

Singh, A. A., Appling, B., & Trepal, H. (2020). Using the multicultural and social justice counseling competencies to decolonize counseling practice: The important roles of theory, power, and action. *Journal of Counseling & Development, 98*(3), 261–271. https://doi.org/10.1002/jcad.12321

Thambinathan, V., & Kinsella, E. A. (2021). Decolonizing methodologies in qualitative research: Creating spaces for transformative praxis. *International Journal of Qualitative Methods, 20*. https://doi.org/10.1177/16094069211014766

Ungar, M. (Ed.). (2021). *Multisystemic resilience: Adaptation and transformation in contexts of change*. Oxford University Press.

Walls, M. L., & Whitbeck, L. B. (2012). The intergenerational effects of relocation policies on Indigenous families. *Journal of Family Issues, 33*(9), 1272–1293. https://doi.org/10.1177/0192513X12447178

Walsh, F. (Ed.). (2009). *Spiritual resources in family therapy* (2nd ed.). Guilford Press.

Walsh, F. (2016). *Strengthening family resilience* (3rd ed.). Guilford Press.

Walsh, F. (2023). Complex and traumatic loss: Fostering healing and resilience. Guilford Press.

Wendt, D. C., & Gone, J. P. (2012). Rethinking cultural competence: Insights from Indigenous community treatment settings. *Transcultural Psychiatry, 49*(2), 206–222. https://doi.org/10.1177/1363461511425622

4

APPROACHING RESILIENCE THROUGH CONTEXTUAL AND SYSTEMIC FRAMEWORKS

Elizabeth R. Watters and Gita Seshadri

Dr. Elizabeth Watters (they/them) is a 28-year-old, White, middle-class, able-bodied, autistic, gender queer, bisexual individual. They are an eye-movement desensitization and reprocessing (EMDR)-trained couple and family therapist who specializes in working with complex posttraumatic stress disorder (PTSD) and providing gender-affirming care for transgender and gender-expansive individuals. Their research focuses on examining the biopsychosocial outcomes following childhood trauma and adversity across key developmental periods, including adolescence, emerging adulthood, and later adulthood. They are particularly interested in examining resilience factors that can mitigate negative outcomes following childhood trauma and adversity.

Dr. Gita Seshadri (she/her) is a South Asian American, middle-class, able-bodied, heterosexual female with a chronic illness. She is a licensed marriage and family therapist who specializes in working with interracial couples and families. She also works with couples and individuals with various life transitions and with those who experience trauma, grief, chronic illness, and substance abuse. Her research focus includes topics centered around women; African American families; sex and sexuality; cultural humility, gender, and

DOI: 10.4324/9781003373513-4

*power; interracial couples and families; process-based research; and trauma.
She seeks to understand how those who have experienced childhood trauma
and hardship find and cultivate resilience and strength within themselves and
their relationships.*

Resiliency theory provides a theoretical framework for understanding
the role of promotive and protective factors and their association with
biological, psychological, and sociological outcomes across developmental stages in at-risk individuals facing significant life stressors or
adversity (Richardson, 2002; Smith-Osborne, 2007). Richardson (2002)
described three waves of resiliency inquiry, including (a) first exploring
characteristics of individuals who thrive in the face of adversity; (b) then
identifying the process of attaining these resilience characteristics or
qualities and examining resilience as a process of coping with stressors
and adversity; (c) and solidifying the concept of resilience as a process
of reintegrating and adapting to the disruption adversity causes, which
requires motivational energy. As phenomenological research led to this
grounded understanding of resilience, literature has provided foundational insight into how resilience and key resilience factors are developmental constructs (Richardson, 2002; Smith-Osborne, 2007).

As the definition of resilience has expanded, scholars have opera-
tionalized three different definitions: trait, outcome, and process (Hu
et al., 2015; Lee et al., 2013; Raghavan & Sandanapitchai, 2020). Trait
resilience conceptualizes resilience as a fixed and stable personality trait
that increases an individual's tendency to positively adjust and adapt to
adverse experiences (Hu et al., 2015; Lee et al., 2013), which researchers
have demonstrated helps protect individuals from the impact of trauma
and adversity (Connor & Davidson, 2003). An example of trait resilience
is using determination to accomplish a goal. A trait is a "function or
behavioral outcome that can conquer and help individuals recover from
adversity" (Hu et al., 2015, p. 18).

Process resilience conceptualizes resilience as a "dynamic process" (Hu
et al., 2015, p. 18) where individuals adapt to and recover from adverse
life events (Luthar et al., 2000). For instance, grieving parents navigate
holding on to a child's memory while letting go of having the child physically present or confront the complicated grief after the death of a child.
Luthar and colleagues (2000) highlighted that process resilience includes

three sets of factors including "(1) attributes of the children themselves, (2) aspects of their families, and (3) characteristics of their wider social environments" (p. 544). In this chapter, we focus on the limitations of trait resilience and the strengths of promoting engaging resilience as culturally and contextually specific processes and outcomes (see Figure 4.1).

Historically, resilience has not always been viewed through these more developmental and systemic lenses. Oversimplistic definitions of resilience are still prevalent as of 2023; for example, resilience has been broadly defined as "a process of adapting well in the face of adversity, trauma, tragedy, threats, or significant sources of stress" (American Psychological Association [APA], 2014, para. 4, APA style. Such definitions have focused on individual traits and attributes that help clients bounce back from adversity (Bryant et al., 2022; Ojukwu et al., 2022). However, this definition limits how clinicians approach resilience through a contextual, systemic lens (Raghavan & Sandanapitchai, 2020). Walsh (1996, 2016) encouraged researchers, academics, and mental health professionals to think about resilience from a systemic perspective; however, more can be done to deepen this conversation. In this chapter, we start with a general critique of resilience and then focus specifically on the oppressive nature of trait resilience.

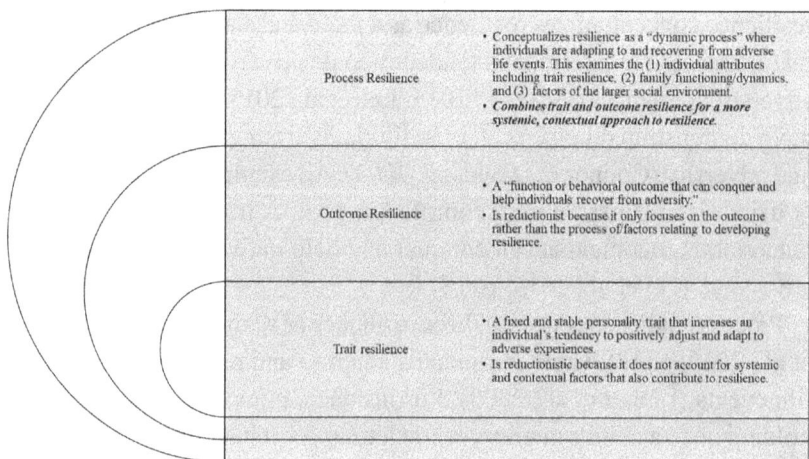

Process Resilience	• Conceptualizes resilience as a "dynamic process" where individuals are adapting to and recovering from adverse life events. This examines the (1) individual attributes including trait resilience, (2) family functioning/dynamics, and (3) factors of the larger social environment. • *Combines trait and outcome resilience for a more systemic, contextual approach to resilience.*
Outcome Resilience	• A "function or behavioral outcome that can conquer and help individuals recover from adversity." • Is reductionist because it only focuses on the outcome rather than the process of factors relating to developing resilience.
Trait resilience	• A fixed and stable personality trait that increases an individual's tendency to positively adjust and adapt to adverse experiences. • Is reductionistic because it does not account for systemic and contextual factors that also contribute to resilience.

Figure 4.1 Types of resilience.

Critique of Resilience

Taking a critical approach to resilience requires acknowledging the concept is not neutral in US society or extant literature (DeVerteuil & Golubchikov, 2016). Resilience has been regularly co-opted by dominant power systems as a governance tool (O'Hare & White, 2013). This co-opted resilience has been used to push inherently privileged, oppressive societal narratives and dominant discourses (Cretney, 2014; DeVerteuil & Golubchikov, 2016; MacKinnon & Derickson, 2013).

Faux resilient phrases such as "pull yourself up by your bootstraps" or "just find a silver lining" minimize the influence of culture and circumstance and provide an empty response to complex situations. Such sayings perpetuate societal narratives that imply if one simply works "hard enough," they can elevate themselves without access to outside support or resources. When resilience carries these subtle but pervasive agendas, it becomes a way to reinforce societal discourses held by those in positions of power to further marginalize, oppress, and discriminate individuals with historically oppressed identities (DeVerteuil & Golubchikov, 2016). Suppose a husband blames his wife for the developmental gaps of their children without realizing they were born prematurely in a patriarchal foreign country where she cannot seek additional medical care because he was not present at birth. The goal of resilience is not to plan for how the children will behave. Rather, the objective is to address injustices by providing parenting supports and removing as many barriers as possible to support family growth and cohesion.

Clinicians should be aware that clients can experience pressure to accept and adjust to their unjust environments instead of acknowledging they are having a normal reaction to a system of oppression. Scholars who have approached resilience through cultural, systemic, and socioecological lenses have highlighted that, because of these narratives surrounding resilience, it is imperative that therapists intentionally deconstruct their perceptions of resilience (Dulin et al., 2018; Ojukwu et al., 2022). Therapists should work practically to (a) be aware of how the current conceptualization of trait resilience is harmful and used to push oppressive societal discourses, (b) deconstruct any internalized narratives they carry so they do not project these onto clients, and (c) help to normalize and deconstruct clients' reactions to harmful ideas about resilience. In the prior example of husband and wife, mental health professionals must acknowledge a certain resilience trait (e.g., determination) will not resolve their children's symptoms. Systemic resilience creates opportunities for the family to focus on dynamics and intersectional contexts (e.g., role of culture, gender, family expectations).

Several meta-analytic studies have demonstrated how higher trait resilience is associated with decreased mental health symptoms, including depression (Hu et al., 2015; Lee et al., 2013; Watters et al., 2023). Yet, most articles synthesized in these meta-analytic studies have included largely heterogeneous study samples that are dominantly white, heterosexual, and affluent (Hu et al., 2015; Lee et al., 2013; Watters et al., 2023). We cannot overgeneralize and apply these findings to the lived experiences of individuals who have multiple oppressed identities in the United States, especially given that individuals with intersecting, marginalized identities face systemic inequalities tied to their ability to experience resilience as a bidirectional interaction between themselves, their family systems, and other systems that contribute to their success in overcoming adversity (Dulin et al., 2018; Ojukwu et al., 2022; Ungar, 2013, 2016). To illustrate how to avoid the pitfalls of overgeneralization, we present and synthesize a case study using our preferred model—contextual family therapy—while incorporating inclusive resilience. Though clinicians may not use the same model, we encourage consideration of this type of integration.

Contextual Family Therapy

Contextual family therapy was founded by Boszormenyi-Nagy (2014) and is an integrated therapeutic model that evolved as an extension of intergenerational family therapy and asserts that four dimensions of reality influence relationships: facts, individual psychology, systemic interactions, and relational ethics (Ducommun-Nagy, 2019; Hargrave & Pfitzer, 2003). Concepts within the theory help define the following family processes:

1. Destructive entitlement, where individuals experience the denial of entitlement from their family of origin, and, in turn, seek what they believed to be owed to them through a different relationship.

2. Parentification captures the process where a child attempts to earn love and acceptance from their parent by taking on the role of a parent or caregiver.
3. Split loyalty includes being loyal to one and simultaneously disloyal to another within a family system.
4. Constructive entitlement includes equal give and take in a relationship and further contributes to a lack of trustworthiness (Goldenthal, 1996; Hargrave & Pfitzer, 2003; Sweeney, 2019).

Additionally, when examining how family systems function, contextual family therapy focuses on two types of relational dynamics: vertical relationships (i.e., relationships between people in different generations) and horizontal relationships (i.e., relationships between people from the same generation).

> **Case Example (Session 1):** A mother–daughter dyad present for therapy. The mother (Mira) is a 45-year-old, able-bodied, cisgender female, heterosexual, Asian American immigrant, small business owner, with a low–middle socioeconomic position. The daughter (Naomi) is a 16-year-old, able-bodied, cisgender female, bisexual, first-generation Asian American with a learning disorder (i.e., dyslexia). Her father (Takeshi) was an able bodied, cisgender male, heterosexual, first-generation Asian American with a chronic illness; however, he had passed away three years prior, when Naomi was 12 years old. The mother–daughter dyad presented to therapy because the daughter became pregnant, and the mother wished her to give the child up for adoption upon its birth. During the intake session, Mira shared she felt lost and frustrated, and though she had never considered therapy before, she did not know what other options she had. Mira reported she "just wanted [her] daughter to make the right decision" and "not throw [her] whole life potential away this young." Mira also shared that Naomi was just acting out because she did not respect her the way that she respected Takeshi. In response to this statement, Naomi shared she felt "misunderstood" and "like a failure," but also shared she felt pressured to make a decision, leaving her feeling "numb" and just wanting to "escape."

Contextual Family Therapy Intervention: Establish a therapeutic relationship to establish and explore loyalty through multidirected partiality. With this family, the therapist would empathize and create a dialogue with Mira and Naomi. The therapist would make attempts to understand the ledger between them and Takeshi's role in the ledger, despite his physical absence in the room.

Integration of Process Resilience: Part of establishing multidirected partiality is also connecting with the family based on their experiences of acculturation by identifying and honoring the inherent strengths and resilience factors related to their cultural and familial practices, traditions, values, and beliefs.

Oppressive Nature of Viewing Resilience as a Trait

With trait resilience, it is important to deconstruct the innately harmful and oppressive nature of viewing resilience through this lens. Approaching resilience as a personality trait implies it is something one either does or does not possess, which is a very reductionist and linear way to conceptualize resilience. This approach blatantly ignores the systemic oppression, marginalization, and barriers embedded in US history and present society for many individuals. Resilience must be viewed from cultural and systemic perspectives (Bermudez & Mancini, 2012; Ungar, 2013). Ungar (2013) concluded that resilience is largely determined by one's environment and ability to promote growth. Resilience needs to be examined within and between populations, as there are similarities and differences between them. Moreover, the resilience one develops is influenced by the level of risk exposure and the protective factors present in their personal and cultural contexts.

Specifically, Cardoso and Thompson (2010) highlighted how, in Latinx communities, resilience is embedded within individual characteristics, family strengths, cultural factors, and community support. Bermudez and Mancini (2012) expanded upon this notion in their book chapter by walking through the specific protective factors present in Latinx families, including "ideals of *personalismo*, which is an emphasis on positive interpersonal relationships, *respeto*/respect, loyalty, *consejos*/advice, *dichos*, and fatalism, which is a form of acceptance, especially of things that cannot change" (p. 219). Additionally, Bryant and colleagues (2022) spoke to how resilience has impacted the Black community in harmful ways by ignoring the histories of slavery, past and present segregation, medical experimentation, and numerous other contextual factors contributing to the allostatic load of Black individuals living with these chronic stressors. Bryant et al. (2022) asserted that practitioners who are

> Committed to engaging in culturally responsive practices . . . in the lives of Black Americans whose health has been compromised by repeated exposure to chronic and acute stress and sheer determination to demonstrate resilience in their everyday lives [and that] responsive practices must be characterized by clinical approaches that are socially and critically informed; grounded in social justice; cocreating reasonable hope.
>
> (p. 20)

We revisit the case using this deepened framework:

Case Example Continued (Sessions 2–3): Mira shared her family of origin dynamics, patterns, and expectations. She disclosed she was the oldest of five children, and her parents expected her to help take care of her younger siblings and help manage the household growing up. By the age of 6, she would help with making family meals, handling chores, and raising her younger siblings. Mira shared that on top of helping with the younger children, she worked hard in school so she could be the first person in her family to seek secondary schooling. She disclosed that as the oldest, her parents also expected her to support them as they aged. She expressed she was used to being the primary emotional caregiver and silent supporter for the family.

Contextual Family Therapy Intervention: In these sessions, the therapist can use an intergenerational genogram to explore the function of destructive entitlement and parentification. Additionally, the genogram can highlight patterns of triangulation, legacies, ledgers, overt and invisible loyalties, and indebtedness.

Integration of Process Resilience: To balance highlighting the mentioned systemic patterns within the family, resilience perspectives can be integrated to highlight intergenerational strength, endurance, commitment to honoring and caring for older generations, and the commitment to improving the quality of life for younger generations.

These key pieces of literature help exemplify the importance of examining resilience through contextual, systemic lenses. We know that one's ability to adapt and overcome hardships is largely influenced by their intersecting identities, along with cultural and contextual variables. For example, Hays's (1996) ADDRESSING framework (i.e., age, disability, religion, ethnicity, socioeconomic status, sexual orientation, indigenous heritage, national origin, and gender) can be employed to fully understand a client's identity and appropriately consider how to integrate process resilience with them. According to Hays, integrating this approach provides clinicians and researchers with a framework for understanding underrepresented groups and oppressive forces by exploring the complexities of intersecting identities in psychology (Hays, 1996, 2008; Kaplin, 2014). This intersectional approach implies that, if an individual is white, cisgender, heterosexual, educated, middle–upper class, abled bodied, and speaks English fluently, they will score higher in trait resilience.

Counter to this approach, individuals who face more systemic barriers, oppression, and marginalization because of their race/ethnicity, gender, sexual orientation, socioeconomic status, developmental or acquired disabilities, national origin/language, and/or religion in US society may appear less resilient. We encourage mental health professionals to think about themselves and their clients in these ways to acknowledge how these social locations can affect themselves and their relationships. Further, the intersection of these locations can be a conglomeration of what affects and integrates into the resiliency process.

The contrast illustrates how society (i.e., the environment in which these individuals live; Ungar, 2013) is built around the needs of privileged, majority individuals. Individuals with multiple oppressed identities do not lack traits related to resilience; however, individuals with multiple oppressed identities have less power, privilege, and resources to dedicate to their growth and help adapt to adversity. As clinicians, researchers, and scholars working in the United States, it is imperative we are aware of the complex, perpetual trauma many individuals face by simply existing in this society as well as their intersections of identities and social locations while interacting with other systems. Without this awareness, we will perpetuate harmful, oppressive narratives when working to foster growth, change, and resilience in clinical settings. By adopting a systemic, contextual approach to resilience, we can value, honor, and emphasize unique cultural and familial strengths of clients from across social locations, rather than devaluing diverse cultural norms that do not align with privileged, majority-centered ideas based on the nuclear family standards that are seen as historically "ideal" in dominant US society.

Case Example Continued (Sessions 4–5): In these sessions, Naomi shared that she was surprised to learn about some of her mother's background, sharing she did not realize how much her mother went through to get to where she is now. She also shared how different her experiences felt being raised as an only child. She shared she felt like her parents expected her to go to college and already knew what she wanted to do with her life but that she did not know what she wanted to be yet. She also shared that she felt pressure to emotionally support her mother and "be perfect" after her father died, but she felt like she was "failing both [her] parents." She shared that she also missed her father and felt like he would have been more supportive and understanding than her mother was being.

Contextual Family Therapy Intervention: In these sessions, the therapist can reframe entitlement and connect it to loyalty and fairness (i.e., balancing the ledger) within the context of their cultural practices, values, and beliefs. This practice will allow both clients to feel heard, be recognized, and thereby empathize with each other (see Figure 4.2).

Integration of Process Resilience: Process resilience can be integrated to help both the mother and daughter appreciate the unique strengths they each possess that have helped them navigate their own unique life stressors, creating new intergenerational legacies.

Case Example Continued (Sessions 6–7): During these sessions, communication became more balanced as both mother and daughter started to accept more influence from each other, which balanced the ledger between them. Mira began to acknowledge the pressure she was putting on her daughter and how she would give her the silent treatment due to her own feelings of loneliness

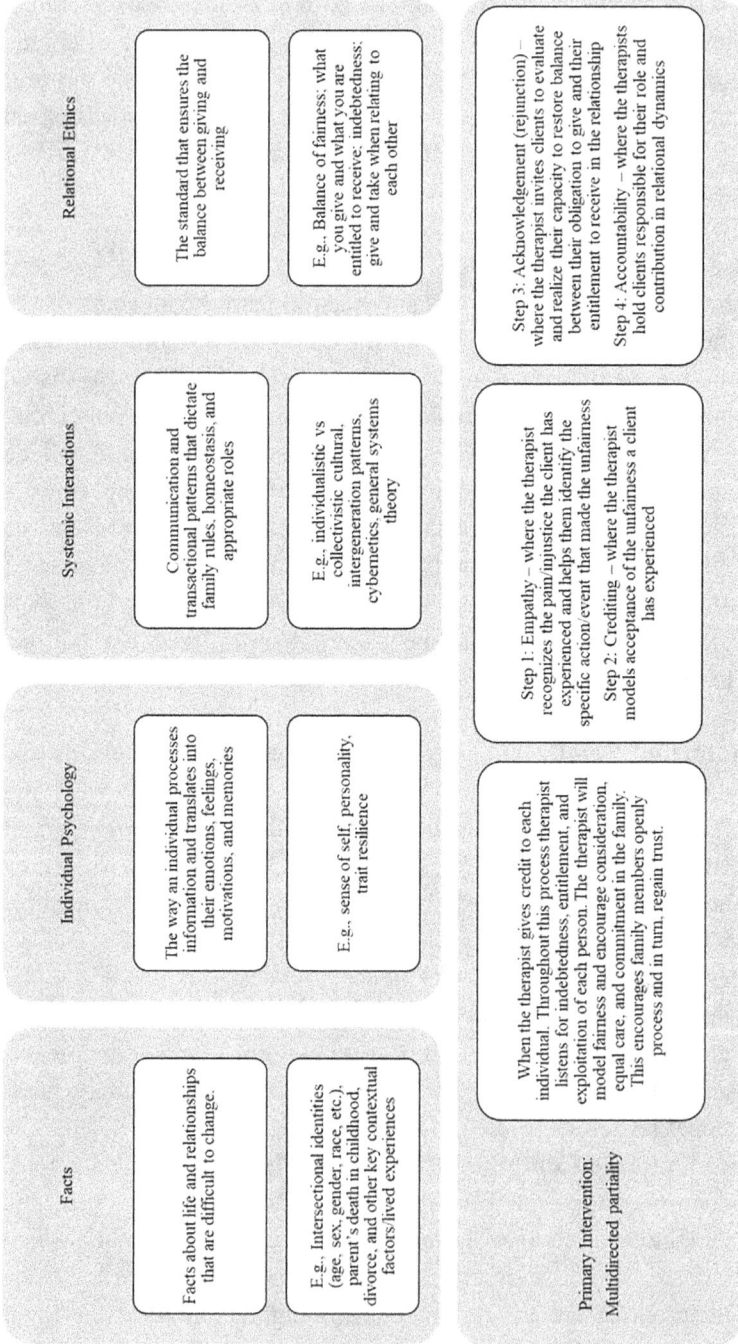

Relational Ethics

The standard that ensures the balance between giving and receiving

E.g., Balance of fairness: what you give and what you are entitled to receive; indebtedness; give and take when relating to each other

Systemic Interactions

Communication and transactional patterns that dictate family rules, homeostasis, and appropriate roles

E.g., individualistic vs collectivistic cultural intergeneration patterns, cybernetics, general systems theory

Individual Psychology

The way an individual processes information and translates into their emotions, feelings, motivations, and memories

E.g., sense of self, personality, trait resilience

Facts

Facts about life and relationships that are difficult to change.

E.g., Intersectional identities (age, sex, gender, race, etc.), parent's death in childhood, divorce, and other key contextual factors/lived experiences

Step 3: Acknowledgement (rejunction) – where the therapist invites clients to evaluate and realize their capacity to restore balance between their obligation to give and their entitlement to receive in the relationship

Step 4: Accountability – where the therapists hold clients responsible for their role and contribution in relational dynamics

Step 1: Empathy – where the therapist recognizes the pain/injustice the client has experienced and helps them identify the specific action/event that made the unfairness

Step 2: Crediting – where the therapist models acceptance of the unfairness a client has experienced

Primary Intervention: Multidirected partiality

When the therapist gives credit to each individual. Throughout this process therapist listens for indebtedness, entitlement, and exploitation of each person. The therapist will model fairness and encourage consideration, equal care, and commitment in the family. This encourages family members openly process and in turn, regain trust.

Figure 4.2 Conceptual illustration of contextual therapy.

and resentment. Naomi realized she was responding to this pressure by trying to earn love and acceptance through conditional, externalizing behaviors. Naomi also had the insight that keeping the secret of her rape was reinforcing her destructive entitlement (e.g., shame, embarrassment, poor self-esteem, pressure to hide her truth).

Contextual Family Therapy Intervention: Through these processes, space can be made for each family member to accept accountability and responsibility for the impact of their roles and previous generational loyalties and acknowledge the impact of social locations and culture—which helps foster hope of exoneration.

Integration of Process Resilience: A deeper reflection on resilience factors, including further acknowledging each client's perseverance and ability to tap into protective factors that helped them come together, can be integrated.

Integrating Resilience Into Contextual Family Therapy

When integrating resilience concepts into research and clinical practices, it is important scholars' and providers' cultural values, beliefs, attitudes, and practices are understood and integrated (Bermudez & Mancini, 2012). If we do not integrate contextual and culturally humble stances proactively, we risk unintentionally harming families who already face systemic marginalization and oppression. As such, we propose integrating resilience with contextual family therapy concepts and interventions, as doing so allows clinicians to examine resilience as a contextual, systemic process that promotes well-being within individuals and family systems.

Walsh (2016) posited:

A family resilience practice approach seeks to identify and involve members who are—or could become—invested in the positive development and well-being of at-risk or troubled youth or adults, believe in their potential, and support their best efforts to make the most of their lives.

(p. 617)

This approach directly maps onto how contextual therapy seeks to (a) assess the legacy (i.e., how relationships are balanced within a system), (b) explore the revolving slate (i.e., patterns of injustice embedded across generations that contribute to a scapegoat/identified patient), and (c) increase merit (i.e., how individual members trust others will contribute equally) and rejunction (i.e., where individuals are invited to explore their own ability to restore balance between what they need/take and give/provide; Boszormenyi-Nagy, 2014; Boszormenyi-Nagy & Krasner, 1987). Ungar (2013, 2016) also highlighted the need for generational and community interventions as ways to look at family resilience and divorce resilience from being an individualistic trait.

In contextual family therapy, conducting a multigenerational analysis with multiple generations entering the therapy room allows for the clients and therapist to explore relational ethics to "resolve the slate" (Sweeney, 2019, p. 93) through rejunctive interventions (e.g., capacity to resolve among entitlement and emotional debts). Contextual therapy interventions can specifically be interwoven with systemic family interventions, such as the cocreation of resilience-oriented maps that highlight multigenerational patterns of resilience and strength (Walsh, 2016). Balance and fairness are based on the obligation and follow through of giving and the entitlement of receiving via communication, boundaries, and trust (Hargrave & Pfitzer, 2003; Sweeney, 2019). In looking at familial and systemic contexts, navigating intersecting identities, and examining resilience as a family process—rather than something that is achieved/possessed or not—clinicians and scholars can help facilitate resilience in family systems in a contextual, systemic way (Ungar, 2013, 2016; Walsh, 2016).

> **Case Example Continued (Session 8):** Through the course of family therapy, Mira and Naomi were able to decide on the best decision for their family regarding the pregnancy. Naomi decided to continue with individual therapy to process her personal trauma and accept her identities (e.g., sexual orientation, ability). Naomi also shared that she needed more space to openly remember and talk about her father, to honor her grief and memories of him. Mira shared that she believed this approach would also help her move through her grief.
>
> **Contextual Family Therapy Intervention:** In the final session, the focus should be on reinforcing the new relational ethics and

balanced ledger to contribute to each client having a restored sense of justice within the family.

Integration of Process Resilience: In the final session, the focus should be on reinforcing family patterns and processes that contributed to the clients' narratives of strength, perseverance, and commitment to healing and understanding each other while honoring their unique lived and traumatic experiences.

Conclusion

Culturally attended therapy moves beyond viewing resiliency solely as a trait that is either possessed or not. By integrating family resilience concepts into contextual family therapy, clinicians and scholars can (a) proactively deconstruct dominant cultural and societal portrayals of—and discourses around—resilience that can reinforce harmful and oppressive narratives and (b) bolster resilient functioning for individuals, couples, and family systems in a culturally curious and contextually driven way. For example, in our case study, dominant discourse dictated that the mother should be ostracized for her response to her daughter; however, approaching the mother–daughter dyad through integrating systemic family resilience and contextual family therapy interventions created a different way forward. Further, by integrating Hays's (1996) ADDRESSING framework, the privileged and oppressed identities could be understood and contextualized when working within this family system specifically. For this family and others, building resilience requires helping them deconstruct these harmful, pervasive narratives and create space for their own suppressed narratives, lived experiences, and cultural and contextual factors that promote well-being in their own lives.

References

American Psychological Association. (2014). *The road to resilience.* APA. https://www.apa.org/topics/resilience/building-your-resilience

Bermudez, J. M., & Mancini, J. A. (2012). Familias fuertes: Family resilience among Latinos. In D. S. Becvar (Ed.), *Handbook of family resilience* (pp. 215–227). Springer. https://doi.org/10.1007/978-1-4614-3917-2_13

Boszormenyi-Nagy, I. (2014). *Foundations of contextual therapy: Collected papers of Ivan Boszormenyi-Nagy, M.D.* Routledge. https://doi.org/10.4324/9781315803852

Boszormenyi-Nagy, I., & Krasner, B. R. (1987). Between give and take: A clinical guide to contextual therapy. *Family Relations, 36*(3), Article 349. https://doi.org/10.2307/583562

Bryant, C. M., Anderson, L. A., & Notice, M. R. (2022). Revisioning the concept of resilience: Its manifestation and impact on Black Americans. *Contemporary Family Therapy, 44*(1), 16–28. https://doi.org/10.1007/s10591-021-09621-6

Cardoso, J., & Thompson, S. (2010). Common themes of resilience among Latino immigrant families: A systematic review of the literature. *Families in Society: The Journal of Contemporary Social Services, 91*(3), 257–265. https://doi.org/10.1606/1044-3894.4003

Connor, K. M., & Davidson, J. R. (2003). Development of a new resilience scale: The Connor-Davidson Resilience Scale (CD-RISC). *Depression and Anxiety, 18*(2), 76–82. https://doi.org/10.1002/da.10113

Cretney, R. (2014). Resilience for whom? Emerging critical geographies of socio-ecological resilience. *Geography Compass, 8*(9), 627–640. https://doi.org/10.1111/gec3.12154

DeVerteuil, G., & Golubchikov, O. (2016). Can resilience be redeemed? Resilience as a metaphor for change, not against change. *City, 20*(1), 143–151. https://doi.org/10.1080/13604813.2015.1125714

Ducommun-Nagy, C. (2019). Contextual family therapy. In J. L. Lebow, A. L. Chambers, & D. C. Breunlin (Eds.), *Encyclopedia of couple and family therapy* (pp. 575–583). Springer. https://doi.org/10.1007/978-3-319-49425-8_361

Dulin, A. J., Dale, S. K., Earnshaw, V. A., Fava, J. L., Mugavero, M. J., Napravnik, S., Hogan, J. W., Carey, M. P., & Howe, C. J. (2018). Resilience and HIV: A review of the definition and study of resilience. *AIDS Care, 30*(Suppl. 5), S6–S17. https://doi.org/10.1080/09540121.2018.1515470

Goldenthal, P. (1996). Doing contextual therapy: An integrated model for working with individuals, couples, and families. W.W. Norton & Company.

Hargrave, T. D., & Pfitzer, F. (2003). *The new contextual therapy: Guiding the power of give and take.* Routledge. https://doi.org/10.4324/9780203501368

Hays, P. A. (1996). Addressing the complexities of culture and gender in counseling. *Journal of Counseling & Development, 74*(4), 332–338. https://doi.org/10.1002/j.1556-6676.1996.tb01876.x

Hays, P. A. (2008). *Addressing cultural complexities in practice: Assessment, diagnosis, and therapy* (2nd ed.). American Psychological Association. https://doi.org/10.1037/11650-000

Hu, T., Zhang, D., & Wang, J. (2015). A meta-analysis of the trait resilience and mental health. *Personality and Individual Differences, 76*, 18–27. https://doi.org/10.1016/j.paid.2014.11.039

Kaplin, D. (2014, October). *Encouraging diversity in psychology*. Association for Psychological Science. www.psychologicalscience.org/observer/encouraging-diversity-in-psychology

Lee, J. H., Nam, S. K., Kim, A. R., Kim, B., Lee, M. Y., & Lee, S. M. (2013). Resilience: A meta-analytic approach. *Journal of Counseling & Development, 91*(3), 269–279. https://doi.org/10.1002/j.1556-6676.2013.00095.x

Luthar, S. S., Cicchetti, D., & Becker, B. (2000). The construct of resilience: A critical evaluation and guidelines for future work. *Child Development, 71*(3), 543–562. https://doi.org/10.1111/1467-8624.00164

MacKinnon, D., & Derickson, K. D. (2013). From resilience to resourcefulness: A critique of resilience policy and activism. *Progress in Human Geography, 37*(2), 253–270. https://doi.org/10.1177/0309132512454775

O'Hare, P., & White, I. (2013). Deconstructing resilience: Lessons from planning practice: Special edition of planning practice and research. *Planning Practice & Research, 28*(3), 275–279. https://doi.org/10.1080/02697459.2013.787721

Ojukwu, E. N., Phillips, J. C., Vance, D. E., & Caine, V. (2022). Thinking with community: A critique of resilience and well-being. *Journal of the Association of Nurses in AIDS Care, 33*(2), 99–102. https://doi.org/10.1097/jnc.0000000000000328

Raghavan, S., & Sandanapitchai, P. (2020). The relationship between cultural variables and resilience to psychological trauma: A systematic review of the literature. *Traumatology*. https://doi.org/10.1037/trm0000239

Richardson, G. E. (2002). The metatheory of resilience and resiliency. *Journal of Clinical Psychology, 58*(3), 307–321. https://doi.org/10.1002/jclp.10020

Smith-Osborne, A. (2007). Life span and resiliency theory: A critical review. *Advances in Social Work, 8*(1), 152–168. https://doi.org/10.18060/138

Sweeney, K. (2019). Contextual family therapy and the evolution of restoration therapy: A practice-oriented approach. In L. Metcalf (Ed.), *Marriage and the family* (2nd ed., pp. 71–94). Springer. https://doi.org/10.1891/9780826161253.0004

Ungar, M. (2013). Resilience, trauma, context, and culture. *Trauma, Violence, & Abuse, 14*(3), 255–266. https://doi.org/10.1177/1524838013487805

Ungar, M. (2016). Varied patterns of family resilience in challenging contexts. *Journal of Marital and Family Therapy, 42*(1), 19–31. https://doi.org/10.1111/jmft.12124

Walsh, F. (1996). The concept of family resilience: Crisis and challenge. *Family Process*, *35*(3), 261–281. https://doi.org/10.1111/j.1545-5300.1996.00261.x

Walsh, F. (2016). Applying a family resilience framework in training, practice, and research: Mastering the art of the possible. *Family Process*, *55*(4), 616–632. https://doi.org/10.1111/famp.12260

Watters, E. R., Aloe, A. M., & Wojciak, A. S. (2023). Examining the associations between childhood trauma, resilience, and depression: A multivariate meta-analysis. *Trauma, Violence, & Abuse*, *24*(1), 231–244. https://doi.org/10.1177/15248380211029397

5

BIOPSYCHOSOCIAL–SPIRITUAL RESILIENCE INTERVIEW

Understanding and Promoting Well-Being
in Patients Living With Medical Conditions

Jackie Williams-Reade

Jackie Williams-Reade, PhD, is a professor of medical family therapy at Loma Linda University in southern California, where she provides clinical training and supervision, conducts and supervises research, and presents nationally on topics related to families and health. Her clinical and research interests include helping better understand and support patients and families living with medical illness, meaning-making and spirituality, and self-of-therapist issues. Jackie's pronouns are she/her, and she identifies as a White, cisgender, straight woman living with a chronic illness. As a professor, supervisor, researcher, and therapist, Jackie values creating a space that centers authenticity, connection, and collaboration.

The biopsychosocial–spiritual (BPSS) interview is based on the biopsychosocial (BPS) model (Engel, 1977) and is a multidimensional approach to understanding an individual's overall health, considering biological, psychological, social, and spiritual dimensions and their interactions. Using a BPSS approach when interviewing patients or families results in information about their strengths and resources; incorporating specific

DOI: 10.4324/9781003373513-5

concepts of systemic resilience could further emphasize their positive and protective factors and processes. This chapter explores the integration of the BPSS model and systemic resilience in the context of individuals diagnosed with medical conditions, highlighting their complementary nature and providing practical suggestions for modifying BPSS assessment to include additional resiliency factors.

BPS Model and Medical Illness

The BPS model, pioneered by Engel (1977, 1980), emphasizes the interplay between biological, psychological, and social factors in determining health outcomes. The BPS model emerged in response to limitations of the traditional biomedical model, which focused primarily on biological factors in explaining and understanding illness. For example, a patient living with chronic pain in the traditional medical context might have been approached solely from a biomedical perspective, with a focus on identifying and treating the underlying physical cause of the pain.

Conversely, the BPS model encourages healthcare professionals to take a more holistic view, which would include assessing not only the physiological aspects of the pain but also the psychological and social factors that may be contributing to the experience and symptoms of pain. Using a BPS perspective, the professional might explore the patient's emotional state, cognitive processes, and coping strategies related to the perception of pain and investigate the patient's social support system, lifestyle factors, and environmental influences that could impact their pain experience. By adopting the BPS model in medical illness, healthcare professionals gain a more comprehensive understanding of the individual's unique illness experience, which allows for the development of personalized treatment plans that address not only the physical symptoms but also the psychological and social factors influencing the patient's well-being.

Integrating Spirituality and Resilience Into the BPS Model

Engel's (1977, 1980) BPS model, which acknowledges the biopsychosocial factors in shaping an individual's health, gains depth and relevance with the incorporation of spirituality as the fourth dimension. Spirituality encompasses a person's search for meaning, connection to something greater than themselves, and their sense of purpose in life. By recognizing and exploring this dimension, mental health professionals can unlock a deeper understanding of their clients' values, coping mechanisms, and resilience. In the realm of mental health, the integration of spirituality into the BPS model holds profound significance. Mental health professionals can attain a more comprehensive understanding of their clients' well-being by recognizing spirituality as a crucial aspect of human experience.

In terms of integrating BPS and resilience, Ungar et al. (2021) discussed systemic resilience in BPS terms: "Individual and collective resilience refers to the process of sustaining well-being by leveraging biological, psychological, social and environmental protective and promotive factors and processes" (p. 1). Acknowledging the BPS dimensions within the broader social and environmental contexts emphasizes these dimensions are not isolated but interact and influence each other. When spirituality is added to systemic resilience, it emphasizes how spirituality also plays a crucial role as a coping mechanism and a source of support, fostering the development of resilience in the face of adversity. By nurturing their spiritual dimension, individuals can draw upon inner strengths and values that empower them to navigate life's challenges, enhancing their capacity for adaptive coping and fostering a sense of coherence amid complex life events.

BPSS Resilience Interview

In the field of medical family therapy, the BPSS interview (Hodgson et al., 2007), an assessment based on the BPS model, is commonly used as an assessment tool to provide a holistic understanding of patients living with a physical health condition and their families (Tyndall et al., 2014). The interview addresses the patient's physical symptoms and medical treatments, thoughts and feelings related to the illness or treatment, sources of support and relationships, and systems of meaning and practices (Wright et al., 1996).

Biomedical and Systemic Resilience

For the purpose of this chapter, I offer a revised interview method that follows the BPSS framework (see Hodgson et al., 2007 for BPSS interview questions) and also integrates systemic resilience questions. This comprehensive approach enhances the assessment process, informs intervention planning based on the patient's ecological systems, and promotes the integration of resilience-enhancing strategies within the patient's broader ecological systems. Next, I outline the BPSS domains and include questions that integrate a resiliency framework. The purpose of each section is included with an example of how a patient might respond and general clinical recommendations.

Purpose

In addition to assessing the biomedical aspects of the patient's health, it is important to incorporate questions that explore the influence of systemic resilience on their well-being. This section aims to understand how the patient's health and illness experience interact with their ecological systems—including family, community, and cultural factors—with an emphasis on systemic resilience.

Possible Questions

- How have your physical health/medical conditions influenced your overall resilience and ability to cope with challenges?
- How do you manage the physical symptoms associated with your medical condition? Are there any strategies or treatments that have been particularly helpful in supporting your resilience?
- Are there any specific biological factors (e.g., genetics, lifestyle choices) that you believe contribute to your resilience or pose challenges to it?
- What surprises or unexpected changes have you noticed in your body's response to your health condition or treatment? How have these changes affected your resilience and well-being?
- Have you or any of your family members experienced similar health issues in the past? How has this influenced your current experience, including your understanding of resilience?
- What does your body need in this moment? How can you best care for your body?
- Where can you find moments of rest for your body when needed?
- How can you create an environment for your body to be more resilient?

Clinical Example and Recommendation

A patient responds to the question, "How has your physical health/medical conditions influenced your overall resilience and ability to cope with challenges?" by stating their chronic pain has significantly impacted their ability to engage in daily activities; they also experience feelings of frustration and helplessness, and the pain has strained their relationships with family and friends. As a response, one could acknowledge the patient's challenges with chronic pain and its effects on their resilience and well-being; explore coping strategies and resources that can help them manage their pain, including pain management techniques; provide psychoeducation on pain's impact on relationships; and explore avenues for increased social support.

Psychological and Systemic Resilience

Purpose

The psychological experience of the patient is closely intertwined with their ecological systems. Questions in this section aim to explore the emotional, mental, and behavioral changes that accompany the patient's illness experience while taking into account systemic resilience factors. It is important to ensure the interviewee feels comfortable discussing their psychological well-being and appropriate follow-up is provided if necessary.

Possible Questions

- How do you think your health condition or illness experience has impacted your emotional and mental well-being? How has your diagnosis or medical condition impacted your psychological resilience?
- Can you identify any psychological strengths or coping strategies that have helped you navigate the challenges associated with your medical condition?
- Can you share thoughts that uplift you and contribute to your well-being? On the other hand, are there thoughts that drain your energy and hinder your ability to take care of yourself?
- Have your thoughts about yourself, your family, and your activities (such as work or hobbies) changed since your diagnosis or health issue?

- What story are you telling yourself about having your medical condition that may be hindering you? What other story can you tell yourself that will enhance your resilience?

Clinical Example and Recommendation

When asked about their psychological resilience, a patient shares that they have found comfort in practicing mindfulness meditation and journaling as coping strategies; however, they also express feelings of anxiety and uncertainty related to their diagnosis, which has affected their ability to engage in activities they once enjoyed. As a response, one could explore the patient's feelings of loss related to their diagnosis, challenge negative thoughts, and foster adaptive coping strategies to help improve their psychological resilience.

Social and Environmental Systemic Resilience

Purpose

This section aims to understand how the patient's social network and environmental conditions impact their health and well-being. Questions are designed to explore the systemic factors contributing to or hindering their resilience. The purpose of this section is to understand the impact that the illness experience has had on one's social network (e.g., spouse, children, siblings, parents, close friends, coworkers) and the environmental conditions that may impact one's health and well-being.

Possible Questions

- How has your support network (family, friends, community) contributed to your resilience during your experience with your medical condition?
- How do you observe the impact of your diagnosis on how you interact with your family, community, or cultural dynamics?
- Who are the significant individuals in your support system? How have these relationships influenced your ability to cope with your illness? Is there anyone you wish would provide more support, and how might you be able to gain their support?

- How can you create space for more community and support in your life? What would that look like to you?
- What parts of your illness are not recognized or respected in your surrounding culture? How can you provide those parts of you with compassion and strength?
- Can you tell me about any challenges you have faced in navigating the healthcare system or accessing medical care? How have you managed or overcome them?
- What support have you received from your family and friends regarding your health condition? How has their support or perspective influenced your resilience?
- Are there any cultural or community resources available to you that enhance your ability to adapt and overcome difficulties?
- How does your physical environment (e.g., home, neighborhood, workplace) impact your well-being and ability to cope with stress? Are there any changes you would like to make in your environment to better support your resilience?

Clinical Example and Recommendation

The patient discusses feeling disconnected from their social network due to their medical condition. They note some friends and family members have seemed uncomfortable discussing their illness, which has led to a sense of isolation. In response, the healthcare professional could encourage open communication with loved ones about their needs and feelings related to the medical condition, which may lead to increased support and understanding. Additionally, exploring opportunities to connect with support groups can foster a sense of belonging and enhance their social resilience.

Spiritual and Systemic Resilience

Purpose

This section explores the patient's beliefs, meaning-making, and sources of strength during their health journey, acknowledging the importance of spirituality in resilience. By understanding the belief systems of patients and families, clinicians can gain insight into the challenges present when making a change, accepting medical intervention, or following up with a recommended treatment plan. Spirituality, faith, or worldview may also be a source of hope and strength for the patient and family members during a time when answers may not be readily available.

Possible Questions

- Are there any spiritual practices or beliefs that have been particularly meaningful or helpful to you during this experience?
- In what ways has your spirituality or belief system supported your resilience in the face of your medical condition?
- What meaning (if any) does this health experience, illness, or injury hold for you?
- Has your health experience influenced your perception of control over certain aspects of your well-being? How can your spirituality help you feel more flexible regarding what you can/cannot control?
- What brings you healing? What helps your spirit feel more resilient? How can you create moments for this in your day-to-day life?

Clinical Example and Recommendation

The patient shares that spirituality has been a source of comfort and strength during their health journey. They found solace in prayer and meditation, which helped them navigate the uncertainty of their medical condition. Responding by acknowledging the importance of spirituality in the patient's resilience, highlighting these valuable insights, and encouraging them to continue nurturing these practices can provide a sense of empowerment and hope and help contribute to their overall spiritual resilience.

Best Practices for BPSS and Systemic Resiliency Integration

A BPSS resiliency framework can provide much-needed support to patients and family members; however, it is important to recognize that applying this framework to this particular population requires specific considerations. In the context of medical illness, patients may interpret resilience as the need to stay strong and positive, leading to potential challenges. I have witnessed well-intentioned family and friends convey messages urging patients to remain strong and positive in their fight against the illness or to "beat" it. Western individualistic norms may influence patients to believe resilience means not seeking outside help.

A mindset that solely focuses on being strong, fixing problems, and handling everything independently can exhaust patients and their families, leaving them more vulnerable to suffering rather than becoming more resilient. To better address resilience in this population, efforts may involve seeking and receiving support, not facing challenges alone, allowing time for healing, advocating for oneself, being flexible in adapting to circumstances, and taking necessary rest periods. The following best practices can guide implementation to help ensure the BPSS resilience interview is used with sensitivity and contextual awareness:

- *Recognize the significance of BPSS factors and ecological systems in shaping an individual's unique illness experience and overall well-being.*

This interview is written to gain the patient's perspective but can be tailored for those in attendance. The interviewer is encouraged to adapt these questions based on the individual's specific context, illness type and phase, overall rapport and comfort, and cultural and personal beliefs. All sections should be approached with sensitivity, and interviewers should ensure patients understand their experiences and beliefs will be respected; the purpose is to understand their unique perspective.

- *Incorporate questions that explore family, community, and cultural contexts, emphasizing their role in fostering resilience as it relates to living with a medical condition.*

These questions aim to explore the patient's systemic resilience within the BPSS framework by promoting a deeper understanding of their strengths, challenges, and resources for fostering resilience. Depending on the context and nature of the person's medical/mental health visit, this interview may be more or less intense for them and their loved ones. If the individual's health appears more serious or vulnerable, the interview may need to be approached more gingerly or directly.

- *Identify and evaluate resilience-facilitating factors and resilience-disrupting factors within the BPSS domains and ecological systems.*

It is important to consider that this interview focuses on resilience and should be used at the appropriate time. I suggest using this interview only after fully exploring the problem to allow a patient or family to share the depth of their experience before focusing on resilience. By asking about resilience too soon, especially in the face of a serious illness diagnosis, clinicians may inadvertently suggest to the patient that they should feel supported and resilient even when in an adjustment or grieving stage. Subsequently, patients may easily think that being diagnosed with an illness or responding with sadness, grief, or anger to an illness is their fault for not being strong or positive enough.

- *Collaborate with clients to leverage their ecological resources for intervention planning.*

This interview may be used as an assessment or intervention, but it should be made clear to the interviewee(s) the purpose of the interview—whether to gather information that will be followed up on later or to explore issues or details that surface—will be addressed. Using the results of this interview to tailor treatment planning and interventions is advised, with continued revisiting of treatment goals to ensure the collaborative relationship is maintained.

Conclusion

By incorporating systemic resilience concepts into the BPSS interview, mental health professionals can gain a deeper understanding of the patient's strengths, challenges, and resources within their ecological systems and promote a more adaptive capacity through tailored interventions that address the multidimensional nature of health and resilience. By embracing this integrated approach, clinicians can contribute to improved health outcomes for individuals and communities by emphasizing the importance of systemic resources and collaboration in promoting adaptive capacity and well-being. These resources include supportive relationships, community networks, cultural practices, healthcare systems, and access to basic needs. By viewing a patient and family's illness experience through this lens and using the BPSS resiliency interview, mental health therapists can provide a fuller understanding and collaborative approach to enhancing overall health and well-being.

References

Engel, G. L. (1977). The need for a new medical model: A challenge for biomedicine. *Science*, *196*(4286), 129–136. https://doi.org/10.1126/science.847460

Engel, G. L. (1980). The clinical application of the biopsychosocial model. *American Journal of Psychiatry*, *137*(5), 535–544. https://doi.org/10.1176/ajp.137.5.535

Hodgson, J., Lamson, A., & Reese, L. (2007). The biopsychosocial-spiritual interview method. In D. Linville, D. Lusterman, & K. Hertlein (Eds.), *Therapist notebook for family healthcare* (pp. 3–12). Hayworth Press.

Tyndall, L., Hodgson, J., Lamson, A., White, M., & Knight, S. (2014). Medical family therapy: Charting a course in competencies. In J. Hodgson, A. Lamson, T. Mendenhall, & D. Crane (Eds.), *Medical family therapy* (pp. 33–53). Springer. https://doi.org/10.1007/978-3-319-03482-9_3

Ungar, M., Theron, L., Murphy, K., & Jefferies, P. (2021). Researching multisystemic resilience: A sample methodology. *Frontiers in Psychology*, *11*, Article 3808. https://doi.org/10.3389/fpsyg.2020.607994

Wright, L. M., Watson, W. L., & Bell, J. M. (1996). *Beliefs: The heart of healing in families and illness*. Basic Books.

6

A SYSTEMIC AND WHOLE-PERSON FRAMEWORK FOR SUPPORTING PHYSICIAN RESILIENCE AND WELL-BEING

Jessica ChenFeng

Jessica ChenFeng, PhD, LMFT (she/her) is an associate professor of marriage and family therapy (MFT) at Fuller Theological Seminary. She has been a practicing MFT for almost 20 years and consults with academic, healthcare, and church organizations to improve the well-being of people within their communities. Her research and clinical work center around social contextual intersections of race, gender, generation, trauma, and spirituality. She resides in southern California with her spouse and two young children. Whenever she gets the chance, she loves reconnecting with her love for analogue: paper planners and stationery, baking, and sewing. Jessica identifies as a cisgender, heterosexual, second-generation Taiwanese American woman.

Physician burnout and resilience continue to be topics of increasing research and concern, with the latest burnout rate at 63% in 2022, a significant increase from 38% in 2020 (Shanafelt et al., 2022). The Accreditation Council for Graduate Medical Education, which regulates resident physician training, requires all residencies to have 24/7 access to a mental health professional for urgent or emergent mental

DOI: 10.4324/9781003373513-6

health issues. Institutions have also continued to develop best practices for alleviating burnout and promoting well-being. Still, these good and necessary efforts may lead some physicians to feel disillusioned by wellness programs, self-care suggestions, and mindfulness workshops when they simply cannot schedule one more responsibility, have relational and physical challenges, have lost their sense of self, or can no longer find the meaning and empathy they need to thrive.

For many years, I served as the associate director of physician vitality at Loma Linda University Health, where my only clinical work was serving physicians. The office's responsibility was to support the well-being of roughly 2,700 physicians and medical trainees. Physicians across all 70 medical specialties received therapeutic support. In this chapter, I offer a resilience-based, systemic, and whole-person framework for working with physicians based on our office's clinical experiences. The learnings I gained while working in the medical community may be applicable across multiple community-based settings.

Systemic Resilience and Physicians

One cannot understand the resilience of physicians apart from a systemic lens. Though this sentiment is true for everyone, it is especially important to understand how physicians have been shaped by, trained, and function as individuals within medical culture and healthcare institutions. Walsh's (2021) dynamic systemic perspective invites clinicians to consider the individual within family, community, and sociocultural systems because such consideration "keeps awareness of the many interdependent influences across and within levels" (p. 266). I specifically address the sociocultural systems that shape physicians' experiences by discussing how attributes of belief systems, organizational processes, and communication and problem-solving processes of the family resilience framework can be applied to understanding physicians within those systems.

Sociocultural Systems and Effects on Physicians

For this chapter, I defined sociocultural systems as the external (i.e., the general population and societal discourses) and internal (i.e., medical culture and systems) variables that affect physicians. In the larger

North American context (i.e., external), there exist certain discourses and beliefs about physicians: primarily, physicians are highly regarded and have historically been respected as medical experts who care for individual and community health outcomes. Because most individuals have been cared for by physicians when in vulnerable health circumstances, it is hard to imagine physicians as vulnerable themselves or as whole persons with their own struggles. Physicians find meaning and fulfillment in their medical practices because they love helping patients, which offers a sense of fulfillment.

It is important to recognize, however, that high standards of meeting patient needs and the assumption of physician invulnerability can become internalized and exacerbate maladaptive perfectionism and impostor syndrome, adversely affecting well-being and prompting burnout. During the COVID-19 global pandemic, when patients were misled by misinformation (Abbasi, 2021), they projected their frustration onto their physicians, directed racism and xenophobia at them, and rejected their counsel—leaving many physicians feeling ignored, unable to accomplish their objectives, and disillusioned. For some physicians, especially physicians of color, it was especially disheartening to see their communities disproportionately affected and feel helpless because of the understandable medical mistrust these communities have experienced due to their own historical racial traumas with the medical system (Vázquez et al., 2023). In addition to the high expectations physicians already hold for themselves, pandemic-related dynamics had a significant impact on the way they internalize their own identities.

There is a hidden curriculum in medicine that has a significant influence on physicians' experiences, perceptions, and standards of practice. In medical school and residency, medical trainees observe and assimilate unofficial, implicit lessons, behaviors, and values. A few of these elements include using clear, collaborative communication, assuming responsibility for mistakes, and acknowledging emotional vulnerabilities. If trainee physicians do not meet unspoken expectations, they may feel inadequate and wonder what went wrong. The trainees also may experience and witness senior physicians lecturing or belittling them or may not hear physicians acknowledge their emotional vulnerabilities following a traumatic medical experience. As a result, the trainees may adopt a number of internalized beliefs about how to conduct themselves:

(a) being emotionally tough (e.g., disregarding and suppressing negative emotions), (b) maintaining an unreasonable and unattainable level of perfection, and (c) attempting to figure things out for themselves. Training in medicine does not always emphasize communication and relational skills that affect patient care and teamwork, so medical trainees may observe and assimilate passive or aggressive communication about expectations and the lack of compassionate handling of mistakes. Many physicians view these implicit values as what "resilience" means, and they spend years learning how to become even better at remaining emotionally unaffected by trauma and growing thicker skin to deal with criticism.

Medical cultures and models have a complex history of biases rooted in social, cultural, and institutional factors. Colonialism, racism, gender bias, and discrimination against LGBTQ+ communities are just a few that have contributed to the foundation of medicine (Jaiswal & Halkitis, 2019; Vázquez et al., 2023). The intersection of these biases has shaped a culture that is largely individualistic, self-reliant, and centered on Western ideals, subsequently contributing to physicians feeling pressured to figure out well-being on their own without encouragement to ask for help or feeling shame when they think they are not "strong" enough. It is necessary to unpack individual-centered belief systems, organizational processes, and communication processes to support systemic resilience for those working in medical contexts.

Belief Systems

The individual-focused system of medicine can affect the way that physicians make meaning of adversity. Mistakes, failures, and challenges can be easily personalized. People may feel as if they are not good enough or fit for the field when facing tough times because they believe they can and should do it all. It is critical for therapists to help contextualize their distress—helping the physician to see that perhaps it is not just about their personal responsibility, but rather that they should consider how they face and feel connected to the medical culture and system around them.

There is a good reason why much of medical training is based on black-and-white, right-or-wrong principles. Clinical decisions affect outcomes in life-and-death situations. Expectations to make the right decisions, fear of making mistakes, and criticism for anything less than perfect can all contribute to developing an inner critical voice. In reflecting on their personal and clinical strengths, physicians often find it difficult to identify and acknowledge these strengths. A binary mindset and all-or-nothing context may contribute to the challenge of cultivating an honest and authentic, positive outlook. Walsh (2021) described this outlook as having hope and an optimistic bias, confidence in overcoming challenges, and acceptance of what cannot be changed. A positive attitude might be defined as avoiding anxiety and negative emotions to survive the next obstacle (e.g., the upcoming board exam or the end of their overnight shifts). This kind of positive outlook requires developing uncertainty tolerance—the acceptance of "both/and"—and recognizing there may be areas of personal and clinical growth while valuing significant achievements and areas of strength.

Organizational Processes

In this section, I apply Walsh's (2021) systemic resilience framework to the assumptions and experiences of physicians. Specifically, I examine the constructs of flexibility, dependability, connectedness, and communication processes. I also offer practical suggestions for increasing resilience.

Flexibility

In Walsh's (2021) systemic resilience framework, flexibility is a foundational organizational process. Adaptation to change allows people and systems to restore and thrive. Leadership that is nurturing, protective, and guides can foster flexibility. Capacity for flexibility is also shaped by organizational processes of dependability, predictability, and mutuality. For example, on a medical team where the faculty or attending physician—in their more senior status—offers clear communication around expectations and models, resident or student physicians have the opportunity to ask for support and to respond authentically and without fear.

Dependability

In medical training, predictability and dependability are not inherent to organizational processes. Residents may experience physically and emotionally grueling residency programs or they might only get holidays off based on seniority; moreover, certain rotations may be particularly challenging, which does not facilitate the dependability and predictability that physicians need to feel nurtured, protected, or valued. Physicians may often feel like they are cogs in a massive medical system wheel, at the mercy of whatever comes their way. Even though predictability is not realistic (e.g., when physicians or their colleagues need to call out sick, in the event of medical emergencies), departments and programs can establish communication protocols (e.g., expressing gratitude, validating frustrations, acknowledging sacrifices) that emphasize the importance of valuing physicians' time and energy so physicians feel as though the medical system supports them.

Connectedness

Mutual support and respect for individual differences are central to connectedness (Walsh, 2021). The medical system does not make it easy for individuals' needs to be identified or valued; for example, taking time off for bereavement or personal reasons often results in physicians feeling guilty that their colleagues have to take over their shifts. It is common for physicians to minimize their own needs for rest and recovery. Authentic relational connection is difficult for physicians because they are exhausted and have low emotional reserves. Social relationships are defined by hierarchy and rank, so relational mutuality is not innate. Senior physicians may demand unquestioning obedience and reprimand subordinates who challenge them. In the medical context, physicians have had little choice but to figure things out on their own instead of relying on institutional support. Administrators and more senior physicians can model genuine care and make concerted regular efforts to connect with colleagues beyond addressing work-related needs. Feeling such a relational connection can go a long way in improving team and workplace morale.

Communication Processes

Communication processes that promote systemic resilience require clarity and open emotional sharing. Having clarity means (a) offering clear, consistent messages, (b) defining and debriefing ambiguous situations, and (c) expressing appreciation and painful feelings. Medical systems can be very fast paced, making communication difficult. When medical learners are uncertain about their clinical decisions or have difficulty reading their senior physicians' nonverbal communication, they may feel internal distress about asking clarifying questions for fear of being reprimanded or being perceived as incompetent or insubordinate.

Particular departments may have administrators who value emotional sharing or debriefing after a traumatic clinical encounter, but discussing painful feelings after a patient's death or other trauma is not typical, and few structured frameworks exist for such discussions (Trivate et al., 2019). Reviewing a case or mortality and morbidity reviews might be perceived as a form of debriefing, but these resources do not usually include emotional aspects or reflections. Positive emotional sharing varies by specialty, gender, and personality. The medical context is full of intense time constraints and a general sense of urgency (e.g., seeing patients, documenting in electronic medical records, signing off approvals, ordering tests), making it difficult to express positive emotions or enjoy social niceties. As such, physicians may benefit from having models of expressing appreciation or verbalizing positive affirmations. Senior physicians can show that it is okay to express emotions of grief when faced with loss, anger around systemic inequities, or other types of "difficult" emotions physicians tend to mask.

There are spaces within medical training and culture where systemic resilience is valued and pursued. In this chapter, I emphasize systemic challenges and barriers to support physician clients in achieving whole-person and systemic resilience. Although I previously suggested interventions, I next offer a supportive framework for how to support physician resilience and well-being through contextual differentiation. This framework is not necessarily standalone, but rather, serves as a clinical process that can be a companion to whatever theoretical frameworks a clinician uses in practice. I highlight establishing contextual awareness, validating and acknowledging dismissed identities, and practicing compassion building and resourcing.

Building Contextual Differentiation to Enhance Resilience

Contextual Differentiation

There is little time, capacity, or support available to physicians to attend to their inner lives and explore systemic resilience. To provide care, clinicians must first help physicians recognize the effects of these external and internal discourses. To accomplish this objective, clinicians can support physicians in developing *contextual differentiation* (ChenFeng, 2018). The ability to distinguish one's own thoughts and feelings from those of one's family is understood as individual differentiation. Being able to identify one's own thoughts and feelings as they are influenced by, intricately connected to, or different from larger social realms is contextual differentiation. Physicians are prone to internalizing and personalizing their negative beliefs about themselves; thus, giving clients a framework for self-compassion and contextualization is critical. When physicians become more aware of how identity and internalized discourses are connected to context, they can release themselves from self-pathologizing thoughts and behaviors, allowing them to choose more freely who they want to be and what kind of community they want to build.

The following is a composite case study of Michelle, a third-year resident physician in internal medicine at an academic hospital in southern California. She was a cisgender, heterosexual, Indonesian Chinese Canadian woman in her late 20s with Buddhist and Christian belief systems. Michelle was a first-generation college and medical school student living in the United States on a work visa. As an only child, she cared for her ailing mother, who lived in Canada. As part of her residency program's mandatory wellness check, Michelle met with one of the therapists in the Office of Physician Vitality as part of a half-day off for her own well-being (Hernandez et al., 2023). She had been in moderate stages of burnout for at least one year, and recent stressors (e.g., working in the intensive care unit during a COVID-19 surge) had exacerbated her symptoms of depression and anxiety.

Establishing Contextual Awareness

Depending on when and where physicians received their training, they may be familiar with the social determinants of health (i.e., conditions and factors that influence people's overall health and well-being, such

as socioeconomic status and access to healthcare) or structural competence (e.g., role of social, economic, and political structures affect health
disparities and outcomes). However, such familiarity does not guarantee
that they are aware of how their own training contexts and sociocontextual identities (e.g., race, gender, socioeconomic status) affect their
well-being and resilience.

The first part of developing contextual differentiation is establishing contextual awareness: "How does medical culture/context shape or
influence my sense of self?" Clinicians may ask questions such as:

- What do you think are the attributes of an ideal physician?
- What kind of expectations do you have of yourself or do you sense
  in the workplace?
- What does it mean to be an Asian American woman physician?

When asked these questions, Michelle shared how she became a chief
resident (considered an honor; a senior resident who is selected to take
on leadership and administrative responsibilities for the residency program) through her diligent, hard work, respect toward the senior residents and faculty physicians, and ability to use her time as efficiently as
possible. I examined how she came to have these traits, how and why
they were valued within medicine, and what about her specific residency
program fostered or reinforced these ideas.

When discussing Michelle's racial, cultural, and gender identity, she
was initially uncertain about what made her experience unique. With
some clinical curiosity, I learned about one particularly traumatic encounter during her last year of medical school when she witnessed a more
senior Asian American female resident experience anti-Asian racism
from a patient, and the mostly White medical team laughed along dismis-
sively as this resident was undefended and humiliated. Michelle shared,
through tears, that nobody ever discussed the encounter, so she learned to
keep her head down, work hard, and try to remain invisible so she would
not have to go through anything similar. It may be helpful to offer reflective comments to connect the client's experience to the context, such as:

> I hear you value hard work and diligence, but I also wonder if you were
> forced to perform diligently and compliantly because the medical envi-
> ronment in which you trained did not know how to support and address

racism faced by Asian Americans. Anti-Asian racism is really real and I wonder about it feeling risky and unsafe to make yourself any more visible for fear of negative attention.

This reflection process is likely to be revisited through the number of experiences (e.g., whether related to sociocontextual identities or experiences of impostor syndrome, anxiety, or burnout) where establishing contextual awareness is beneficial to reduce the personalization of critical and negative thinking. In Michelle's case, this exercise gave her permission to see that she was not simply "a bad leader" or that she was "not good at being outspoken and direct." She had contextual experiences that limited her development of these traits.

Validating and Compassion Building to Promote Resilience

The next phase of contextual differentiation is to validate and build compassion. In supporting physicians in recognizing their perceived incompetence or anxiety as not just an individual issue but perhaps a result of sociocultural systems and discourses, their first reaction may be something similar to "But if that's the case, why can't I get over it?" *Providing validation to physicians involves letting them know that what they are experiencing is normal, perfectly okay, and not a sign of being weak or bad.* Physicians rarely discuss their emotional vulnerabilities with one another, so they often may feel as though they are the only ones going through their situation because many colleagues appear to be doing just fine. A useful validation tool is to cite research on physician impostor syndrome, burnout, depression, and anxiety rates. In addition, sharing that physicians tend to internalize this kind of stress and highlighting the significant impact that medical training and culture have on physician well-being can alleviate self-criticism. This phase might also include exploring Michelle's family-of-origin dynamics and the effects of model minority racialization that have contributed to her self-criticism.

Lack of self-compassion in medicine is caused by a number of factors, making this an important area for development. Compassion building differs from validation in that it involves admitting and accepting what is felt rather than denying and judging it. This step is a significant one in moving toward self-compassion. Because physicians are socialized to constantly improve and work on their "faults," when they learn that they "should not" feel bad about themselves, they, too, want to correct it. Acknowledging that what they are feeling and doing does not have to be categorized as "bad" or "good" supports their ability to cope with uncertainties. Physicians can benefit from Neff's (Neff & Germer, 2018) work and website on self-compassion.

Resourcing

As discussed, medical training and culture emphasize individualistic frameworks of self-reliance and "mental toughness," as opposed to emotional vulnerability and interdependence. It takes significant work for physicians to learn how to recognize personal needs and reach out for support. Resourcing is the antidote to the lack of contextual awareness and the expectation that one must solve everything on their own. I believe that an essential act of *resourcing* is learning how to navigate social relationships and connected systems for the purpose of increasing meaningful connections and interdependence.

In resourcing, physicians explore their support systems and identify relationships where trust can be built or where connections can be deepened. Physicians understand how hard it is to become excellent in their clinical skills or to pass board exams but have often not been taught or modeled how to establish and maintain meaningful relational connections. Students and residents often lose touch with old friends or family simply because their schedules are so demanding, and their nonphysician friends and family do not understand the demands of their medical training. In addition to communicating their work demands, physicians must also express their desire to connect with their families and friends. It might be helpful for clinicians to model phrases such as: "I will be starting to work night shifts for the next 6 weeks, and I am sad to miss some of our family gatherings" or "It would be great if we could get together on my days off. Are you open to planning for that?" or "I recently finished my medical training and began a new position where I have much more control over my schedule. I know it's been a while; would you be open to planning regular hikes or outings like we used to?"

Resourcing also includes learning about and connecting with supportive systems. Physicians are not always aware of how to access mental health providers or if their institution offers Employee Assistance

Programs or specific clinical support. It may not occur to many physicians that they could and should ask for time off for significant mental health concerns or bereavement. The clinician can gently guide them in navigating such systemic questions and finding the right person or office who can offer nonjudgmental guidance. Beyond individual physicians trying to figure out the system, the hope is that institutions have established clear pathways for physicians to not only know how to reach out for support but also to have support embedded into their work lives. As an example, programs can institute wellness days for their resident physicians and offer regularly scheduled wellness checks, which takes the stigma and burden off of individual physicians (Hernandez et al., 2023).

As a chief resident, Michelle had limited time on her days off and usually spent them resting or catching up on chores. She knew her vacation weeks in advance, so she began planning how and with whom she wanted to spend it. She worked hard until her week of vacation, then crashed and spent most of the time alone or with her parents. Planning vacations in advance was a new experience, and imagining what she would like to do and how she would like to feel gave her some hope and power. Although Michelle acknowledged that she may not be able to have regular meals with friends or participate in the same social events as peers her age, she could take small steps to feel less like her entire life was at the mercy of her residency schedule.

Conclusion

Cultivating a physician's contextual differentiation requires the process of considering how the context of medical training (along with family dynamics and social contexts) can provide many experiences for building character and personal resilience but can also contribute to challenges in developing systemic resilience. Increasing contextual differentiation will enable physicians to detangle from harmful and limiting ways of being, celebrate interdependence and social support, and promote whole-person flourishing. The work of building contextual differentiation is applicable in any other setting in that it is a useful framework for supporting individuals in understanding their relationship to the systems around them. Those considering this work would benefit from deepening their own personal relationship to and understanding of societal systems and discourses that influence their lives.

References

Abbasi, J. (2021). COVID-19 conspiracies and beyond: How physicians can deal with patients' misinformation. *Journal of the American Medical Association*, *325*(3), 208–210. https://doi.org/10.1001/jama.2020.22018

ChenFeng, J. L. (2018). Integration of self and family: Asian American Christians in the midst of White Evangelicalism and being the model minority. In E. Wilson & L. Nice (Eds.), *Socially just religious and spiritual interventions: Ethical uses of therapeutic power* (pp. 15–26). Springer. https://doi.org/10.1007/978-3-030-01986-0_2

Hernandez, B. C., ChenFeng, J. L., Schill-Depew, A. E., & Lee, S. (2023). A biopsychosocial-spiritual wellness check program for internal medicine residents: A brief report. *Families, Systems & Health: The Journal of Collaborative Family Healthcare*, *41*(1), 54–60. https://doi.org/10.1037/fsh0000727

Jaiswal, J., & Halkitis, P. N. (2019). Towards a more inclusive and dynamic understanding of medical mistrust informed by science. *Behavioral Medicine*, *45*(2), 79–85. https://doi.org/10.1080/08964289.2019.1619511

Neff, K., & Germer, C. (2018). The mindful self-compassion workbook: A proven way to accept yourself, build inner strength, and thrive. In I. Itvzan (Ed.), *The handbook of mindfulness-based programs: Every established intervention, from medicine to education* (pp. 357–367). Routledge.

Shanafelt, T. D., West, C. P., Dyrbye, L. N., Trockel, M., Tutty, M., Wang, H., Carlasare, L. E., & Sinsky, C. (2022). Changes in burnout and satisfaction with work-life integration in physicians during the first 2 years of the COVID-19 pandemic. *Mayo Clinic Proceedings*, *97*(12), 2248–2258. https://doi.org/10.1016/j.mayocp.2022.09.002

Trivate, T., Dennis, A. A., Sholl, S., & Wilkinson, T. (2019). Learning and coping through reflection: Exploring patient death experiences of medical students. *BMC Medical Education*, *19*(1), Article 451. https://doi.org/10.1186/s12909-019-1871-9

Vázquez, E., Juturu, P., Burroughs, M., McMullin, J., & Cheney, A. M. (2023). Continuum of trauma: Fear and mistrust of institutions in communities of color during the COVID-19 pandemic. *Culture, Medicine, and Psychiatry*. https://doi.org/10.1007/s11013-023-09835-3

Walsh, F. (2021). Family resilience: A dynamic systemic framework. In M. Ungar (Ed.), *Multisystemic resilience* (pp. 255–270). Oxford University Press.

7

SYSTEMIC RESILIENCE AND ABOLITION

Developing Individual and Communal
Capacities to Respond to Harm and Violence

Maggie Baisley

*Dr. Maggie Baisley is a European-American, neurodivergent, queer woman
raised in a primarily middle-class, patriarchal, and politically conservative
environment. Dr. Baisley is in a public marriage with a queer woman; they
coparent two young children. At 24 years old, she was involved in a fatal car
accident, which thrust her into the carceral system. Her later clinical work with
veterans processing sexual trauma and labor rights efforts reinforced the urgent
need to build democracy and dignity into institutions. Dr. Baisley cofounded
an organization called Reclaim Justice Movement, which seeks to collectivize
and build life-affirming systems through the spread of restorative justice and
transformative justice practices.*

The purpose of this chapter is to explore the resilience-informed possibilities of taking an abolitionist stance as a mental health professional, both
personally and professionally. As a European-American, queer, neurodivergent, middle-class woman with a background in clinical psychology,
I discuss the intersection of punishment, political power, trauma, and the

DOI: 10.4324/9781003373513-7

ideology of abolition in the context of clinical practice. Specifically, this chapter examines childhood experiences of punishment and how they shape adult views on punishment. I challenge punishment in relationships and family policing by aligning abolition and nonpunitive parenting as an act of resilience. I offer restorative and transformative justice (TJ) practices as alternatives to support the role of mental health professionals in challenging oppressive practices. Ultimately, I call on mental health practitioners to adopt an abolitionist stance in their work and lives.

The term "abolition" emerged from the slavery abolition movement and described the two-part movement to (a) dismantle and eliminate the prison-industrial complex and (b) build life-affirming communities and institutions. The prison-industrial complex describes the "overlapping interests of government and industry that use surveillance, policing, and imprisonment as solutions to economic, social and political problems" (Critical Resistance, n.d., para 2). The tough-on-crime ideology that posits more punishment will lead to more safety is largely not empirically supported (Baumgartner et al., 2021; Chalfin & McCrary, 2017). The United States is the most incarcerated country per capita in the world and the second most incarcerated in number (World Prison Brief, n.d.). The American Public Health Association (2020) published a policy statement calling for abolition as an urgent public health intervention.

The American Psychological Association (APA, 2022) has continued to move in a different direction, again publishing a statement advocating for police reform to reduce violence against marginalized communities; however, there has been no indication that interventions such as body cams, implicit bias training, and mental health crisis training for police officers work effectively (Vitale, 2021). Some mental health practitioners have continued to advocate for abolition and have called for dismantling the prison-industrial complex (Drustrup et al., 2022; Kim, 2018; Klukoff et al., 2021; Richie & Martensen, 2019). All realms of life—from individual functioning to parenting norms—are susceptible to influence by carceral logic (i.e., practices of policing and imprisonment; Martensen, 2020). As activists and thinkers, Kaba and Meiners (2014) put simply, carceral logic is "a punishment mindset, crept into nearly every government function, including those seemingly removed from prisons" (para. 4). In this chapter, I discuss how carceral logic might lead a parent to rely on monitoring and punishment for unwanted children's behaviors. When a trainee makes a mistake or does something wrong, then a supervisor might turn to reporting, documenting, and eventually punishing the behavior. Mental health providers must examine how structures outside the clinic get replicated inside clinics and within individuals.

I argue abolition and systemic resilience are related. Building the capacity of interdependent and interconnected individuals, families, and communities to adapt and thrive in ever-changing environments is a foundation of systemic resilience (Ungar, 2018, 2021). Developing systemic resilience requires the ability to engage in conflict and respond to harm productively. Violent and punitive state interventions, which overemphasize punishment and legalistic thinking, undermine communities' attempts to determine their own directions and also de-skill individuals in responding directly to harm (Gash & Harding, 2018). The abolition movement invites clinicians to examine carceral thinking and respond creatively to interpersonal harm through practices related to TJ (Kim, 2011, 2021).

Childhood, Punishment, and the Emergence of Abolition-Oriented Parenting

To achieve the collective resilience necessary for abolition, as clinicians, we must start with ourselves and our own experiences. In a carceral world, people associate punishment with justice and fairness; for example, one widely used therapy for sexual trauma centers on how confusion exacerbates post-trauma symptoms as victims struggle to understand how something bad could happen to a good person (Resick & Schnicke, 1992). Believing in justice and the connection between good behavior and good outcomes leads traumatized individuals to blame themselves and search for what they did to deserve such violence. Most people learn this belief about justice from an early age. Parents may have offered candy for good behavior and time-outs or spankings for bad behavior under an ideology that different types of behavior should be tied to punishment. The following prompt, inspired and largely based on the work by (Project Nia, n.d.), can help folks sort through the mechanics of punishment and examine its impact, particularly on people with limited resources and power:

> Think of a time when you were a child, and your caretakers or other authority figures punished you. What was it like? What did you

feel? What behavior was punished? How did the punishment affect your behavior?

In groups, I often start with my own example of a childhood punishment memory:

> I was in fifth grade and walking to be picked up from school. I got in a verbal fight with my brother, which led to him punching me in the stomach a few times. I became enraged and slapped him across the face, much harder than he had been punching me. The parent who was picking us up saw me slap him, left me at the school, and brought my brother home. I felt ashamed and like I was a monster. I do not even remember how I got home. As I grew up, I still did not know what to do when I experienced anger, especially toward others. Into my adulthood, I noticed I was often scared whenever I was angry.

This childhood punishment exercise helps draw attention to the universal experience of *power over punishment* (i.e., done by people with significantly more power and resources)—all participants with whom I have worked, regardless of class, race, gender, or other identities, have been able to think of an example. As children, we are hopelessly dependent on our caregivers, who act as gatekeepers to all resources (e.g., food, hygiene, travel, toys). In my example, I was reliant on an adult to travel back to my house, and this travel was withdrawn as punishment for bad behavior. Puerto Rican activist, writer, and poet, Levins Morales (1999), stated:

> Childhood is the one political condition, the one disenfranchised group through which all people pass. The one constituency of the oppressed in which all surviving members eventually stop being members and have the option of becoming administrators of the same conditions for new members.
>
> (p. 51)

The grassroots abolition group *GenerationFIVE*—named for its goal of eliminating childhood sexual abuse in five generations—refers to this quote as illustrative in understanding the political relationship between parents and children (*GenerationFIVE*, 2017). Taking these ideas a step further, how an individual is treated when vulnerable and dependent shapes a lot about how they think others deserve to be treated. I start with a childhood memory exercise because, when I start in childhood, it is easy to see how an individual might be committed to the idea that punishment is necessary for bad behavior and how such a concept does not really work in practice.

Self-Reflection Questions

- What are your views on punishment? How have your own experiences of punishment shaped your views?
- What does "behave" mean to you? How does your definition align with a developmental understanding of children? How does your definition relate to emotion regulation?
- How would you define the role of parents in children's lives? What are you responsible for?

Alignment of Abolition and Nonpunitive Parenting: Awareness and Respect Within Political Power Differences

Individuals learn punitive instincts as children and then become parents or caretakers. Social media has exploded with gentle parenting resources; for example, one news article identified that the hashtag #gentleparenting has been used more than 4 billion times (Cheong, 2023). Interestingly, this news article identified gentle parenting as "controversial" because the approach focuses on "communication and respect" (Cheong, 2023, para. 1). Treating children and their needs and desires with respect is, unfortunately, controversial. Gentle parenting, popularized by parenting book author Ockwell-Smith (2016), is defined generally as a philosophy that focuses on nonpunitive strategies to balance the needs and priorities of children and their caretakers.

However, scholarly research has not focused attention on gentle parenting with the same fervor as popular media, and some researchers have critiqued the overemphasis of these positive strategies as not validated empirically (Larzelere et al., 2017). Punishment is generally defined as the use of an unpleasant response to reduce a behavior (American

Psychological Association, n.d.). Punishment may control behavior in some immediate situations; however, according to a narrative review of 69 studies, physical punishment, in particular, creates more problematic behavior over time (Heilmann et al., 2021). Importantly, obedience and behavioral outcomes from fear of punishment are often disconnected from an individual's understanding of why they engage in the behavior or why it is harmful. As an alternative, gentle and trauma-informed parenting models emphasize trust and connection; when a parent asks their child to stop doing something, the child may respond accordingly because they learned to trust the parent's guidance. Regardless of the efficacy of physical punishment or punishment in general—which is questionable at best—we mental health professionals and social scientists must ask a broader question of how this approach aligns with our values.

The surge in interest in and controversy over nonpunitive parenting philosophies such as gentle parenting has revealed a possible shift from carceral values and thirst for abolition. These positive parenting philosophies have challenged the idea that harmful or inconvenient behavior comes from a lack of punishment. People may still feel generational tensions; for instance, my parents' generation as adults witnessed the most rapid expansion of incarcerated people the State (i.e., the ruling government) had ever conducted in the tough-on-crime era of the 1990s (Baumgartner et al., 2021). It is no wonder that carceral logics seeped into family and parental relationships as I again note the fractal systems and the ways in which families become a microcosm for the State regarding surveillance and punishment. In its place, consider how to incorporate practices more consistent with abolition values like creativity, connection, and respect toward children. At the same time, as clinicians, we must avoid engaging in punitive practices, informally surveilling others, and pursuing parenting perfection while we try to engage in these respectful parenting practices (e.g., Henderson et al., 2010).

Case Example: "But How Will They Learn to Behave?"

Alex said he came to therapy due to job-related stress. Therapy shifted toward focusing on painful memories of being physically beaten by his stepfather for seemingly mundane mistakes (e.g., forgetting his homework at school). As Alex and I processed these memories, Alex expressed relief at uncovering long-repressed feelings. Thinking he had come a long way in validating the harm his stepfather caused, I was shocked when he casually said he spanks his kids when they misbehave, sometimes leaving bruises. When I asked him in a curious way about why he spanks his kids, he responded, "How else will they learn what is right?"

Self-Reflection Questions

- What feelings and reactions come up for you when a client discloses they use punitive tactics on their children to address "misbehavior?" How do your reactions change according to the tactic?
- How might you encourage creativity and imagination for the client in considering other, more effective responses?

In helping clients process and recover from childhood trauma, we, as mental health providers, contribute to the capacity for an abolitionist future. As these providers, we can take this contribution a step further by considering how we can support clients in developing their skills to manage stress and respond respectfully and creatively to their children's behavior.

Mandatory Reporting and Creative Alternatives: From Family Policing to Family Power

Mandatory reporting is a concrete way mental health providers promote the carceral system. Presler (2021) described the self-perpetuating feedback loop of healthcare reporting of family violence and the criminal legal system, whereby healthcare providers defer to the legal system to address safety, and the legal system defers to providers for their decisions (Presler, 2021). Melton (2005) described the history of mandatory reporting for child abuse as a "policy without reason" (p. 1). The widespread policy emerged in the 1960s and spread quickly to all 50 states under the guise of child safety. Melton (2005) highlighted:

> In societies in which the majority of children lack fulfillment of basic material needs, a requirement to report and investigate the families in which parents may be neglecting is almost certain ultimately to overwhelm the child protection system and to distract policymakers from attention to the core problem.

(p. 13)

As of 2023, prevalence estimates have suggested that most people never report child abuse cases and interpersonal violence in general to the police (Xie & Baumer, 2019). People often turn to other resources and strategies to address violence, possibly due to awareness of how punitive State intervention can worsen stressful circumstances. The family policing system removes over 250,000 children from their homes each year (US Department of Health and Human Services, 2021) and investigates families of an estimated 37% of all children and more than half of all Black children (Kim et al., 2017). Qualitative analyses have conveyed stories of fear and trauma from parents subjected to state violence and scrutiny (McTavish et al., 2017). The child welfare system is connected intimately with the criminal–legal system and the police. For example, in a historical analysis of child welfare investigating the overrepresentation of Black families, Williams-Butler (2022) pointed out the Eurocentric methods for evaluating parenting and the connection to the police:

> From its very foundation, CPS had an interdependent relationship with the criminal justice system, or carceral State, with the goal of punishing parents deemed unfit by using the power of the law to inflict State-led punishment.
>
> (p. 6)

Family violence, in general, is a public health issue, not a criminal one. Providing robust social services, meeting basic material needs, and enlisting the support of a caring community to promote accountability show promise in preventing and responding to abuse. As of 2023, unprecedented legislation has cast gender-affirming care for trans children as child abuse and used the politicization of trans kids to expand mandatory reporting laws even further (Harrell et al., 2023). From this review of mandatory reporting and the persistent underreporting of child abuse, mental health providers must respond to the abuse of children with a full political understanding of their positions and consider imaginative, abolition-based approaches.

Personal Example: Neighbor Intervention

I was outside one morning to take my 3-year-old to daycare, and he had gotten into the habit of running down the sidewalk to the next street. He reveled in the game of chase and the frantic attention he received when he ran. This morning, he ran far down the street. I was recently postpartum and could not keep up. He was about to turn the corner, and I desperately screamed in vain for him to come back. Another parent, taking their kids to school on bikes, pedaled ahead, got off their bike, and stood in front of my son. They said, "No. Mom," and gestured toward me. I was so relieved at this small yet impactful intervention. My neighbor, with whom I had not associated before that moment, took a share in the responsibility for my child's safety.

Self-Reflection Questions

- What does your community do to keep kids safe?
- How would you know if child abuse were occurring within your neighborhood?
- How might you intervene if you suspected abuse and did not have the option of calling the police?
- What are your reactions to the family policing system? What challenges you when you consider imagining a different approach?

How Punishment Becomes Infused in Relationships and the Promise of Abolition

As discussed previously, children may learn to conflate punishment and justice at an early age. Whereas clinicians may be aware and knowledgeable about racism, sexism, classism, ableism, homophobia, and transphobia, we may lack a broader political analysis of how the prison-industrial complex relates to these structural forces of oppression. In addition, we may turn to other forms of punishment to address everyday conflict. Punishments, though an understandable desire, often do not lead relationships toward resolution or repair. What would it look like for us as therapists to practice nonpunitive approaches toward each other and help our clients sort through their punitive instincts? Next, I provide an example of how carceral and legalistic thinking might emerge in trauma-focused therapy. Through this example, I consider the constraints of carceral thinking for healing and abolitionist alternatives.

Case Example: Sexual Harm and Title IX

Ryan sought therapy for feeling generally tired and depressed. They also stated they experienced a sexual assault a few weeks ago. As their therapist, it is important to look the disclosure at face value and assume its truth, having always been taught to believe survivors as a feminist practice. However, when Ryan shares more details about the sexual assault, the sense arises that the sexual interaction with a peer seemed more like a misunderstanding and a harmful sexual experience to Ryan. Ryan said they were considering reporting the sexual assault to the Title IX office at their school.

Considering an Abolitionist Response

- Ryan used the term "sexual assault," which is a criminal−legal term, not a clinical one, with implications about intent and invoking a legalistic perpetrator−victim framework (e.g., Gash & Harding; Baisley et al., 2022). As therapists, we may feel pressured to validate the labels folks use to describe their experiences. However, when we consider the pressures to overstate harm to receive validation, we might engage in the conversation differently.

Case Example: Supervisee Performance Issues

Julia supervises Shauna, a clinical psychology student. After a few weeks at her new externship site, Shauna has struggled to keep up. Julia talks with her about the importance of submitting her notes on time. Shauna acknowledges this conversation but fails to keep up with the notes over the next couple of weeks. Julia feels frustrated and worried about the possible impact on her role, as she is responsible for Shauna's work. She considers reporting her behavior to her school's director of clinical training and giving her a negative evaluation.

Considering an Abolitionist Response

- First, we may question the supervisor's instinct to address Shauna's behavior using a punitive evaluation before she understands why Shauna's notes might be late. This instinct might be understood as carceral logic—a rule is broken, and punishment is needed. What could an abolitionist response look like? Such a response might start with examining the purpose of documentation and administration, which is tied to the criminal legal system, liability, and a for-profit healthcare system. This contextualization can help supervisors avoid overstating the importance of notes and examine how their anxiety might shape an instinct for punishment and use of authority.

- Still, documentation remains a part of the profession, so a supervisor might take more steps to understand why Shauna's notes are late. What is her process? What does her schedule look like? What does genuine understanding and support look like? In many settings, students work multiple jobs to make ends meet; they may also be exploited and forced to see more clients than they are able to engage with meaningfully. To challenge carceral logic in this scenario, one must avoid individualizing the issue and understand the total context of a person's behavior.

Restorative and Transformative Justice Practices

The project of dismantling and disrupting the carceral state and building life-affirming institutions and communities is closely aligned with restorative justice and TJ frameworks that offer roadmaps for responding to harm and conflict. Restorative justice is a westernized term that describes a paradigm of responding to harm created and inspired by indigenous cultures worldwide (Zehr, 2015). Many countries have federal restorative justice programs, which can exist in diverse formats (e.g., school-based, in prisons) and functions (e.g., diversion or independent from the criminal–legal system). The concept of TJ is a political paradigm that promotes responding to harm in nonpunitive ways and preventing institutional violence. TJ practitioner Mingus (2022) defined the paradigm:

> TJ is a political framework and approach for responding to violence, harm and abuse. At its most basic, it seeks to respond to violence without creating more violence and/or engaging in harm reduction to lessen the violence. TJ can be thought of as a way of "making things right," getting in "right relation," or creating justice together.

Transformative justice responses and interventions 1) do not rely on the state (e.g., police, prisons, the criminal legal system, I.C.E. [Immigration and Customs Enforcement], foster care system (though some TJ responses do rely on or incorporate social services like counseling); 2) do not reinforce or perpetuate violence such as oppressive norms or vigilantism; and most importantly, 3) actively cultivate the things we know prevent violence such as healing, accountability, resilience, and safety for all involved.

(para. 6)

TJ emerged as an antidote to distortions of restorative justice as it became more entrenched within the power structure of institutions (Kim, 2018, 2021). TJ thinkers and activists have highlighted the limitations of the restorative justice paradigm when used in places such as prosecutors' offices and university Title IX offices, as it is used as a simple adjunct to an overarching carceral, punitive system. One TJ advocate and social worker, M. E. Kim, published an open-access Creative Interventions Toolkit that provides hundreds of pages of content regarding community responses to harm (Creative Interventions, 2023). Project Nia (n.d.), an abolitionist organization based in New York, also produced videos to help everyday people consider how they respond to conflict, including basic practices like apologizing after doing something harmful. Restorative justice and TJ practitioners around the world have developed and tested creative methods for responding to conflict and harm that do not rely on punishment.

Abolitionist Mental Health

The mental health profession must also be examined at a systems level. Mental health professionals engage with carceral institutions of every kind and are often used to further justify these institutions (Klukoff et al., 2021). For example, psychologists conduct screenings of refugees to assess whether they are indeed traumatized and worthy of refugee political status. Social workers and psychologists populate the Department of Defense, federal and state prisons, and police departments. Solutions to inhuman conditions and violence often include adding mental health providers for an appearance of humanity without challenging or changing violent structures and policies.

Social workers, scholars, and activists, Richie and Martensen (2019) stated an understanding of abolition requires three conceptual tasks:

1. Understand the ways that crime and build-up of punitive systems and responses are politically and socially invented.
2. Acknowledge the expansion of the prison industrial complex directly relates to taking resources away from social programs and services.
3. Understand and explore the ways in which the term "mass incarceration" is a misnomer and covers up the more targeted nature of prosecution and imprisonment.

These concepts guide my thinking on the prison-industrial complex in a general sense. Abolition involves a dance of conceptualizing how the current system remains the status quo and considering practical steps forward. In terms of daily practice and program development, formerly incarcerated person and social worker Dr. James and social worker Rasmussen have called upon social workers to consider specific, critical questions to guide next steps. As mental health providers, we may ask these questions repeatedly as we are challenged or tempted to engage in practices that further entrench a carceral system that maintains the status quo:

Reflection Questions

- Does the work shift power, give voice, mobilize, and include the leadership of impacted people?
- Does the work dismantle dichotomies of good versus bad, violent versus nonviolent, or deserving versus undeserving?
- Does it work against the expansion and legitimization of carceral systems? Or the narratives that fuel them?
- Does it provide financial relief for impacted people without compromising their agency?
- Is the work trauma-informed and rooted in a historical analysis of oppression?
- Is the work committed to an evolving process of decolonization and inquiry toward its ways of knowing, being, and acting?
- Perhaps most importantly, is the work self-actualizing—meaning are we moving toward the cocreation of a society that puts us out of business? (Rasmussen & James, 2020, para. 13).

Many programmatic examples align with these practices, especially peer support efforts and de-professionalization of mental health services. Consider programs such as the Trans Lifeline, which is run completely by peers and will not connect callers to the police without consent. Other programs, like CAHOOTS (Crisis Assistance Helping Out On The Streets), which started in Eugene, Oregon, shift mental health crisis calls to medical personnel instead of the police. In addition, mental health providers can create fractal change on the individual and interpersonal levels as we engage in creative conversations and ideas about conflict and nonpunitive strategies.

Summary and Way Forward

This chapter hopefully ignites some ideas and further dialogue about abolition, or maybe helps by revisiting familiar concepts. Through personal and clinical examples, I discussed the connection between systemic resilience and abolition, with the capacity to effectively respond to harm and conflict as foundational to a resilient community. I talked about early childhood exposure to punishment and the universal experience of political marginalization experienced through childhood. I then discussed how childhood experiences might reinforce a mythology of justice as punishment, emphasizing the need to examine carceral logics or the instincts to punish and invoke institutional power to address unwanted behavior from individual to system levels. I then opened the possibilities of an abolitionist mental health paradigm. What could these ideas mean going forward? As mental health providers, we can begin by noticing and exploring carceral logic in ourselves and others that pervade our institutions. Rather than surveilling and punishing these logics, we can become creative and compassionate in creating alternatives. Leaning on restorative justice and TJ models helps us as clinicians learn a new—and old—way to relate to ourselves and others.

Educational Resources

Note: The following resources are predominantly North American and collected by nonmental health professionals. The United States incarcerates more people per capita than any other country in the world. In response to a national history of genocide, slavery, and incarceration of specific marginalized groups, the United States also has a rich abolition movement; however, abolition is a global effort, with groups across the world building creative responses to their local instances of violence and relearning strategies of their ancestors prior to colonization.

Bay Area Transformative Justice Collective (BATJC). BATJC is an Oakland, California-based abolitionist, transformative justice group that grew from *GenerationFive* with a mission to eliminate child sexual abuse using nonstate, noninstitutional interventions. Their website has various resources, including "podmapping" worksheets to consider how you might engage in accountability for your behavior or engage in mutual aid with others. https://batjc.wordpress.com/

Creative Interventions Toolkit. The Creative Interventions Toolkit is a comprehensive, open-access toolkit for responding to harm. The toolkit is currently in English and Spanish, and soon to be translated into French and German. Physical copies are available to order through AKPress. www.creative-interventions.org/toolkit/

Movement for Family Power. Movement for Family Power is a New York-based group focused on ending family punishment. Their website offers analysis, news, and descriptions of their efforts. www.movementforfamilypower.org/

Project Nia. Project Nia is a New York-based group focused on supporting youth and providing general education on transformative justice. They also produced a series of short, accessible videos dialoguing about aspects and skills relevant to transformative justice. https://project-nia.org/mission-history

Piepzna-Samarasinha, L. L., and Dixon, E. (Eds.). (2020). *Beyond survival: Strategies and stories from the transformative justice movement*. AK Press. This anthology series presents stories of the messiness of efforts to respond to and prevent further interpersonal violence.

Purnell, D. (2022). *Becoming abolitionists: Police, protests, and the pursuit of freedom*. Astra Publishing House. This book offers the nuts and bolts to gain a working knowledge of the connections among Black Lives Matter efforts, liberatory education, and abolition.

Schulman, S. (2016). *Conflict is not abuse: Overstating harm, community responsibility, and the duty of repair*. Arsenal Pulp Press. This book provides an analysis of how the carceral system removes nuance from conflict and requires individuals to overstate harm to get needed support and validation.

References

American Psychological Association. (n.d.). Punishment. In *APA dictionary of psychology*. https://dictionary.apa.org/punishment

American Psychological Association. (2022). *APA resolution on psychology's role in addressing the impact of, and change required with, police use of excessive force against people of color and other marginalized communities in the United States*. www.apa.org/about/policy/resolution-policing.pdf

American Public Health Association. (2020). *Advancing public health interventions to address the harms of the carceral system* [Policy statement]. www.apha.org/policies-and-advocacy/public-health-policy-statements/policy-database/2021/01/14/advancing-public-health-interventions-to-address-the-harms-of-the-carceral-system

Baisley, M. C., Tucker, A., & McDonnell, C. (2022). Healing from sexual harm: Transcending criminal-legal thinking. *The Military Psychologist*, 37(2), 1–37. www.militarypsych.org/wp-content/uploads/TMP_V37_i2_AD_FINAL_Summer2022.pdf

Baumgartner, F. R., Daniely, T., Huang, K., Johnson, S., Love, A., May, L., Mcgloin, P., Swagert, A., Vattikonda, N., & Washington, K. (2021). Throwing away the key: The unintended consequences of "tough-on-crime" laws. *Perspectives on Politics*, 19(4), 1233–1246. https://doi.org/10.1017/S153759272100164X

Chalfin, A., & McCrary, J. (2017). Criminal deterrence: A review of the literature. *Journal of Economic Literature*, 55(1), 5–48. https://doi.org/10.1257/jel.20141147

Cheong, C. (2023, May 6). Meet TikTok's "gentle parenting" influencers. The viral genre is rife with controversy, but creators say they're misunderstood. *Insider*. www.insider.com/gentle-parenting-tiktok-creators-controversy-explained-interviews-2023-4

Creative Interventions. (2023). *Creative Interventions toolkit*. www.creative-interventions.org/toolkit/

Critical Resistance. (n.d.). *What is the PIC? What is abolition?* https://critical-resistance.org/mission-vision/not-so-common-language/

Drustrup, D., Kivlighan, D. M., & Ali, S. R. (2022). Decentering the use of police: An abolitionist approach to safety planning in psychotherapy. *Psychotherapy, 60*(1), 51–62. https://doi.org/10.1037/pst0000422

Gash, A., & Harding, R. (2018). # MeToo? Legal discourse and everyday responses to sexual violence. *Laws, 7*(2), Article 21. https://doi.org/10.3390/laws7020021

GenerationFIVE. (2017). *Ending child sexual abuse: A transformative justice handbook.* https://transformharm.org/resource_author/generation-five/

Harrell, S., Jordan, S., & Wahab, S. (2023). From exceptionalism to relationality: Responding to mandatory reporting in Texas anti-trans directives. *Affilia, 38*(1), 13–19. https://doi.org/10.1177/08861099221136632

Heilmann, A., Mehay, A., Watt, R. G., Kelly, Y., Durrant, J. E., van Turnhout, J., & Gershoff, E. T. (2021). Physical punishment and child outcomes: A narrative review of prospective studies. *The Lancet, 398*(10297), 355–364. https://doi.org/10.1016/S0140-6736(21)00582-1

Henderson, A. C., Harmon, S. M., & Houser, J. (2010). A new state of surveillance? Applying Michel Foucault to modern motherhood. *Surveillance & Society, 7*(3–4), 231–247. https://doi.org/10.24908/ss.v7i3/4.4153

Kaba, M., & Meiners, E. (2014, February 24). *Arresting the carceral state.* https://jacobin.com/2014/02/arresting-the-carceral-state/

Kim, H., Wildeman, C., Jonson-Reid, M., & Drake, B. (2017). Lifetime prevalence of investigating child maltreatment among US children. *American Journal of Public Health, 107*(2), 274–280. https://doi.org/10.2105/ajph.2016.303545

Kim, M. E. (2011). Moving beyond critique: Creative interventions and reconstructions of community accountability. *Social Justice, 37*(4), 14–35. https://myreader.toile-libre.org/uploads/My_52f01c9f371e1.pdf

Kim, M. E. (2018). From carceral feminism to transformative justice: Women-of-color feminism and alternatives to incarceration. *Journal of Ethnic & Cultural Diversity in Social Work, 27*(3), 219–233. https://doi.org/10.1080/15313204.2018.1474827

Kim, M. E. (2021). Transformative justice and restorative justice: Gender-based violence and alternative visions of justice in the United States. *International Review of Victimology, 27*(2), 162–172. https://doi.org/10.1177/0269758020970414

Klukoff, H., Kanani, H., Gaglione, C., & Alexander, A. (2021). Toward an abolitionist practice of psychology: Reimagining psychology's relationship with the criminal justice system. *Journal of Humanistic Psychology, 61*(4), 451–469. https://doi.org/10.1177/00221678211015755

Larzelere, R. E., Gunnoe, M. L., Roberts, M. W., & Ferguson, C. J. (2017). Children and parents deserve better parental discipline research: Critiquing the evidence for exclusively "positive" parenting. *Marriage & Family Review, 53*(1), 24–35. https://doi.org/10.1080/01494929.2016.1145613

Martensen, K. M. (2020). Review of carceral state studies and application. *Sociology Compass, 14*(7), Article e12801. https://doi.org/10.1111/soc4.12801

McTavish, J. R., Kimber, M., Devries, K., Colombini, M., MacGregor, J. C. D., Wathen, C. N., Agarwal, A., & MacMillan, H. L. (2017). Mandated reporters' experiences with reporting child maltreatment: A meta-synthesis of qualitative studies. *BMJ Open, 7*(10), Article e013942. https://doi.org/10.1136/bmjopen-2016-013942

Melton, G. B. (2005). Mandated reporting: A policy without reason. *Child Abuse & Neglect, 29*(1), 9–18. https://doi.org/10.1016/j.chiabu.2004.05.005

Mingus, M. (2022, January). *Transformative justice 101.* University of California Los Angeles, School of the Arts and Architecture. www.wac.ucla.edu/announcements/archive/2022/winter/january/mia-mingus-transformative-justice-101

Morales, A. L. (1999). *Medicine stories: History, culture, and the politics of integrity.* South End Press.

Ockwell-Smith, S. (2016). *The gentle parenting book: How to raise calmer, happier children from birth to seven.* Little, Brown Book Group.

Presler, C. (2021). Mutual deference between hospitals and courts: How mandated reporting from medical providers harms families. *Columbia Journal of Race and Law, 11*(3). https://doi.org/10.7916/ybfy-v131

Project Nia. (n.d.). *Educational resources.* https://project-nia.org/educational-resources

Rasmussen, C., & James, K. J. (2020, July 17). *Trading cops for social workers isn't the solution to police violence.* Truthout. https://truthout.org/articles/trading-cops-for-social-workers-isnt-the-solution-to-police-violence/

Resick, P. A., & Schnicke, M. K. (1992). Cognitive processing therapy for sexual assault victims. *Journal of Consulting and Clinical Psychology, 60*(5), 748–756. https://doi.org/10.1037/0022-006X.60.5.748

Richie, B. E., & Martensen, K. M. (2019). Resisting carcerality, embracing abolition: Implications for feminist social work practice. *Affilia, 35*(1), 12–16. https://doi.org/10.1177/0886109919897576

Schulman, S. (2016). *Conflict is not abuse: Overstating harm, community responsibility, and the duty of repair.* Arsenal Pulp Press.

Ungar, M. (2018). Systemic resilience. *Ecology and Society, 23*(4). www.jstor.org/stable/26796886

Ungar, M. (2021). *Modeling multisystemic resilience: Multisystemic resilience, adaptation and transformation in contexts of change.* Oxford Scholarship Online. https://doi.org/10.1093/oso/9780190095888.003.0002

U.S. Department of Health and Human Services. (2021). *The AFCARS report.* www.acf.hhs.gov/sites/default/files/documents/cb/afcarsreport28.pdf

Vitale, A. S. (2021). *The end of policing.* Verso Books.

Williams-Butler, A. (2022). Intersectionality and structural gendered racism: Theoretical considerations for Black women, children, and families impacted by child protective services in the United States. *Critical Social Policy, 43*(3), 514–535. https://doi.org/10.1177/02610183221125322

World Prison Brief. (n.d.). *Highest to lowest—prison population total.* Retrieved March 21, 2023, from www.prisonstudies.org/highest-to-lowest/prison-population-total?field_region_taxonomy_tid=All

Xie, M., & Baumer, E. P. (2019). Crime victims' decisions to call the police: Past research and new directions. *Annual Review of Criminology, 2*(1), 217–240. https://doi.org/10.1146/annurev-criminol-011518-024748

Zehr, H. (2015). *The little book of restorative justice: Revised and updated.* Simon and Schuster.

8

RESILIENCE AS A SECURE ATTACHMENT PATTERN

Eli Harwood

Eli Harwood. MA, LPC, is a psychotherapist and author of the book, Securely Attached: Transform Your Attachment Patterns Into Loving, Lasting Romantic Relationships. *She is the co-clinical director at The PASS Center, an attachment-focused therapy clinic in Denver, Colorado. Eli is also the creator of Attachment Nerd, an online resource to support the greater community in learning how to cultivate secure patterns in their attachment relationships. Eli has three children, one partner, two cats, too many plants, and identifies as a cis-female, European American clinician in her early 40s.*

Clients seeking therapy are typically trying to overcome something painful, traumatic, or confusing. Many clients feel stuck or detached from themselves and their relationships. As clinicians, our job is to help them discover or reconnect to their resilience.

As an attachment-focused clinician, I define resilience as the *relationally learned* ability to move through a state of suffering or pain into a state of regulation. As psychologist Samson summarized so succinctly,

DOI: 10.4324/9781003373513-8

"The capacity for self-soothing is born out of hundreds and hundreds of instances of being soothed by someone else" (as cited in Groysman, 2020, para. 11). People first learn emotional coping strategies in relationship to early caregivers and then in ongoing ways with whomever they create close relationships thereafter. How we talk to ourselves, how we respond to our fears and pains, how we treat our bodies, and what we do when we are scared and overwhelmed are all patterns we establish in attachment relationships. The same is true for the development of our self-concept. In the book *A Compelling Idea*, Shroufe (2020) summarized self-concept by saying, "The patterns and quality of the organized infant-caregiver system will become the core of the child's emerging self as he or she progressively becomes a more active participant in relationships and internalizes roles previously played by the caregiver" (p. 49).

In an ideal attachment experience, a caregiver successfully functions in three important ways. The first is as a safe haven—a place to be held, protected, and regulated. The second is as a secure base—a social launch pad that allows a child to feel confident venturing away in small intervals to explore the world around them, knowing there is somewhere safe to return if trouble arises. The third is as a place of identity and belonging.

As therapists, many of us know firsthand that not all caregivers are capable of offering a safe haven, a secure base, and a positive identity and sense of belonging to their children—which lends itself to children adapting their attachment instincts to accommodate their caregivers' inabilities. The children instead develop insecure–anxious–ambivalent, insecure–anxious–avoidant, or insecure–disorganized attachment patterns. Forty percent of infants worldwide experience an inadequate attachment relationship with their caregivers, leading to insecure attachment patterns and correlative struggles with learning achievements and negative behaviors (Moullin et al., 2014). Unless there exists an intervention of a healing relationship, these struggles for resilience often continue into adulthood.

When assessing for an adult client's past and present attachment patterns, I assess their attachment patterns both historically and presently, and I ask the following questions to help my client(s):

1. What do you remember about the way your caregivers responded to you when you felt emotionally tender or distressed as a child?

2. If the experiences were not comforting, how did you cope with the pain on your own?
3. Were your caregivers able to express affection and delight toward you? If not, how did that affect you as a child?
4. Did you experience any traumatic loss or abuse in regard to your caregivers?
5. What beliefs and relational habits toward self and others emerged inside of your mind and body in relation to your attachment experiences?
6. Are there any transformative positive or negative close attachment relationships in your adulthood that have changed the trajectory of how you feel and relate?
7. If we are able to help you heal the pain from your attachment experiences, what would you like to be able to do and feel differently in your close relationships moving forward?

My steps in establishing increased resilience with my clients are designed to help them (a) identify insecure attachment patterns, (b) process the pain beneath those patterns, and (c) learn a secure pattern of relating. Clients who have built secure attachments can see the life that exists alongside loss, circumstance, wounds, or oppression. Despite the troubling issues they experience, they see themselves with dignity and have a solid sense of self-worth. The clients can open their hearts, minds, and relationships to what is good and beautiful around them.

Individuals are boosted into resilience when they can actively reach for support when in tender states (e.g., lonely, sad, scared, ashamed, lost) and then allow it to soothe them and change their body state and internal narrative about whatever was distressing them. These two skills—reaching and receiving or internalizing—contribute to the inner narrative and resilient mindset that one will be okay and deserves care, support, and healing, leading to resilience (Sroufe et al., 2005).

As Walters and Seshadri advocated in Chapter 3, building resilience is a process. My metaphor for this attachment-based work begins with the adage that you can give a person a fish or you can *teach them how to fish*. As clinicians, we want clients to leave our care with the skills necessary to:

1. Know where to find fish—identify the safe, loving, nurturing people in their lives.
2. Know how to effectively cast a line in the water—actively reach for others in times of need and distress.
3. Know how to reel in the catch—receive care and soothing from others.
4. Cook and eat the fish—let the care from others internalize into positive self-worth and a pattern of treating oneself with great respect and nurture.

This process of learning a secure attachment pattern (i.e., learning how to fish) is different for everyone. Each person's unique attachment history plays into their readiness to fish. Thus, I present the four attachment patterns and share clinical goals and resources for encouraging change within each pattern. Attachment awareness fits well in many different relationships and forms of therapy. A client can learn these skills in individual, couple, and family settings. Clinicians can take attachment-informed ideas and apply them to their models of change and interventions. To begin, I share how a secure attachment pattern develops to get a sense of what we are trying to help clients (and ourselves) learn.

Secure Attachment Development

A secure attachment pattern develops in the context of a relationship with a caregiver who is highly warm, highly attuned, and highly responsive. This relational experience regulates a child both physiologically and psychologically. A person with a secure attachment experience believes relationships are a place for support and care; they instinctively and actively seek out others when in a state of tender need or distress (Ainsworth et al., 1978). This process of reaching and receiving care internalizes into a strong sense of self-worth, such as, "My needs matter, and I am worthy of support and love."

Recognizing Secure Attachment Patterns in the Therapy Context

- An individual adult client opens up emotionally during a session, receives attuned empathy from the therapist, and reports feeling relief as a result.

- A parent and child interact, the child shares some difficult emotions with the parent, and the parent responds with compassion and soothing support.
- In a couple's session, one person discusses an internal struggle affecting their mood or behavior, and the other person remains receptive and present to that vulnerable sharing. The struggling person melts physically and emotionally into the arms of their sweetheart.

Helping a Child in Therapy Use a Secure Attachment Pattern

When working with children in therapy, I prefer to keep family members in the therapy room for interactive therapy to bolster the therapeutic value in their relationship instead of having the child develop bonds with me. The therapy focuses on helping the child share their emotional world with their secure caregiver and using the strength of that relationship as the container for whatever stressor the child encounters. One of my favorite lines to families with children in therapy is:

> My goal is not to become the therapeutic force in your child's life, but to help you identify your family and individual strengths and needs to empower *you* to be the therapeutic connection they need in this particular struggle or scenario. After all, I see them once a week, but you are with them day in and day out.

Individual Therapy and Secure Attachment Patterns

When individual, adult clients come to therapy with a secure attachment pattern from childhood or one they learned from previous healing relationships, they tend to respond quite readily to the empathy and interventions we offer. There is little emotional complexity for them to seek or receive care. The client made the appointment (i.e., reach), and they leaned into the therapeutic offerings (i.e., soothe). It makes "sense" in their nervous system to use the resilience of connection. In this case, our primary role as the therapist is to mirror and validate the client's emotional states and support them in identifying their correlating needs and desires.

Systemic Therapy and Secure Attachment Patterns

Adults with secure attachment patterns actively bid for connection with their partners, friends, family, and therapists when they are in a state of dysregulation or distress.

In couples therapy, clients with secure patterns open up to their partners and ask for help in articulated and direct routes of communication. If a client with a secure pattern partners with someone with an insecure or disorganized (i.e., unresolved) attachment pattern, the therapist may need to help educate them about attachment trauma and how to mitigate the expectations of their loved ones while that person learns to heal and trust the secure love they have to offer.

Insecure, Ambivalent Pattern Development

An insecure–anxious-ambivalent or resistant attachment pattern develops when a caregiver is only able to respond to their child with warmth and attunement *intermittently*. Such inconsistency may be a result of mental health issues the caregiver is navigating, substance abuse patterns, a domestic violence dynamic at home, a stressful work environment, and so on (Scher & Mayseless, 2000). A person with an anxious–ambivalent attachment pattern struggles to feel soothed and calm in their close relationships. Their early experiences taught them attachment figures are not consistently available, so they have learned to rely on their hypervigilant scanning of others to feel protected from potential emotional or literal abandonment. Although these folks fixate strongly on their close relationships, they struggle to feel safe and secure in them.

Insecure-Anxious-Ambivalent Patterns in the Therapy Context

- An individual adult client will easily talk about painful or anxious topics during a session and even cry and ask for help. Yet, when the therapist offers empathy, insights, or support, the client continues to stay stuck in dysregulation and does not yet know how to receive care and let their guard down enough to be seen and soothed.
- In family therapy, a parent talks about wanting to be there for their child, and the child reports that "sometimes, sort of," their parent is

able to be there for them. Then, in session, when the child is upset and asks for support in some way, the parent responds with their own emotional upset, interfering with the soothing process.

- In couples therapy, after working to identify what Client A wants from Client B, Client B offers the requested need; yet, instead of feeling soothed and supported, Client A disqualifies the bid for connection, saying, "It doesn't count if I have to ask for it. You're only doing it because we're in therapy" (i.e., protest behavior).

Helping a Child in Therapy With an Ambivalent Attachment Pattern

When I have assessed a child is exhibiting an ambivalent or resistant pattern of anxious preoccupation and is fixating on their caregiver but not soothing in their presence, the first intervention needs to be with the parent—discussing their past and present stressors and helping them identify obstacles that have rendered them unavailable at times or intermittently responsive. Helping the parent understand the tantamount importance of being consistent in their emotional responsiveness will best help the child relax and begin to feel safe enough to learn how to soothe.

Individual Adult Therapy and Ambivalent Attachment Patterns

In individual therapy, the adult has the ability to share what they are suffering through and how they want their experience to be different. When offered empathy, tools, or insight, the client will usually bat away attempts to soothe them. They have never learned to receive and let down their guard in the places they most long to do so (i.e., close caring relationships).

For a client with this resistant or ambivalent pattern, therapists need to be patient as they learn to internalize consistent empathy and care. If the therapist pushes them to soothe or projects their need for movement in the therapy, they can unconsciously recreate the unpredictable caregiver this client internalized as a child. After spending significant time building trust and seeing the client can begin to internalize the therapeutic relationship as a new model for connecting, therapists can also highlight the fear the client has about letting down their guard and let care soothe them, followed by encouraging them to begin to relinquish control over the connections they desire.

Couples and Family Therapy and Ambivalent Attachment Patterns

Often, a person with an ambivalent or resistant pattern motivates a system to enter therapy. This individual is plagued with the pain of feeling constantly insecure in their relationship dynamic and wants things to change. During the therapy process, even when the other family members make genuine attempts to meet this person's requests, nothing seems to satisfy them. In this situation, the work of the therapist is to invite them gently to slow down and work on absorbing what is being offered. It is also important to communicate to the other parties that the issue is not that this person does not want to be soothed but that they do not know how—returning to those historical stories about their childhood and the reasons their nervous system adapted with hypervigilance.

Insecure-Avoidant Pattern Development

Insecure-anxious avoidant (i.e., dismissive) patterns develop when a caregiver invalidates, ignores, or consistently misses their child's emotional needs and tender cues (Benoit, 2004). As a result, the child learns that keeping emotional needs private is the most effective way to cope with their pain. Instead of seeking their caregiver for coregulation support, they *distract themselves and dissociate from their emotional states*. In this state, the child is not "less" attached or even less interested in closeness; rather, the child has learned that avoiding sharing their emotional needs is the most effective way to maintain proximity with their caregivers.

Unlike secure and resistant infants, the avoidant child has not developed the skill of reaching for others. Although the child can appear calm and soothed on the outside, they are not actually in a calm state; they are relying on numbness to cope with their dysregulation.

Insecure-Avoidant Attachment Pattern in Therapy

- In individual therapy, this person struggles to find the words to describe what is happening in their internal world and in their relationships. They may look "calm" on the outside but struggle internally, unsure of how to rely on others.
- In family therapy, parents may dismiss a child's pain or narrative as an attempt to help them feel better, saying things like, "You're okay,

you'll be fine, you're a tough kid" in moments where the attuned response would be, "I can see how much you are hurting, or I am so glad you shared that with me, so I know what you are going through."

- In couples therapy, a client may present a stoic or blank face, even in the middle of tense or emotional content. Their partners often complain of being unable to tell if they care or know what they feel.

Helping a Child in Therapy With an Insecure-Anxious-Avoidant Attachment Pattern

Avoidant children need emotional support and attunement as much as those who are actively seeking support. A goal in family therapy is to help the parent of this child learn to access, understand, and tolerate their emotional world and the emotions of others. As the parent begins to value emotional connection, as the therapist, we also want to help them to supportively communicate to their child that feelings are an opportunity for connection, not a burden. Emotion-focused games can be a great way to break the ice with avoidant or dismissive family systems. By beginning the dialogue about feelings in a lighter way, it feels less threatening while developing a shared language about body states.

Individual Therapy and Insecure Avoidant Attachment Patterns

The avoidant (i.e., dismissive) attachment pattern makes leaning into therapy an uncomfortable process. The primary avoidant instinct is to ignore and dismiss emotional cues and pain, so just by being in therapy, this client loses their primary coping skill, leaving them feeling worse (i.e., more) than before they entered the process. It takes time for a person with an avoidant pattern to begin to see the gain that comes with feeling their feelings and sharing their pain. The client has to learn the difference between numb and calm, which means feeling the pain between those two body states.

I think of this work as titrating emotional tolerance. I do not want to throw this person into the deep end of their painful life experiences, as they do not yet know how to swim. Little by little, I want to reflect back to their feeling states and help the client see it can lead us to feel more endeared by the emotions, not more burdened by them.

Couples and Family Therapy and Insecure-Avoidant Attachment Patterns

One of the most important insights necessary to supporting someone with an avoidant attachment pattern is understanding they do not avoid because they do not want closeness—they avoid because *that* is how they maintained the highest level of closeness possible with their early caregivers. Such an interpretation is essential to help family members understand the client's tendency to isolate from others when struggling. Similar to individual therapy, as therapists, we want to help this person increase their window of tolerance for tender emotions and relational needs so they can increase their resilience through the use of relationships and connection to their body. Though the client can come across as nonfeeling or calloused due to restricted emotional expression on their face and in their voice, we want to advocate for their partners and family members to understand why they learned this coping pattern and what lies beneath it. We also need to help the client see and absorb that when they open up and let themselves be emotionally transparent, they become *more* connected to their family members rather than *less* resilient.

Disorganized Attachment Development

With the previously mentioned secure, avoidant, and ambivalent attachment experiences, a child is able to develop a *coherent pattern*, such as reaching out and seeking shelter in the arms of a caregiver (Reijman et al., 2018). Avoiding and numbing is a pattern, as is hypervigilance and scanning for loss. Even though the second two patterns are considered insecure, they are also considered coherent and organized.

Children who do not exhibit the aforementioned patterns are considered disorganized or disoriented in their attachment system. The child with a disorganized attachment category has experienced a caregiving deficit far beyond inadequate; they have experienced a frightening caregiver or caregiving environment. In these cases, the caregiver has acted erratic, abusive, psychotic, or neglectful to the basic needs and safety of the child (Carlson, 1998).

A disorganized (i.e., unresolved) attachment process develops because a caregiver, meant to be a haven during distressing fear, is the *catalyst* of the distressing fear (Granqvist et al., 2017). If the caregiver is the threat, the child has nowhere to seek refuge. This situation results in a shutdown or scrambling of the child's attachment drive, leading to a pattern of serious dissociation and activation of the fight, flight, freeze, and fawn response when facing distressing scenarios. The child does not feel safe running toward the caregiver when scared, so they rely on more primitive survival responses from their parasympathetic nervous system: fight, flight, freeze, faint, and fawn.

These children are often labeled as behaving badly and receive subsequent punitive treatment at home, school, and other locations of caregiving. Their behavior feels scary because they are scared and do not trust that anyone is safe enough to run to. As they grow into adults, these children are categorized as having an unresolved attachment pattern. They continue to live in a survival mode in terms of relationships and struggle to feel safe in any close relationships—or anywhere else for that matter.

Disorganized Attachment Patterns in Therapy

- In individual therapy, folks with disorganized and unresolved attachment patterns often struggle with deeply seeded self-hatred that sounds like "I deserve this" or "Why would anyone love me?" Alongside that disorganized sense of self-worth is a disturbed and often distorted idea of the intentions of others. The individual will anticipate people will use, harm, and abuse them, or misinterpret ill intent as a result of actual experiences of harm, abuse, and ill intent in their early years from their caregivers, and often, from later toxic relationships.
- In family therapy, unresolved caregivers will talk about their children in highly negative ways and accuse them of being "ungrateful and spoiled" or share they are "trying to ruin my life." They struggle to

see the dignified meaning underneath their child's dysregulation and resulting behavior.

- In couples therapy, disorganization can appear in the forms of struggles to interpret intent in the other partner or dissociation and shutdown in contexts of bids for connection or vulnerable disclosures.

Helping a Child in Therapy With a Disorganized Attachment Pattern

Children with a disorganized pattern need to be given as much predictability as possible. Clinicians should keep therapy on the same day, at the same time, and explain exactly what will happen if they are sick and need to cancel an appointment. The clinicians should also give the children free rein over whatever safe and soft toys and games they have but must remain clear about what is and is not safe play and how they will handle it if something unsafe happens.

If the child's caregivers are in a stable place, clinicians should help them understand how to create a predictable structure at home as well. Strategies include creating visual calendars and daily schedules that help the child anticipate what is coming, giving ample time before transitions, and discussing the process for transitions. This child is unsure they are safe and needs as many anchors in their school, home, and treatment environments as possible.

Individual Therapy and Disorganized Attachment Pattern

I believe a disorganized attachment pattern is synonymous with complex posttraumatic stress disorder. When folks with this pattern are brave enough to seek therapy, they are generally in a rough spot. The client will usually feel stronger—both positive and negative—feelings about their therapist and that relationship. The work is hard for them and can be hard on the therapist, too, but it does not mean they cannot progress and learn to feel safer and more worthy of love.

Clinicians should continue to offer the individual empathy and understanding and work for a long time on grounding skills and resourcing their nervous system before diving into trauma work. It may take years for this person to feel safe and fully ready to lean into close relationships. The therapeutic relationship may be the client's safest relationship for a long time before they can internalize that safety and begin to trust others with it.

Couples and Family Therapy and Disorganized Attachment Patterns

When someone with this attachment pattern comes into therapy within a system, I usually see a system that revolves around that person's woundedness. The person could be the parent, partner, or child, but their struggle to feel safe and the disorganized responses to that lack of safe feeling tend to put everyone else into a heightened state of fear. The key is to create trust with the person who is unresolved in their style without justifying the reactions to their feelings and projecting them into the family system. Then, I find a way to begin to gain their investment in doing their own personal work to process their traumas and make sense of their reactions based not only on their present interactions but also on how their past has affected those interactions. This work takes an incredible amount of attunement on the therapist's part and endearment toward the person with the disoriented pattern.

Conclusion

Whether working with an individual trying to learn a secure partnership, a couple stuck in a gridlocked pattern of disconnection, or a family working through the presence of a trauma or a generational pattern, an attachment-focused lens will give everyone a dignified way through. It is through identifying relational patterns that the therapist can assist everyone in the session to cast their line for connection, reel it in, and receive care from their closest relationships. Clients can then experience an entirely new level of resilience by using the support of those closest to them through secure, attached relationships.

Through relational attunement and supportive responses to pain, therapists may give someone their first experience of emotional resilience. Such an experience may initially confuse them, but if we continue to be curious and compassionate to help them identify the connection between their current patterns and their past pains, their attachment system will grab hold of our care and start to write an entirely new narrative—one that will bring them closer to people, themselves, and the hope of a connected future.

Table 8.1 Family Therapy Attachment Patterns and Goals

Attachment patterns in children	Relational experience with caregiver	Coping response to that experience	Play/family therapy goals
Secure	Caregivers are warm, attuned, and responsive to child.	Child learns to trust their body cues and reach for others in moments of distress.	Encourage and validate parents in using secure patterns to help children process life traumas, oppression, etc.
Avoidant	Caregivers are consistently emotionally misattuned to child.	Child learns to ignore their body cues and distract themselves in moment of distress.	Help parents learn to notice and tolerate emotions in themselves and their children. Increase receptivity and responsiveness to feelings.
Ambivalent	Caregivers are inconsistent in their availability or effectiveness to soothe child.	Child learns to vigilantly scan their caregiver for change and protest comfort.	Help parents identify barriers to consistency and acknowledge them with children in an appropriate way. Identify supports and solutions to increase availability and establish greater trust.
Disorganized	Caregivers are relationally frightening to the child.	Child has high trauma responses toward dissociation and enters sympathetic fight, flight, freeze, faint when in distress.	Establish trauma-informed individual care for the parent, and do not do family therapy until the parent is stable enough to be a safe presence for the child. Assess for abuse and neglect and try to identify other safe caregivers in children's lives who can help scaffold the family while the parent works to heal.

Table 8.2 Adult Individuals' and Couples' Attachment Patterns and Therapy Goals

Adult attachment pattern	Relational pattern toward attachment figures (partners, friends, and children)	Beliefs/instincts in regard to tender needs and distress	Areas for growth and learning in therapy
Secure-Free-Autonomous	Is relationally warm, open, and able to navigate emotions with a generally calm presence.	Believes their needs matter and tends to communicate needs directly and then receive care with ease.	Ongoing nuances of understanding emotional states and effective relating, especially in complex contexts.
Dismissive	Is relationally distant and sometimes cold. Struggles to open up and retreats when strong emotions enter the scene.	Believes that emotions are a burden and that it is kinder to swallow feelings and avoid than share with others.	Emotional awareness and tolerance in both self and others as well as learning to verbalize and share emotions.
Preoccupied	Tends toward enmeshment and hypervigilance within close relationships. Seeks copious amounts of reassurance but struggles to trust it.	Believes that they are not good enough to be loved consistently and that they need to constantly stand guard for potential loss. Struggles to trust the love others give.	Receptivity to care and soothing, body settling, and direct communication of needs.
Unresolved	Struggles to understand the intent of others and often feels caught between fear of harm or abuse and fear of abandonment.	Believes that they are unsafe and unworthy of being safe. Believes that others have mal-intent and cannot possibly genuinely care for them.	Finding safe people and space and learning to emotionally regulate. Trauma processing and internal self-narrative editing.

Recommended Resources

Resources for Attachment-Focused Interventions in Family Therapy
Norris, V., & Lender, D. (2020). *Theraplay–The practitioner's guide*. Jessica Kingsley Publishers.

Powell, B., Cooper, G., Hoffman, K., & Marvin, B. (2013). *The circle of security intervention: Enhancing attachment in early parent-child relationships*. Guilford publications.

Resources for Children With Attachment Trauma
Perry, B. D., & Szalavitz, M. (2017). *The boy who was raised as a dog: And other stories from a child psychiatrist's notebook—What traumatized children can teach us about loss, love, and healing*. Hachette UK.

Purvis, K. B., Cross, D. R., & Pennings, J. S. (2009). Trust-based relational intervention: Interactive principles for adopted children with special social-emotional needs. *The Journal of Humanistic Counseling, Education and Development, 48*(1), 3–22. https://doi.org/10.1002/j.2161-1939.2009.tb00064.x

Books for Building a Secure Attachment Pattern in Adulthood
Harwood, E. (2023). *Securely attached*. Penguin Random House.

Tatkin, S. (2012). *Wired for love: How understanding your partner's brain and attachment style can help you defuse conflict and build a secure relationship*. New Harbinger Publications.

Books for Adults With Attachment Trauma
Perry, B. (2021). *What happened to you? Conversations on trauma, resilience, and healing*. Flatiron Books.

Van Der Kolk, B. (2015). *The body keeps the score: Brain, mind, and body in the healing of trauma*. Penguin Books.

Accessible Attachment Theory Books
Karen, R. (1998). *Becoming attached: First relationships and how they shape our capacity to love*. Oxford University Press.

Shroufe, A. (2020). *A compelling idea: How we become the persons we are*. Safer Society Press.

References

Ainsworth, M. D. S., Blehar, M. C., Waters, E., & Wall, S. (1978). *Patterns of attachment: A psychological study of the strange situation*. Lawrence Erlbaum.

Benoit, D. (2004). Infant-parent attachment: Definition, types, antecedents, measurement and outcome. *Paediatrics & Child Health, 9*(8), 541–545. https://doi.org/10.1093/pch/9.8.541

Carlson, E. A. (1998). A prospective longitudinal study of attachment disorganization/disorientation. *Child Development, 69*(4), 1107–1128. https://doi.org/10.1111/j.1467-8624.1998.tb06163.x

Granqvist, P., Sroufe, L. A., Dozier, M., Hesse, E., Steele, M., van Ijzendoorn, M., Solomon, J., Schuengel, C., Fearon, P., Bakermans-Kranenburg, M., Steele, H., Cassidy, J., Carlson, E., Madigan, S., Jacobvitz, D., Foster, S., Behrens, K., Rifkin-Graboi, A., Gribneau, N., & Spangler, G. (2017). Disorganized attachment in infancy: A review of the phenomenon and its implications for clinicians and policy-makers. *Attachment & Human Development, 19*(6), 534–558. https://doi.org/10.1080/14616734.2017.1354040

Groysman, V. (2020, May 18). *Sleep training babies, crying it out, sleep without training methods explained by infant mental health specialist.* Talkin Sleep. https://talkinsleep.com/sleep-training-babies-crying-it-out-sleep-without-training-methods-explained-by-infant-mental-health-specialist/

Moullin, S., Waldfogel, J., & Washbrook, E. (2014). Baby bonds: Parenting, attachment and a secure base for children. *Sutton Trust.* www.bl.uk/collection-items/baby-bonds-parenting-attachment-and-a-secure-base-for-children

Reijman, S., Foster, S., & Duschinsky, R. (2018). The infant disorganized attachment classification: "Patterning within the disturbance of coherence." *Social Science & Medicine, 200*(200), 52–58. https://doi.org/10.1016/j.socscimed.2017.12.034

Scher, A., & Mayseless, O. (2000). Mothers of anxious/ambivalent infants: Maternal characteristics and child-care context. *Child Development, 71*(6), 1629–1639. https://doi.org/10.1111/1467-8624.00253

Shroufe, A. (2020). *A compelling idea: How we become the persons we are.* Safer Society Press.

Sroufe, L. A., Egeland, B., Carlson, E. A., & Collins, W. A. (2005). *The development of the person: The Minnesota study of risk and adaptation from birth to adulthood.* Guilford Publications.

9

CULTIVATING SYSTEMIC RESILIENCE OF BLACK ADOLESCENTS WITH DISORDERED EATING

Targeting Belief Systems as a Mechanism
for Change

Ashley A. Hicks and Casey C. Levy

Ashley A. Hicks, PhD, IMFT-S, is a clinical associate professor of human development and family science at The Ohio State University. She is a licensed, independent marriage and family therapist, clinical supervisor, researcher, consultant, speaker, and registered yoga teacher. Her clinical practice and research focus on adolescent/family development in marginalized communities; adolescent eating disorder treatment and recovery; and the creation, delivery, and evaluation of culturally appropriate mental health services for diverse populations. Ashley is the current director of The Ohio State University's Couple and Family Therapy Clinic. Ashley is a cisgendered, able-bodied, Black, queer, Christian, US citizen, middle-class, English-speaking woman.

Casey C. Levy, MD, MPH is an assistant professor of clinical pediatrics at The Ohio State University Medical Center practicing within the Division of Adolescent Medicine at Nationwide Children's Hospital in Columbus, Ohio. She completed her pediatric residency and chief residency at Children's Hospital of the King's Daughters in Norfolk, Virginia, before completing her fellowship in

DOI: 10.4324/9781003373513-9

adolescent medicine in Columbus, Ohio. During her fellowship, she obtained her Master of Public Health from The Ohio State University, developing a passion for program development and upstream intervention. Dr. Levy is currently Medical Director for the Adolescent Medicine Eating Disorder Services at Nationwide Children's Hospital, spearheading the growth and development of high-quality, evidence-based medical care for youth with eating disorders as they journey toward recovery. She identifies her social location as a middle-aged, cisgendered, able-bodied, White, neurotypical, heterosexual, Christian, US citizen, English-speaking, female adolescent medicine physician.

Black adolescents experience disordered eating (DE) and eating disorders (EDs) at similar rates to other races and ethnicities but are half as likely to be diagnosed or receive treatment (Deloitte Access Economics, 2020). Anti-Black stereotypes contribute to decreased recognition of DE, delaying the start of treatment and compromising care provided to Black adolescents. This chapter introduces a family resilience approach to working with Black adolescents who experience DE and their families. The text highlights individual and family belief systems as a primary source of systemic resilience and an important focus for clinical intervention. We combine existing knowledge of Black adolescents' resilience with evidence-based treatment for EDs to apply to DE interventions. Application of this approach and examples of clinical interventions are also provided.

DE refers to food- and diet-related behaviors that do not meet diagnostic criteria for a clinical ED but can impair physical and psychosocial functioning (Neumark-Sztainer et al., 2011). DE behaviors include restrictive, compulsive, irregular, or inflexible eating patterns, limited food variety, dieting, binge eating, self-induced vomiting, or other purging behaviors (e.g., laxative misuse). DE behaviors often begin during adolescence and can persist over time, sometimes developing into diagnosable EDs. Consistent DE in adolescence significantly increases the likelihood of continued DE and/or development of an ED into young adulthood (Neumark-Sztainer et al., 2011). EDs have the second highest mortality rate of all mental health disorders, and an estimated 29 million people in the United States will have an ED in their lifetime, equating to a 6.4% lifetime prevalence (Deloitte Access Economics, 2020).

Although DE is commonplace in the United States, significant disparities exist in recognition, assessment, and intervention. Black adolescents and families must contend with stereotypes concerning DE that are often based on body weight, body shape, racism, and stigma shaped by Euro-centric cultural and societal norms regarding whose bodies are valued in society. Black, Indigenous, and People of Color (BIPOC) persons are less likely than White persons to be asked about a DE or ED by a doctor (Becker et al., 2003). Black adolescents are half as likely to be diagnosed and treated for Eds, compared to other races and ethnicities, despite experiencing EDs at similar rates (Deloitte Access Economics, 2020). Earlier onset of anorexia nervosa (AN) in Black individuals lengthens the disease duration, and Black populations have reported greater social and role functioning impairment compared to White individuals with EDs (Marques et al., 2011; Taylor et al., 2007).

Despite the prevalence, impairment, and future health implications of DE among Black adolescents, there are a dearth of empirical and clini-cal data available. Given the impact of systemic racism and inadequate recognition of DE in Black people, this literature gap is both expected and unacceptable. Black individuals are significantly less likely to be assessed for and diagnosed with EDs across all healthcare settings. Even if assessment and ED diagnosis occur, Black individuals have reported lower treatment utilization than their White counterparts (Marques et al., 2011). If the healthcare community is unable to recognize, diagnose, and treat Black youth with EDs, then there will be no study participants to help better understand the unique treatment needs for DE or ED in Black youth. As such, though clinicians can identify effective interventions for adolescent DE and EDs, the ability to generalize these outcomes to Black adolescents is tentative, at best. More commonly, Black adoles-cents are left unrecognized and undiagnosed to deal with DE in isola-tion. Such a reality further restricts visibility to healthcare providers and society of the experience of DE in Black adolescents and perpetuates the belief that DE and EDs in Black adolescents are less common and less severe than White counterparts.

To understand the current, negligent care state most thoroughly for Black adolescents with DE, it is important to understand anti-Blackness as a primary risk factor for DE among Black youth. Anti-Blackness is a cultural paradigm that defines assumptions that undergird per-sonal, cultural, and collective worldviews as a society (Dumas, 2016). Anti-Blackness positions Black people as socially dead and thus not considered human by broader society (Patterson, 1982). The result is anti-Black racism—the systematic and structural authorization of the dehumanization of Black lives (Liu et al., 2023). Anti-Blackness creates an environment of ongoing adversity for Black adolescents. Black adolescents must navigate through prejudice and discrimination across multiple contexts while engaging in a primary task of adolescence—identity development. For example, Black girls have been found to make meaning about their ethnic–racial identity (ERI) in response to stereotypical and biased messages about race received from family, peers, schools, and classrooms (Mims & Williams, 2020).

Black adolescents experience multiple manifestations of anti-Blackness in their daily lives. In this chapter, we identify three specific manifestations of anti-Blackness and their relationship to DE and systemic resilience for Black adolescents: (a) White supremacy, (b) adultification, and (c) fat phobia. White supremacy is the ideology that White people are superior to others. This ideology is used to maintain cultural, social, political, historical, and institutional dominance by White people (Liu et al., 2023). The reality that most clinical and empirical data related to DE and ED for all people, especially adolescents, are based on White patients and communities is one example of how White supremacy influences understanding and interventions related to DE—essentially removing Black people and their experiences from the conversation. Adultification is racial bias where Black children are treated as adults, expected to be more mature, and viewed as more culpable than their White peers (Epstein et al., 2017; Goff et al., 2014). Racial discrepancies also exist in psychiatric diagnoses of Black children and adolescents, such that Black youth are more likely to be diagnosed with disruptive behavioral disorders, compared to White youth, who are more likely to be diagnosed with mood disorders (Mauldin et al., 2022; L. Nguyen et al., 2007). Such a discrepancy is one way in which adultification manifests itself in healthcare. In DE and ED treatment, adultification of Black adolescents—especially girls—can occur when providers view Black girls' lack of adherence to treatment plans or clinical recommendations as intentionally defiant and treatment interfering, compared to White girls whose behaviors may be more often attributed to (a) problems related to malnutrition, (b) a diagnosed or undiagnosed EDs, or (c) comorbid mental health concerns such as depression or anxiety. Fat phobia is defined as a pathological fear of fatness and is comprised of negative attitudes and stereotypes related to larger bodies maintained by a fear of being fat or around fat people (Robinson et al., 1993).

For Black adolescents, fat phobia is inextricably linked to anti-Black racism, colorism, and White supremacy. Especially when a Black adolescent body is larger and darker, devaluation and dismissal of DE are commonplace due to an idealization of thinness and Whiteness by US society (Harrison, 2021; Strings, 2019). Previous studies have found differential experiences of patients with EDs based on race (Becker et al., 2003; Marques et al., 2011). For example, Black women with binge-eating disorder are less likely to receive treatment for an eating problem than White women, although both groups are just as likely to receive treatment for a weight problem (Pike et al., 2001).

The stigma associated with being Black in a large body, in general, or when compared to that of White individuals, is a direct contributor to the inadequate recognition of DE behaviors (Brochu, 2018; Strings, 2019). In addition to a broad societal stigma that minimizes recognition of DE in Black youth, cultural stigma exists within the Black community about DE and ED, resulting in an erroneous belief that restrictive eating, dieting, and purging behaviors among Black adolescents do not reach a level to trigger concern (Armstrong, 2009; Bordo, 2013). Additionally, the history of food insecurity for Black people in the United States has impacted cultural understandings of the role of food in Black life. Social determinants such as access to food, healthcare, economic stability, and social-community context also contribute to the unique challenges of Black persons', especially adolescents', abilities to be seen, heard, and supported when grappling with DE (Bidopia et al., 2023; Goode et al., 2022, 2023).

This chapter combines knowledge about resilience of Black adolescents with best practices and evidence-based treatment for EDs to offer practitioners practical conceptualizations and interventions when working with Black adolescents presenting with DE. The mainstay of adolescent ED treatment is family based treatment (FBT), which relies heavily on family and kinship to support youth through treatment (Lock & Le Grange, 2005). FBT cedes making food and eating decisions to caregivers until the adolescent can learn to make these decisions safely in the future. FBT starts treatment with the underlying tenet that caregivers are the most important source of treatment support, and the ED is a crisis needing urgent intervention (Lock & Le Grange, 2005). To support the recovery and well-being of Black adolescents with DE, we use a family resilience approach (Walsh, 2015) rooted in a foundation of FBT (Lock & Le Grange, 2005). This multisystemic approach considers individual, family, and system-level processes influencing the ability of Black adolescents to sustain their well-being and address DE by using psychological, social, cultural, and physical resources.

A Family Resilience Approach to DE With Black Adolescents

Belief systems, organizational processes, and communication processes are three aspects of family functioning that promote resilience (Walsh, 2015). This chapter focuses on examining belief systems as the basis for clinical intervention with Black adolescents with DE. Our discussion focuses on key processes within this domain: meaning making and positive outlook specifically related to their relevance to clinical practice with Black adolescents with DE. We offer interventions and clinical activities that help practitioners provide resilience-focused, multisystemic, culturally relevant, and effective care for Black adolescents struggling with DE.

Culturally and Relationally Relevant Meaning Making

The ability to make meaning or make sense out of one's struggles is important for resilience. Individuals and families experiencing adversity may feel out of control and overwhelmed, which is true for those who engage in DE. Clients with DE often feel a sense of secrecy, shame, and guilt related to their thoughts and behaviors. For Black adolescents, this shame or secrecy may be heightened due to the cultural and medical stigmas associated with DE and the size and shape of Black persons (Strings, 2019). If the healthcare community assumes that Black adolescents do not experience DE, then Black adolescents who experience these symptoms may feel increasingly misunderstood and invisible, interpreting these symptoms as personal or moral failings.

Just as Black adolescents are absent examples of appropriately recognized DE and treatment, Black families are absent a framework for recognition and treatment of DE or ED in Black youth. Black caregivers and families may develop an internalized sense of failure or shame, given that success and well-being of the children are established cultural values, and DE treatment might threaten these values. Having feelings of shame and failure, coupled with marginalization due to anti-Black racism, can make it difficult for family members to identify DE and may prevent them from seeking or receiving support. Healthcare professionals may perceive Black individuals' and families' lack of awareness or minimization of DE as treatment resistance, interference, or indifference—leading to a lack of empathy, missed educational needs, unrecognized diagnoses, unidentified treatment needs, and underdevelopment of the crucial therapeutic alliance between family members and providers (Roberts & Chaves, 2023). To best understand all of the facets of work in a family system, we introduce B, a 15-year-old Caribbean Black woman living in the Midwest just starting out in therapy. We refer to B and other client examples throughout this chapter to best illustrate various topics.

> Consider B, who initiated therapy due to symptoms of depression, low self-esteem, and concerns about DE and a possible ED. B lives with her older sister, her primary caregiver. Her sister believes the eating issues were caused by "American culture" and that if she could just stop comparing herself to "thin, White girls," she would be fine. Feeling responsible for her eating difficulties, B began to disconnect from her treatment providers. Within a couple of sessions, B expressed that treatment was no longer needed and stated she was no longer having any trouble eating. Recognizing the importance of caregiver support, the therapist then tried to build an alliance with B's sister to assist her in identifying B's DE behaviors and possible ED. According to the sister, the therapist was wrongly focusing on eating concerns as opposed to the true problem: her sister's need to be "American." With these unaligned treatment directions, the treatment sessions focused more on discussing clinical relevance of DE symptoms instead of developing symptom management strategies. After four sessions, sister and B thanked the therapist and stated that all issues had been addressed and requested termination of services shortly after they began.

To enhance meaning and promote wellness (Walsh, 2015), professionals working with youth such as B and her sister must be willing to help them explore DE symptoms as a crisis that is meaningful, comprehensible, and manageable. DE will often happen with no apparent trigger or etiology, and even if DE progresses to ED, the cause is rarely apparent or clear (Lock & Le Grange, 2005). When approaching treatment through an FBT lens, clinicians acknowledge the presence of DE but also recognize we may never understand why or how this behavior developed, and the why or cause is not needed to improve this health concern. Rather, initial treatment focuses on improvement of nutritional deficits and DE behaviors to correct any functional impairment. Although FBT methodology avoids addressing the cause as a starting point for treatment, for families like B and her sister, these questions must be brought up and discussed, which may need to occur before formulating subsequent treatment steps. Discussing causal or explanatory attributions related to DE symptoms such as "How could this happen?" and "Why do you think this may be important our clinical work together?" improves transparency of provider concern and can be especially important for Black families who may be distrustful of the healthcare system and providers. Once there is a transparent conversation about the etiology, or lack thereof, of DE and health concerns associated with DE, then DE can be identified as a treatment goal that can be used to align and unite B and her sister. Recognizing the psychological and physical benefits of consistent, appropriate nutritional intake is a comprehensible and manageable step toward helping B early on in treatment if these benefits are framed and educated on early in treatment planning.

As discussed previously, we can see how Black individuals may see DE as a rare occurrence in their community. Not only does the under-recognition of DE and health implications interfere with treatment theoretically, but in B's case, the belief that DE does not affect the Black community undermined, disrupted, and prematurely terminated her care. Clinicians could, instead of focusing on the cause or prevalence of DE, discuss the impact of anti-Blackness—in B's case, specifically White supremacy and fat phobia—and its effect on health, weight stigma, and marginalization on Black adolescents' mental health, emphasizing the connection to DE symptoms. B's therapists must deconstruct B's and her sister's beliefs about the "thin ideal" and relate this mindset as a possible contributor to B's DE symptoms. This dialogue promotes a client-centered alliance and helps identify behaviors to work on in treatment. For example, asking B questions such as (a) "How do you feel about your body?" (b) "Tell me how others (peers, family, society) see your body?", and (c) "What comments have been made about your body by family, friends, or your community?" open space for dialogue about individual body image and the client's understanding of external perceptions of their body that may be influenced by anti-Black—specifically, White supremacist—adultified, and fat phobic ideals. Following up this set of questions with "Do you ever change your eating to change your body?" may allow the therapist to identify current DE behaviors and their relationship to anti-Blackness. Additionally, we recommend validating B's sister's assertion that B needs to stop comparing herself to "thin, White girls" while naming how systemic racism, White supremacy, and fat phobic beliefs are foundational to this dynamic.

Fostering Positive Outlook and Identity

Positive outlook is necessary for resilience (Walsh, 2015). Strength-based approaches are important for Black adolescents and families because they draw on innate resources that have been successful in managing previous adversity, and they use those same resources to address DE. For example, spirituality can offer inspiration for Black adolescents and their loved ones to envision a world of new possibilities where DE is not a primary actor in their lives. Circular questioning can be used to assist in this process, and all members of the system can be asked to respond to the questions "What would life look like without the presence of DE?" and "How would I/we respond if the pressure to (eat/restrict/compensate/fit the mold) was absent?"

For Black adolescents and their families, creating conversations to develop or augment shared meanings regarding DE symptoms should include the adolescent, the caregivers, an extended network of family and friends, and relevant healthcare professionals. The goal of this collective treatment team is to support the interruption and ultimate remission of DE symptoms and increase overall adolescent well-being. From a place of shared understanding, therapists can use the adolescent's and their family members' various strengths to foster a positive outlook characterized by hope, confidence, and encouragement. Black adolescents and families can foster positive outlooks by promoting racial/ethnic identity and cultural socialization through dialogue and storytelling.

During one session with B and her sister, the therapist asked the sister to discuss her experience related to how her body was visualized after moving to the United States. B's sister remembered vividly how, in their previous home, all the kids in her school had braids and looked similar to her, so she felt she could be just like the other girls. Upon moving to the United States, B's sister recounted how she entered her high school classroom and looked into a room full of faces that were different than hers. She felt different immediately and noted this feeling made her uncertain of how to act, dress, speak, or exist in this new environment. B noted that growing up primarily in the United States in their current neighborhood, she never felt like she fit in or looked like her friends. She was amazed to hear that her sister had that experience before in school in their home country, and said she wished she could have that now. B's sister reflected that the difference in their experiences in school and life probably made them have different outlooks on how they viewed themselves.

From this conversation, the therapist learns that B and her sister have a shared experience of uncertainty regarding body image, self-esteem, and belonging connected to their experiences of immigration and acculturation in the United States. Using this shared experience, the therapist can further explore the differences and similarities between B's outlook, her sister's current outlook, and the previous outlook held by B's sister as a teen. Differences in acculturation strategies adopted by the sisters might account for differences in their outlook and sense of self. From conversations with the family, we assume B's sister adopted an integration or biculturalism strategy to acculturation (i.e., adopting the receiving culture while retaining the heritage culture), which is associated with more favorable psychosocial outcomes (A. M. D. Nguyen & Benet-Martínez, 2013) and B adopted an assimilation strategy (i.e., adopting the receiving culture while discarding the heritage culture; Berry, 1980). The therapist can help facilitate conversations within this family unit and encourage ongoing conversations with extended kinship networks about how B's sister and others were able to adjust successfully to their new environment. Additionally, the therapist can discuss how B and her sister can draw from their positive experiences in their home country and in the United States to help support a more positive self-image and build confidence that changes can be made to improve B's overall well-being and decrease DE behaviors and related health complications. To take a more in-depth look into the conversation with B and the provider, see Table 9.1 for examples of provider questions, client responses, and clinical insights.

Racial and Ethnic Socialization: Dialogue and Storytelling as Intervention

Black youth experience the highest rates of perceived racial discrimination of any youth in the United States (Nagata et al., 2021). Ethnic–racial pride and identity have been identified as a source of resilience for Black youth in the face of prejudice and discrimination. ERI is defined as "a multidimensional, psychological construct that reflects the beliefs and attitudes (which) individuals have about their ethnic–racial group memberships, as well as the processes by which these beliefs and attitudes develop over time" (Umaña-Taylor et al., 2014, p. 3). ERI is associated with adaptive psychosocial, health, and academic outcomes for Black adolescents (Rivas-Drake et al., 2014). In fact, ERI and pride have been identified as protective factors against obesity-related concerns (i.e., fears of gaining weight, concerns about body shape and weight, emphasis on weight and dieting behaviors) among Black youth with high body mass indexes, regardless of gender (Lisse et al., 2022).

Given the protective nature of ERI, supporting the development or maintenance of a strong positive racial identity in Black adolescents with DE is an important support for remission of DE or ED symptoms in Black youth. Clinicians working with Black adolescents must be willing and able to discuss previous intentional and unintentional racial socialization from parents, peers, and larger systems (e.g., schools, communities, and media) and the influence these systems have on ERI development, DE, and treatment. The clinician must also incorporate these concepts into evidence-based practices such as FBT. Moreover, the entire caregiving team must engage in and enhance conversations related to recovery and intentional positive ERI development to ensure culturally responsive treatment. By engaging Black adolescents in intentional racial and cultural socialization, they can learn about and develop a sense of belonging to their cultural community, which will help them recover from DE.

Table 9.1 Examples of Possible Questions, Sample Answers, Concerns, and Insights for Clinical Conversations About DE With Black Adolescents by Topic and Theme

Theme/ Topic	Provider questions	Sample answers	Concerns revealed and follow-up possibilities
Eating and Nutrition	How do you feel about your nutrition?	*I feel my eating is better now.*	Concern that eating has been a problem in the past.
			Follow-up: You mention eating is better now, when was it not better?
	On average, how many times per day are you eating?	*I eat once per day.*	Concern for underfueling.
			Follow-up: Can you give me a range of how many times you ate in a given day over the last week?
	How do you know when to eat in the day? Do you get hungry, or do you follow more of a schedule for your eating?	*I eat dinner because my sister makes me eat dinner. I don't like feeling hungry, so I will often chew gum or drink water to keep from feeling it in the day. I do not eat unless I am very hungry.*	Concern for lack of hunger signals or lack of consistent fueling. Concern for chewing gum or drinking water to avoid feeling hungry or eating.
	Are there health concerns in your family that impact your food or eating choices?	*My Grandmother has high cholesterol, so I know I need to eat only low-fat foods, and my sister has high blood pressure, so I know that salt is bad for that so the less salt the better.*	Client prioritizes health and wants to take care of their body. Client does pay attention to the health and medical recommendations of those around them.

	Is anyone worried or concerned about your nutrition?	*My sister is worried, but I keep telling her I'm fine.*	Concern that client isn't recognizing a concerning nutritional situation. Follow-up: Can you tell me why your sister is worried about your eating? Bringing in sister's perspective works well here too.
	Have you tried any diets for weight loss?	*I tried keto once and also am interested in intermittent fasting.*	Concern that dieting is happening and research of diets is also occurring. Follow-up: What places do you go or sources do you use for research like this?
Eating and nutrition	Does your mood impact your eating?	*It does—sometimes when I am very upset, I cannot eat; when I am stressed, my body just doesn't want food; and sometimes, when I am sad, eating makes it worse.*	Hearing that nutritional intake seems variable given mood or stress level with concern that we have already heard indictors of under fueling. Is there a primary anxiety/stress difficulty or mood difficulty impeding eating versus eating being independently an issue. Follow-up: Tell me more about the stress in your life. You mentioned that sadness makes it hard to eat—what makes you sad?

(Continued)

Table 9.1 (Continued)

Theme/ Topic	Provider questions	Sample answers	Concerns revealed and follow-up possibilities
Body image	What do you consider physically desirable in a human body?	*I think a slender, graceful, light-skinned, ballerina-like girl is pretty and muscled, strong boys are handsome.*	Hearing a drive for thinness, perfectionistic tendencies, and colorism all intersecting for this client.
	Do you feel that your body size or shape is concerning?	*I think that I was too big before and now I look and am better. I see the people around me, and I don't want to be so large.*	Recognizing indications of fat phobia and drive for thinness that are steeped in anti-blackness.
	Tell me how others see your body.	*They see an overweight Black girl.*	Hearing the intersection of race, gender, body image concerns, and disordered eating behaviors.
			Follow-up: Tell me more about why and how others see you as overweight, Black, and a girl.

	What comments have been made about your body by family, friends, or your community?	*My family tells me I'm beautiful, but they have to say that. My friends talk about how they want to lose weight and get a thigh gap. My church and folks around tell me I look good since I lost some weight. People ask me what I did to lose the weight so that they can try too. I follow this girl on social media who has lost a lot of weight, and she has great tips and motivation for me.*	Hearing validation of disordered eating. Concern for social media influencing eating, nutrition, and body image. Follow-up: How do you feel when people comment on your weight and weight changes?
Body Image	Does your body appear healthy?	*I think I am more healthy now after having lost weight than before when I was so overweight.*	Hearing that weight equates to health for this client. Follow-up: What makes you feel healthier now about your body?
Community and societal factors	How do the people around you keep themselves healthy?	*They walk in the neighborhood or park during the daytime and cook at home for meals.*	Hearing that eating out is not preferred and that exercise is important. Follow-up: Tell me more about how you and your sister cook or make food? Do you like to go out to eat?

(Continued)

Table 9.1 (Continued)

Theme/ Topic	Provider questions	Sample answers	Concerns revealed and follow-up possibilities
	Is your community healthy?	*A lot of people where I live are overweight, and that's not healthy. I also know a lot of people eat fast food because it's cheap and easy to get.*	Noting the Anti-Blackness element of fat phobia and ranking of nutritional value of food with fast food at the bottom of the list. Follow-up: Do you ever eat fast food? What do you know about fast food's nutritional value?
	Do you live near a grocery store?	*We live pretty far from a big grocery store and so we get our groceries from the convenience store on the corner. We sometimes will go to the grocery store, but it's usually only every now and then that we do that—my sister has to be off work and we have to have time to take the bus there and back.*	Taking into account the systemic racism impact of the location of foods and food availability. If you will be asking this client and family to spend time getting new foods may be time and resource extensive for them. Follow-up: Tell me a bit about the foods you purchase from the store near you.

Do you see your doctor regularly? Have they recommended anything related to your health?	*I see my doctor when I'm sick or if I need shots. When I came in before, they told me that my weight was starting to get too high and I should stop drinking all soda pop, juice, and make sure to be active.*	Recognizing the racism and implicit bias frequent to the experiences of Black clients related to healthcare and health education provided. Follow-up: How you feel talking to doctors?
Do you feel that you look like others in your community?	*I look like my cousins and relatives, who are all overweight. I am glad that my skin isn't as dark as my neighbor's, but I do wish I had a waist as skinny as hers.*	Identifying the influence of colorism, fat phobia and beliefs about what is desirable physically for a human body.

One intervention that can be used to promote ERI is dialogue and storytelling (Banks-Wallace, 2002), which can assist Black adolescents in healing relationships that may have been damaged because of DE. Relationships that commonly require repair when DE is present are one's relationship with food, self, and loved ones. Historically, Black storytelling has been used as a means of redefining what is considered normal or "ideal" and can serve as an affirmation of the experiences of Black people in Black bodies who struggle with internalization of the "thin ideal" and other stereotypes about Black bodies that contribute to the maintenance of DE symptoms.

Dialogue and storytelling should focus on relational resilience, reaffirming that the youth is not alone in dealing with DE or ED symptoms or the subsequent anti-Blackness they face as a result of living within today's societal context. The clinician should allow the adolescent to tell and hear stories from their own family of origin and their broader kinship and social networks. These stories can take the form of oration, poetry, music, or essay. Storytelling can promote racial and ethnic pride through the learning of history and traditions by facilitating intergenerational conversations about health, healing, weight, and self-esteem. By sharing and learning about family and cultural resilience and considering collective and individual trauma, Black adolescents may be able to identify their inherent strengths, which can be used to overcome DE.

Consider L, a 13-year-old Black female, and her mother, who come to see a new therapist to discuss eating, nutrition, and concern for an ED. L reported that she had seen another therapist before but said that they "didn't get [her]." L comes from a close family who she described as "loud and supportive." Mom shared that they are a very health-conscious family, and the entire family engages in health and weight loss challenges together annually. The therapist provided psychoeducation to Mom and L about DE. They discussed the importance of focusing on sufficient fueling rather than limiting fueling and how human bodies grow and develop consistently throughout adolescence.

Therapist, L, and Mom work together to make sure L is eating frequently enough. To best support L's efforts, the therapist discussed having Mom direct all food and eating decisions. L expressed concern that Mom would "give [her] too much food" and that Mom would not eat healthy enough when she was not participating in the family competition. The therapist redirected L's concerns by saying L knows her Mom has her best interest at heart and would never want to hurt her, to which L agreed. L and Mom decided the competition may make it harder for Mom and L to focus on sufficient eating. In place of the competition, the therapist invited L and Mom to develop a written, oral, or visual representation of their family's story about food, eating, and resilience. Mom became tearful, discussing that she felt she had to focus on weight loss for L because of their family history of health concerns such as obesity, diabetes, and hypertension. Mom noted concerns surrounding L's behaviors when working toward weight loss and how weight loss efforts very rapidly were the focus of L's life. The therapist encouraged L and Mom to consider family stories or experiences around food and eating that were positive and not focused on weight loss or health concerns. Mom shared with L her great grandmother's story of being a cook and restaurant owner in the South. Mom expressed that her love for cooking and sharing food comes from her own grandmother's story. L was surprised by this information, as her great grandmother died before her birth, and Mom had never shared this story. Mom shared with L great grandma's recipe cards that were passed down to her from her own mother and were "falling apart" from old age. The family brought these cards to the next therapy session, and the therapist, L, and Mom discussed how "special" having these family recipes is and how the family might incorporate some of these recipes into their family meals. Mom decided to discuss with extended family how to channel their health motivation and family stories into a self-care and physical activity challenge. L was excited to share what she and Mom learned about how to define health and well-being.

Clinicians can help Black adolescents create counterstories that challenge medical, cultural, and racial stigmas associated with DE on individual and family systems. These counterstories illuminate the lived experiences and knowledge of Black adolescents and their families who have struggled or are struggling with DE. Once developed, these counterstories can also serve as resources for other Black and marginalized persons experiencing DE or ED.

At a larger systems level, clinicians can intentionally engage in understanding their clients' stories and counterstories as a means to move toward third-order thinking (McDowell et al., 2019). Third-order thinking asks the clinician to shift how they understand their clients' experiences in relationship to broader sociocultural systems and "create space to take apart, inspect, and disrupt" anti-Blackness (e.g., White supremacy, adultification, and fat phobia) and consider multiple possibilities and perspectives that may be contributing to or maintaining DE. Such work requires clinicians to become aware of the societal context and power processes present in FBT and society at large and the impact of those processes on how Black adolescents navigate their lived experience, including seeking care. In *Not All Black Girls Know How to Eat: A Story of Bulimia*, Armstrong (2009) detailed one Black woman's experience with DE and an ED and her road to recovery while navigating the racial, cultural, and financial barriers to recovery. Armstrong shared her counterstory of learning how her legacy of strong, independent Black ancestors impacted her willingness to seek help and her attempts to navigate a hostile healthcare system. Sharing stories such as this with family members and loved ones—and even the adolescents themselves when clinically appropriate—can be used to increase provider and client awareness of how power, privilege, and oppression influence Black adolescents' experience with DE and recovery.

Providing culturally relevant care requires ongoing consideration of providers' social location, experiences, beliefs, and practices. Anti-Blackness, including White supremacy, fat phobia, adultification, colorism, and dehumanization are ingrained in the collective socialization process of the United States. All providers must grapple with how they have accepted and resisted these realities and how they influence one's clinical practice. Of particular importance when working with DE is the development of self-awareness related to the intersection of weight bias, racism, gender, and beliefs about what it means to be healthy (Harrison, 2021; Mauldin et al., 2022).

Conclusion

Black adolescents navigate a world where their bodies are classified as wrong, and they are told to strive for an unattainably thin, White ideal. In response to this racist ideal, people may engage in DE, which may negatively affect their physical, psychological, and mental health. Although some evidence has supported the use of FBT in treating DE and ED (Couturier et al., 2013; Lock & Le Grange, 2005; Rienecke,

2017), there remains a lack of research on the effectiveness of this type of treatment for Black adolescents. To support the development of resilience for Black adolescents experiencing DE, we employ a family resilience framework and integrate how meaning making, belief systems, and cultural responsiveness can support clients. Our recommendations include creating meaning within the diagnosis of DE and ED and using dialogue and storytelling to promote resilience. A stronger therapeutic alliance and treatment engagement may be created by discussing the effects of anti-Blackness, White supremacy, systemic racism, and weight bias openly. Finally, Black adolescents and their families have tremendous inherent resilience owing to their daily, lived experiences, so DE treatment may be most effective when using these strengths as a foundation in treatment.

We offer a series of tips for clinicians new to addressing DE in clinical practice that are useful for all populations and have specific relevance for working with Black adolescents.

- Be curious and do not assume. Ask lots of questions. Clarify details carefully.
- Clients and caregivers may be unaware how DE can impact both physical and mental health. Caregivers might be unaware of the intensity of DE behaviors that are occurring in the client.
- Be open and accepting and recognize that all people and family units have varied natural food cultures. These food cultures may be different than yours and still not be disordered, or they may feel typical to a client/caregiver and be very concerning.
- Social and structural elements impact food availability, nutritional choices, and availability of caregivers for supervision at meal or snack times.
- Provider appearance with regard to race, gender, body size/shape, age, etc., and patients' perceptions of the provider are likely to influence engagement and openness with the conversation.
- Consider this topic can be sensitive for clients and caregivers and is sometimes accompanied by strong emotional reactions. As caregivers are tasked with providing appropriate nutrition as a basic care element, any perception of negative judgment may be met with defensiveness, sadness, defeat, anger, or avoidance.

- Clients and caregivers have received many different messages in their lives about nutrition, health, body size, and eating, which may alter their assessment of the information presented or questions raised.
- Consider asking permission to start a conversation about nutrition and eating.
- Be aware clients may "test out" statements or information to see if the clinician will ask more questions, express concern, or appear unconcerned.
- DE can happen in the setting of an ED, and it can happen due to other mental health concerns. As such, DE can be a symptom of a therapeutic target or an independent therapeutic target.
- DE will make patients struggle to make therapeutic gains due to biochemical and neurologic changes the body undergoes while experiencing inadequate nutritional intake. In this way, DE may also be an amplifier of other mental health concerns or impede therapeutic progress if not addressed.

Future work in this area should include an exploration of Black adolescents and their families' experiences in seeking and receiving treatment for DE and ED. Quantitative studies may provide more detailed information about the predictors, trajectories, and prognoses of DE for Black adolescents and further inform development of more culturally sensitive interventions. Qualitative investigations, interviews, focus groups, and direct observations that focus on factors that promote resilience and recovery for Black adolescents can be used to help in the development of assessment protocols and trainings to support and increase the provision of effective clinical care and clinician development.

References

Armstrong, S. C. (2009). *Not all black girls know how to eat: A story of bulimia.* Chicago Review Press.

Banks-Wallace, J. (2002). Talk that talk: Storytelling and analysis rooted in African American oral tradition. *Qualitative Health Research, 12*(3), 410–426. https://doi.org/10.1177/104973202129119892

Becker, A. E., Franko, D. L., Speck, A., & Herzog, D. B. (2003). Ethnicity and differential access to care for eating disorder symptoms. *International Journal of Eating Disorders, 33*(2), 205–212. https://doi.org/10.1002/eat.10129

Berry, J. W. (1980). Acculturation as varieties of adaptation. In A. M. Padilla (Ed.), *Acculturation: Theory, models, and some new findings* (pp. 9–25). Westview Press.

Bidopia, T., Carbo, A. V., Ross, R. A., & Burke, N. L. (2023). Food insecurity and disordered eating behaviors in children and adolescents: A systematic review. *Eating Behaviors, 43*, Article 101731. https://doi.org/10.1016/j. eatbeh.2023.101731

Bordo, S. (2013). Not just "a White Girl's Thing": The changing face of food and body image problems. In C. Counihan & P. Van Esterik (Eds.), *Food and culture: A reader* (pp. 265–275). Routledge.

Brochu, P. M. (2018). Weight stigma is a modifiable risk factor. *Journal of Adolescent Health, 63*(3), 267–268. https://doi.org/10.1016/j.jadohealth. 2018.06.016

Couturier, J., Kimber, M., & Szatmari, P. (2013). Efficacy of family-based treatment for adolescents with eating disorders: A systematic review and meta-analysis. *International Journal of Eating Disorders, 46*(1), 3–11. https://doi. org/10.1002/eat.22042

Deloitte Access Economics. (2020, June). *The social and economic cost of eating disorders in the United States of America: A report for the strategic training initiative for the prevention of eating disorders and the academy for eating disorders.* www.hsph.harvard.edu/striped/report-economic-costs-of-eating-disorders/

Dumas, M. J. (2016). Against the dark: Antiblackness in education policy and discourse. *Theory Into Practice, 55*(1), 11–19. https://doi.org/10.1080/0040 5841.2016.1116852

Epstein, R., Blake, J. J., González, T., & Georgetown University Law Center on Poverty and Inequality. (2017). *Girlhood interrupted: The erasure of black girls' childhood.* Georgetown Law Center on Poverty and Inequality.

Goff, P. A., Jackson, M. C., Di Leone, B. A. L., Culotta, C. M., & DiTomasso, N. A. (2014). The essence of innocence: Consequences of dehumanizing Black children. *Journal of Personality and Social Psychology, 106*(4), 526–545. https://doi.org/10.1037/a0035663

Goode, R. W., Godoy, S. M., Olson, K., Berg, S., Agbozo, B., Gwira, R., Xu, Y., Wolfe, H., Bhutani, J., & Alexander, R. (2023). "If I start panicking over having enough, then I start eating too much": Understanding the eating behaviors of SNAP recipients in larger bodies during COVID-19. *Eating Behaviors, 49*, Article 101741. https://doi.org/10.1016/j.eatbeh.2023.101741

Goode, R. W., Webster, C. K., & Gwira, R. E. (2022). A review of binge-eating disorder in Black women: Treatment recommendations and implications for healthcare providers. *Current Psychiatry Reports, 24*(12), 757–766. https://doi.org/10.1007/s11920-022-01383-8

Harrison, D. L. (2021). *Belly of the beast: The politics of anti-fatness as anti-blackness*. North Atlantic Books.

Lisse, A. A., Hochgraf, A. K., & McHale, S. M. (2022). Weight concerns in Black youth: The role of body mass index, gender, and sociocultural factors. *Journal of Research on Adolescence, 32*(4), 1341–1353. https://doi.org/10.1111/jora.12692

Liu, W. M., Liu, R. Z., & Shin, R. Q. (2023). Understanding systemic racism: Anti-blackness, white supremacy, racial capitalism, and the re/creation of white space and time. *Journal of Counseling Psychology, 70*(3), 244–257. https://doi.org/10.1037/COU0000605

Lock, J., & Le Grange, D. (2005). Family-based treatment of eating disorders. *International Journal of Eating Disorders, 37*(S1), S64–S67. https://doi.org/10.1002/eat.20122

Marques, L., Alegria, M., Becker, A. E., Chen, C. N., Fang, A., Chosak, A., & Diniz, J. B. (2011). Comparative prevalence, correlates of impairment, and service utilization for eating disorders across US ethnic groups: Implications for reducing ethnic disparities in health care access for eating disorders. *International Journal of Eating Disorders, 44*(5), 412–420. https://doi.org/10.1002/eat.20787

Mauldin, K., May, M., & Clifford, D. (2022). The consequences of a weight-centric approach to healthcare: A case for a paradigm shift in how clinicians address body weight. *Nutrition in Clinical Practice, 37*(6), 1291–1306. https://doi.org/10.1002/ncp.10885

McDowell, T., Knudson-Martin, C., & Bermudez, J. M. (2019). Third-order thinking in family therapy: Addressing social justice across family therapy practice. *Family Process, 58*(1), 9–22. https://doi.org/10.1111/famp.12383

Mims, L. C., & Williams, J. L. (2020). "They told me what I was before I could tell them what I was": Black girls' ethnic-racial identity development within multiple worlds. *Journal of Adolescent Research, 35*(6), 754–779. https://doi.org/10.1177/0743558420913483

Nagata, J. M., Ganson, K. T., Sajjad, O. M., Benabou, S. E., & Bibbins-Domingo, K. (2021). Prevalence of perceived racism and discrimination among US children aged 10 and 11 years: The Adolescent Brain Cognitive Development (ABCD) Study. *JAMA Pediatrics, 175*(8), 861–863. https://doi.org/10.1001/jamapediatrics.2021.1022

Neumark-Sztainer, D., Wall, M., Larson, N. I., Eisenberg, M. E., & Loth, K. (2011). Dieting and disordered eating behaviors from adolescence to young adulthood: Findings from a 10-year longitudinal study. *Journal of the American Dietetic Association, 111*(7), 1004–1011. https://doi.org/10.1016/j.jada.2011.04.012

Nguyen, A. M. D., & Benet-Martínez, V. (2013). Biculturalism and adjustment: A meta-analysis. *Journal of Cross-Cultural Psychology, 44*(1), 122–159. https://doi.org/10.1177/0022022111435097

Nguyen, L., Huang, L. N., Arganza, G. F., & Liao, Q. (2007). The influence of race and ethnicity on psychiatric diagnoses and clinical characteristics of children and adolescents in children's services. *Cultural Diversity and Ethnic Minority Psychology, 13*(1), Article 18. https://doi.org/10.1037/1099-9809.13.1.18

Patterson, O. (1982). *Slavery and social death: A comparative study.* Harvard University Press.

Pike, K. M., Dohm, F. A., Striegel-Moore, R. H., Wilfley, D. E., & Fairburn, C. G. (2001). A comparison of black and white women with binge eating disorder. *American Journal of Psychiatry, 158*(9), 1455–1460.

Rienecke, R. D. (2017). Family-based treatment of eating disorders in adolescents: Current insights. *Adolescent Health, Medicine and Therapeutics,* 69–79.

Rivas-Drake, D., Seaton, E. K., Markstrom, C., Quintana, S., Syed, M., Lee, R. M., Schwartz, S. J., Umaña-Taylor, A. J., French, S., Yip, T., & Ethnic and Racial Identity in the 21st Century Study Group. (2014). Ethnic and racial identity in adolescence: Implications for psychosocial, academic, and health outcomes. *Child Development, 85*(1), 40–57. https://doi.org/10.1111/cdev.12200

Roberts, K. J., & Chaves, E. (2023). Beyond binge eating: The impact of implicit biases in healthcare on youth with disordered eating and obesity. *Nutrients, 15*(8), Article 1861. https://doi.org/10.3390/nu15081861

Robinson, B. B. E., Bacon, L. C., & O'Reilly, J. (1993). Fat phobia: Measuring, understanding, and changing anti-fat attitudes. *International Journal of Eating Disorders, 14*(4), 467–480. https://doi.org/10.1002/1098-108x(199312)14:4<467::aid-eat2260140410>3.0.co;2-j

Strings, S. (2019). *Fearing the Black body: The racial origins of fat phobia.* New York University Press. https://doi.org/10.18574/nyu/9781479891788.001.0001

Taylor, J. Y., Caldwell, C. H., Baser, R. E., Faison, N., & Jackson, J. S. (2007). Prevalence of eating disorders among Blacks in the National Survey of American Life. *International Journal of Eating Disorders, 40*(S3), S10–S14. https://doi.org/10.1002/eat.20451

Umaña-Taylor, A. J., Quintana, S. M., Lee, R. M., Cross, W. E., Jr., Rivas-Drake, D., Schwartz, S. J., Syed, M., Yip, T., Seaton, E., & Ethnic and Racial Identity in the 21st Century Study Group. (2014). Ethnic and racial identity during adolescence and into young adulthood: An integrated conceptualization. *Child Development, 85*(1), 21–39. https://doi.org/10.1111/cdev.12196

Walsh, F. (2015). *Strengthening family resilience.* Guilford Publications.

10

FOSTERING SYSTEMIC RESILIENCE IN FOSTER AND KINSHIP CARE

Yolanda Wearing and Raquel Martin

Yolanda Wearing's intertwined identities are Black, cisgender, heterosexual, and woman. Living and working in Philadelphia, one of the most densely populated cities in the United States, has provided her with a unique lens to perceive the world. For over two decades, Yolanda has dedicated herself to the field of social work, striving to be an unwavering advocate for marginalized and oppressed families and youth.

A 34-year-old cisgender, heterosexual Black woman, wife, and mother born and residing in the United States, Dr. Raquel Martin has dedicated her professional journey to the specialty of Black mental health and connects deeply with liberation psychology. Throughout her career as a professor, scientist, and licensed clinical psychologist, Dr. Martin has passionately advocated for herself and her community. Her endeavors aim to challenge and reshape systems that perpetuate harm to marginalized and oppressed groups. She works toward creating spaces where Black voices resonate with authenticity and power. Beyond her professional commitments, Dr. Martin is devoted to sculpting a safer world for her children, family, and community, anchoring her advocacy in the pursuit of well-being and equitable representation in all spheres of life.

DOI: 10.4324/9781003373513-10

Child protective services is a system that often operates to safeguard youth and support families (Crosson-Tower, 2018; Myers, 2008). A safety threat or an event that puts a child at risk of hurt, harm, or danger must occur for child protective services to intervene. These are not times when individuals present their best selves; rather, in these situations, the parent will exhibit many emotions, ranging from anger, denial, grief, and sometimes acceptance. Depending on their age, the child is likely confused, scared, oppositional, and pulled in different directions. The foster parent or kinship caregiver likely wants to help but may not have the tools to know how, tasking the social worker with managing the situation with ease. The purpose of this chapter is to provide clinicians and social workers with insight into the context of the foster and kinship care system while also offering resilience-based skills and resources that can be used to support these families.

Although each individual will look at the child protective services system differently, clinicians' interventions have to be ones that build systemic resilience within all involved parties, including themselves. Building systemic resilience is important because children, biological parents, and foster parents or kinship caregivers must be taught to bounce back from difficult experiences and learn from them. In addition, clinicians operating in child protective services must make a practice of building resilience within themselves to address and intervene with a trauma-informed approach to get to the crux of what brought the family to the attention of child protective services in the first place. These practitioners must also eventually assist in the child's and biological parents' success when child protective services intervention is no longer required.

In the realm of resilience, the significance of nurturing and preserving family relationships is clear. Integrating a child into their family network offers immediate backing and promotes enduring resilience, anchoring the child in a matrix of relationships that can care for, steer, and shield them. The connections found through family finding significant and supportive relationships are important to building resilience in the child by increasing the number of supports and connections the child has and on whom they can rely. These connections also can assist the clinician in combating the feeling of abandonment a child may have while in foster care—as a child may be resistant to being placed with strangers in an unfamiliar home—by presenting individuals who want to build a relationship with the child. Recommendations from a case study provide examples of ways to manage this stressful transition. Best practices related to placing children have resilience constructs embedded (e.g., "identify and build positive connections"; Office of Children & Families in the Courts, 2023, para. 3).

Clinicians must address issues that caused the child's removal from the home. While the preferred goal is reunification, it is important to understand that reunification will not be the goal in scenarios that would jeopardize the child's safety (LaBrenz et al., 2020). To bolster resilience-oriented relationships, clinicians can use concurrent planning. This strategy outlines two simultaneous plans when a child enters foster care: (a) a plan for reunification with the family and (b) a plan for adoption if reunification is not possible.

Foster care and kinship care consists of a triad between birth parent, child, and foster parent, and relationships between and among these groups must be addressed simultaneously. For the birth parent, clinicians need to examine what safety threats led to the child's removal from the home. Where are the parents' protective capacities? Are they absent or diminished? Does this parent want to take responsibility for their child entering foster care? Whether the removal was due to inadequate housing, a parent's inability to keep the child safe, a parent's drug or alcohol problem, or their inability to address and treat their mental illness, the outlined problem or barrier needs to be addressed immediately. The sooner the problem or barrier is identified, the sooner a plan to remediate the issue can be formulated and the barrier(s) removed. Addressing barriers and problem solving in a timely manner cultivates resilience, which allows the birth parent and child, if age appropriate, to see the problem and lay out a specific, measurable, attainable, realistic, and timely strategy to approach and solve it.

The Family Service Plan (FSP) is a document that captures this information. The FSP outlines goals and objectives that will address barriers to reunification and assist in removing them, while reminding all parties of their roles and functions and keeping all parties on task. All parties must participate in developing an FSP to give it credibility. Best practice dictates that the social worker or clinician keep in contact with the birth parent frequently; for example, weekly home visits, telephone calls, and or text messages. Frequent contact between the birth parent and the foster care social worker goes against state regulations that outline one home visit per month between the foster care social worker and the birth parent. These visits play a huge part in keeping the parties engaged in addressing the problems that led to the child's removal. Furthermore, a parent will need assistance navigating the child protective services system.

Case Study: Cultivating Resilience in Multiple Layers of a Foster Care System

The following case study gives tips on how social workers can build resilience with members of the triad which consists of the child, birth parent, and the foster/kinship parent (also called resource parent). Mr. and Mrs. King are new kinship caregivers. Their 15-year-old nephew, Jared, has been placed into their home, and he has a history of staying in multiple foster care placements. When meeting with Jared and the Kings, the foster care social worker should give everyone the opportunity to ask questions of one another and have an open dialogue about how the new living situation will look (e.g., establishing a daily routine and curfew; handling school, medical, and dental care; outlining Jared's allowance and a visitation schedule with his natural parent[s] and siblings).

Bolstering Resilience with the Foster Care Child

In the presence of Mr. and Mrs. King, the foster care social worker should explain the child's rights and responsibilities when being placed in their care and explain the kinship caregivers' rights and responsibilities for taking care of Jared. The foster care social worker should also speak with Jared alone to allow Jared to express himself independently of the Kings. The foster care social worker should ask Jared the following questions that center resilience constructs such as belonging and safety (Brendtro et al., 2019).

- How are you feeling?
- Do you feel safe with the Kings? (If Jared feels unsafe, he should contact the foster care social worker immediately.)

- What are your hopes and dreams?
- Have you been able to communicate with your parents and friends? How often?
- Are you interested in participating in extracurricular activities in or outside of school?
- What are the foods she likes and dislikes?
- What does you like to eat for breakfast, lunch, and dinner?
- What is your wake-up time and bedtime?
- What are your favorite television shows or video games to play?
- What school do you attend, and what grade is she in?
- What are your most and least favorite academic subjects?
- Do you need anything?

For Jared and other children who are placed in care, clinicians need to examine children's views of why they were removed from their parent(s) and placed with strangers. Each child will need time to adjust to new people, new surroundings, and, in some instances, a new school, which means developing new friendships. If age appropriate, children need to be informed of the plan to have them return to their home of origin. Children can participate in this process by attending the FSP meeting and being allowed input into the objectives and goals that are generated. Increased participation of children in the decision-making processes while involved with the child welfare system can lead to the promotion of care effectiveness (Ten Brummelaar et al., 2018) and greater esteem development (van Bijleveld et al., 2020).

It is essential to remember that the child was accustomed to living with their parent(s) and sibling(s) and now has been placed with a stranger. As such, establishing a daily routine is imperative and should involve visiting their parent(s) and sibling(s) for routine medical and dental care and remaining in and attending their schools of origin. Children also need to participate in telephone contact with their parents as early and as often as possible. If the child's transition to their new foster home is not going well, individual and family therapy may need to be implemented. Depending on the child's age, a referral to a therapeutic nursery may be appropriate.

It is important for the child to know they have a voice and are being heard. Furthermore, this approach ensures the child knows they are an active participant in the planning that will take place during their time in foster care. Such a process allows the child to feel comfortable expressing their feelings with the social worker or clinician, which will eventually include sharing or expressing their feelings with the foster parent or kinship caregiver. Finally, the social worker or clinician must share with the child, biological parent, and foster parent or kinship caregiver the child's rights while in foster care. It is empowering when a child knows explicitly how they can and cannot be treated while in the foster or kinship care home. Crisis plans that outline emergency procedures should be used in conjunction with regular visits from the social worker to future encourage safety and support.

Promoting Resilience with the Foster Care or Resource Parents

Concurrent with building a clinical relationship with Jared, the child in foster care, the social worker should speak with the foster caregivers or resource parents—in this case, the Kings—and ask them the following questions while paying attention to building connections, open communication, and support (Walsh, 2016).

- How are you both feeling?
- Are there any changes that had to be made to accommodate Jared? If so, how comfortable were you in making these changes?
- How is your relationship with Jared's parent(s)?
- What forms of discipline will be used with Jared?
- How will you react? What is the plan for when Jared exhibits externalizing behaviors or unhealthy coping behaviors?

The foster parent's role and function for children in the foster care system—along with their relationships with the birth parent and child—play an important part in building systemic resilience. From the moment the child is placed, the foster parent will need to transition the child to their new surroundings. The foster parent must speak with the child about their likes and dislikes; establish a daily routine that includes school attendance, medical and dental care, and mental health care; and, most importantly, ensure the child can communicate with their parent via phone and in-person visits. The foster parent and birth parent will need to speak with one another about the child and establish a relationship. The foster care social worker can aid in this transition by introducing the birth parent to the foster parent and remaining as the bridge to their interactions. The foster care social worker must be careful to address the needs of the triad because all three will need to act together for the child's needs.

The foster or resource parent can aid with the child's transition by giving the placed child choices (e.g., what color or cartoon character sheets go onto the bed, what toiletries the child will use, and pictures or decorations that will go into the room). If the child has a picture or pictures of their parent or sibling, these can be placed in the room. The resource parent should also know when the child can speak with and visit the natural parent and siblings and establish a daily routine of contact. This step will go a long way to ensure the birth parent, siblings, and child remain engaged with one another.

The resource parent should also know when the child's last medical and dental appointments took place and verify the child's medical and dental care are current within the first 60 days of their placement. To establish continuity of care, the child's school, medical, and dental care providers should not change unless necessary for the child's protection. Children and birth parents need to see as many familiar faces as possible during this time, medical professionals included. Furthermore, these consistent connections promote stability and resilience at a time when the child's and biological parents' lives are in flux with the involvement of new people (e.g., foster parents, kinship caregivers, social workers, therapists, attorneys).

Foster parents will need support with the new child in their home. They will need to learn communication techniques to interact with birth parents and foster children in a manner that will create a safe space for the placed child and the birth parent to begin to interface with one another while being separated. Communication skills are incredibly important; one study investigating characteristics among foster parenting that led to increased stability found over 40% of participants expressed experiencing difficulty communicating effectively with their foster children (Crum, 2010). Additionally, this study found a positive correlation between limit setting and placement disruption. Specifically, foster parents who established rigid and firm rules were less likely to seek input from their foster children, and those who perceived their parenting role as being in charge had a greater likelihood of placement disruptions. This is incredibly concerning, given the impact that placement disruptions have on children (Crum, 2010). Instability within child placement can lead to an increased risk of behavior problems, limit the child's ability to form a secure attachment with an adult, decrease chances of both reunification and adoption, and potentially increase the risk of poor executive functioning and academic achievement (Leathers et al., 2019).

Therefore, in addition to strong communication skills, foster parents will need to learn and incorporate techniques that are nonphysical in nature and lead with love and understanding to decrease placement instability. Finally, foster parents will need to learn behavior management skills. Placed children largely come from homes where they have experienced varying degrees of abuse and neglect, and this trauma can take many forms when a child is placed into foster care. (Kilpatrick & Holland, 2008). The trauma may present as opposition or outright defiance; foster parents need to learn how to react to the many emotions displayed by the placed children and understand they may not be the true target. The foster parents will need to assist the child in channeling their emotions in a positive way and need their assigned social worker to guide them in this process. The social worker can outline training for the foster parent to pursue and also assist the foster parent in locating a respite provider if they do not have a provider already. Foster parents will also need to have the support of other foster parents. It is imperative foster parents have their own support network to surround themselves with individuals who can provide opportunities for respite, to vent, and to bounce ideas off.

Being a foster parent can be difficult and can lead to compassion fatigue, burnout, and secondary traumatic stress (Ottaway & Selwyn, 2016). Foster parents must navigate many physical, emotional, and psychological demands on their time and energy; the relationship between birth parent and placed child has to be managed to avoid as much negative triangulation as possible, with competing demands for foster parent's time. For example, foster parents must be available (a) to participate in visits made by the social worker, child advocate, and other child protective services team members; (b) to see to the medical, educational, and social needs of the child; (c) to take mandatory training to remain a certified foster parent; and (d) to take care of their own physical, emotional, and psychological needs. This situation will prove arduous if the foster parent has a spouse or partner, biological children, or employment outside of the home. To properly serve families and provide the most appropriate support and resources, social workers and clinicians must be on the lookout for signs the foster parent is overwhelmed. Here are possible ways social workers can provide assistance to foster parents to decrease their likelihood of feeling overwhelmed:

- Encourage the foster parent to outline their support network.
- Ask the foster parent to consider having the child placed into respite for a weekend.
- Put the foster parent in contact with a foster parent support group.
- Assist the foster parent with providing transportation to or from medical, dental, school, mental, and family visits.
- Take the time to listen to the foster parent.
- Insist the foster parent engage in daily self-care activities; assist the foster parent in securing daycare, extracurricular, and summer activities for the placed child.

Amplifying Resilience with Birth Parents

Birth parents need support with navigating new relationships and situations while their child or children are in foster care (e.g., foster parents, foster care social workers, court-appointed attorneys, county social workers). When providing services to a child who will enter foster care, clinicians must first speak with the birth parent or caregiver to establish whether kin may be able to care for the child in lieu of the parent. Kin does not solely mean a biological relationship—such support can come from a neighbor or someone with whom the birth family or child has a relationship or is familiar and who is willing to allow the child to be placed into their home.

In addition, birth parents still need to remain abreast of their child's medical, dental, and educational needs or progress while their child remains in foster care. If their child is medically fragile or has behavioral difficulties, birth parents will need to become involved with other individuals accordingly.

Supervised visits between the birth parent and their child must occur as soon as possible once a child has been removed from their home of origin. A visitation schedule must be outlined, followed, and shared with all parties. The parties include but are not limited to the birth parent, child if/ when age appropriate, foster/kinship caregiver, and the foster care social worker. This approach is not only best practice but a legal requirement. If siblings were removed and separated from one another, sibling visits need to occur in conjunction with parental visits. Supervised visits should continue until an assessment is made that allows a child to participate in unsupervised visits with their parent(s). When a birth parent or sibling visit is missed, the meetup must be rescheduled in no more than seven business days. Birth parents must also be able to speak with their child via telephone and know the location where their child resides.

A Strength-Based Approach to Navigating Next Steps

Family reunification can be viewed through multiple perspectives, including the lenses of law, policy, and practice. In terms of law, there is a codified assumption that children fare better with their biological parents. Regarding policy, initiatives have been put in place to prioritize a parent's right to rear their children (e.g., the Indian Child Welfare Act of 1978, the Adoption Assistance and Child Welfare Act of 1978, and the Adoption of Safe Families Act of 1997; Wulczyn, 2004). There is no one way to ensure a child, birth parent, or foster or kinship caregiver is fully prepared for reunification; however, the following steps are recommended to bolster focusing on strengths and cultivating resilience:

Step 1: The FSP

The FSP needs to be reviewed to ensure all or the majority of the goals and objectives outlined for the birth parent have been achieved or are in the process of being completed before or shortly after the child is reunified. Furthermore, the problems or issues that led to the child's removal must be rectified. This provides clarity and clear communication among systems.

Step 2: Progression for Visits

There must be a progression for visits between the birth parent and the child. Visits will begin as supervised by a social worker or visitation coach and subsequently increase to unsupervised, community, day visits; overnight visits; and finally, court-approved reunification. Throughout this process, the social worker or visitation coach must assess the parent–child interaction and determine whether these visits are progressing and remain appropriate for the child. In addition, a home safety walk-through assessment at the birth parent's home must be conducted monthly by a social work team member to ensure the home environment is safe enough for the child to visit and eventually return. At each phase of these visits, the social worker provides counsel to all parties and ascertains how the visits are progressing from the child's, birth parents', and foster parents' points of view.

Step 3: Navigating Triad Difficulties

It is not uncommon for the child, birth parent, and foster or kinship caregiver to each manifest their difficulties with the reunification process (Collins et al., 2008). For example, the child may become defiant before a family visit or soon after returning to the foster or kinship care home from a familial visit. The social worker must consider: Is the child fearful of returning home? Does the child feel disloyal to the birth parent or foster/kinship parent?

Birth parents may also be afraid to have their child return home full-time, which can be displayed by the birth parent purposely sabotaging reunification efforts. For example, a birth parent may not call to confirm a visit attendance or decide to no-show at visits altogether. Relatedly, foster or kinship care parents may be afraid of the child returning to their birth parent due to their own feelings of impending loss or grief they are afraid to address. These and other issues need to be addressed immediately by the foster care social worker. Having meetings with the birth parent and foster or kinship parent together and individually after each family visit provides an opportunity for parents to outline points of stress, discuss progress and areas for improvement, and prepare all parties for the next visit. In addition, having the birth parent interact with the child at points other than a scheduled visit (e.g., accompanying the foster or kinship parent and child to medical appointments or inclusion in parent–teacher conferences) will increase contact and ensure the birth parent remains included in the child's care.

Step 4: Sharing the Reunification Date

The reunification date should not be a surprise to anyone. The child (if age appropriate), birth parent, and foster parent should be given at least 30 days' notice when the child will be reunified. This time will allow the birth parent to prepare for the child's arrival and the foster or kinship parent time to prepare for the child's departure.

Step 5: Aftercare Plan and Aftercare Services

Right before or immediately after the child is reunified with the parent, an Aftercare Plan needs to be outlined with the birth parent to formalize a support system to aid the parents. The plan will outline how the services the child received while in placement (i.e., medical, education, behavioral health) will continue after reunification. Services for the family can include reconnecting the birth parent with medical insurance, enrolling the child for SNAP benefits, securing childcare, locating summer activities, locating a parent support group, and providing community linkages so the birth parent can secure needed resources locally and independently (The City of Philadelphia Department of Human Services, 2017). An aftercare worker, social worker, or a member of the case management team will provide case management services, including home visitation for up to 12 months or until the birth parent voluntarily discontinues aftercare services. For the city of Philadelphia, for example, home visits in the first and second quarters are held twice a month; in the third and fourth quarters, visits decrease to once a month and include a check-in call. Services also include financial assistance and the provision of concrete goods for the family when needed.

Considerations for Clinical Workers

Clinicians involved in foster care work must have the time and space to meet with their supervisor to share concerns, discuss, and secure counsel when issues arise between members of the triad consistently. It is easy for practitioners to succumb to vicarious trauma, given their large caseload size and the compliance and paperwork-driven nature of working in child protective services. We believe that knowing the difference between a crisis, what is urgent, and what is important—and how to address each situation—is a key factor in the case management process.

Foster care workers need a support system to allow them to focus on ensuring the safety and permanency of the children they serve. Social workers have a higher likelihood of burnout due to their role in human service work, which has high emotional expectations. Additionally, many organizational factors contribute to burnout in this field, including lack of agency, low support, and high caseloads (Lloyd et al., 2002; Newell & MacNeil, 2010). The emotional impact of difficult decisions may get in the way of a foster care social worker's primary role, which is to focus on the child's safety and permanency. Foster care workers have a number of intricate and important roles, such as completing safety and risk assessments, attending court to provide testimony, and conducting home safety walk-through assessments in the birth parent's home. These responsibilities, although imperative for the well-being of the client, might get pushed to the side momentarily when workers are bogged down with clerical tasks, such as submitting requests for and providing concrete goods; providing transportation to and from medical, dental, or mental health appointments for clients; or uploading case documents. Foster care social workers should have a team of ancillary workers responsible for those tasks and allow the social worker to focus on the safety and permanency work with the child and the family.

Conclusion

In navigating the intricate landscape of child protective services, it becomes evident that layers of history, structural nuances, and human narratives are deeply interwoven. The evolution of foster and kinship care illuminate society's enduring commitment to its most vulnerable people—a commitment made richer by the author's vast experiences and invaluable insights. Beyond theoretical discourse, the authors' wealth of experience translated into myriad practical applications grounded in real-world challenges and solutions. Systemic resilience is more than an academic concept; it is a tangible reality mirrored in the lived realities of case workers, children, birth families, and placement families alike.

Each voice of those involved in these situations provides a unique insight into the trials and triumphs intrinsic to the system. Although the provision of tangible resources stands as a testament to the system's efforts, the unwavering drive to advocate for children's safety and foster their autonomy shines through, significantly influenced by the authors' relentless pursuit to safeguard children. In concluding this chapter, it is essential to acknowledge the progress made and the milestones ahead. Driven by the passion and expertise of dedicated professionals like the authors, there is an ever-present hope that, armed with knowledge and experience, we can continuously refine and enhance child protective services for a brighter, safer future for every child.

References

Brendtro, L., Brokenleg, M., & Van Bockern, S. (2019). *Reclaiming youth at risk: Futures of promise* (3rd ed.). Solution Tree.

The City of Philadelphia Department of Human Services. (2017). *The improving outcomes for children system transformation community umbrella agency practice guidelines.* www.phila.gov/documents/community-oversight-board-data-report/

Collins, M. E., Paris, R., & Ward, R. L. (2008). The permanence of family ties: Implications for youth transitioning from foster care. *American Journal of Orthopsychiatry, 78*(1), 54–62. https://doi.org/10.1037/0002-9432.78.1.54

Crosson-Tower, C. (2018). *Exploring child welfare: A practice perspective* (7th ed.). Pearson.

Crum, W. (2010). Foster parent parenting characteristics that lead to increased placement stability or disruption. *Children and Youth Services Review, 32*(2), 185–190. https://doi.org/10.1016/j.childyouth.2009.08.022

Kilpatrick, A. C., & Holland, T. P. (2008). *Working with families, an integrative model by level of need* (5th ed.). Pearson.

LaBrenz, C. A., Fong, R., & Cubbin, C. (2020). The road to reunification: Family-and state system-factors associated with successful reunification for children ages zero-to-five. *Child Abuse & Neglect, 99*, Article 104252. https://doi.org/10.1016/j.chiabu.2019.104252

Leathers, S. J., Spielfogel, J. E., Geiger, J., Barnett, J., & Voort, B. L. V. (2019). Placement disruption in foster care: Children's behavior, foster parent support, and parenting experiences. *Child Abuse & Neglect, 91*, 147–159.

Lloyd, C., King, R., & Chenoweth, L. (2002). Social work, stress and burn-out: A review. *Journal of Mental Health*, *11*(3), 255–265. https://doi.org/10.1080/09638230020023642

Myers, J. E. (2008). A short history of child protection in America. *Family Law Quarterly*, *42*(3), 449–463.

Newell, J. M., & MacNeil, G. A. (2010). Professional burnout, vicarious trauma, secondary traumatic stress, and compassion fatigue. *Best Practices in Mental Health*, *6*(2), 57–68.

Office of Children & Families in the Courts. (2023). *Family finding–revised*. https://ocfcpacourts.us/childrens-roundtable-initiative/family-engagement-initiative/family-finding/

Ottaway, H., & Selwyn, J. (2016). "No-one told us it was going to be like this": Compassion fatigue and foster carers. *Fostering Attachments*. https://doi.org/10.13140/RG.2.2.33955.45606

Ten Brummelaar, M. D., Harder, A. T., Kalverboer, M. E., Post, W. J., & Knorth, E. J. (2018). Participation of youth in decision-making procedures during residential care: A narrative review. *Child & Family Social Work*, *23*(1), 33–44. https://doi.org/10.1111/cfs.12381

van Bijleveld, G. G., Bunders-Aelen, J. F., & Dedding, C. W. (2020). Exploring the essence of enabling child participation within child protection services. *Child & Family Social Work*, *25*(2), 286–293. https://doi.org/10.1111/cfs.12684

Walsh, F. (2016). Family resilience: A development systems framework. *European Journal of Developmental Psychology*, *13*(3), 1–12. http://doi.org/10.1080/17405629.2016.1154035

Wulczyn, F. (2004). Family reunification. *The Future of Children*, *14*(1), 95–113. https://doi.org/10.2307/1602756

11

GRIEF AND RESILIENCE AFTER THE DEATH OF A DOG

Jennifer Golbeck

Jennifer Golbeck, PhD, is a professor in the College of Information Studies at the University of Maryland, College Park. Her research includes work on the intersection of social media, psychology, and artificial intelligence. She is the coauthor of The Purest Bond *(with Stacey Colino), which is about the science behind people's bond with their dogs. Her pronouns are she/her, and she identifies as a White, cisgender, bisexual woman.*

Resilience is critical for grieving and healing in the face of loss. Although most dog owners—and pet owners generally—consider their pets part of the family, managing their end of life and the grief that follows is quite different. Dog owners generally know their dogs will live shorter lives compared to humans. The owners are responsible for managing the end of their dog's life and, often, making a choice about euthanasia (Walsh, 2023). Roughly 80% of dogs die via euthanasia (Lewis et al., 2018). In a pet's last days, owners often must deal with anticipatory grief. These

DOI: 10.4324/9781003373513-11

issues lead to guilt around the choices the dog owners made and uncertainty about if those choices were correct.

After a dog's death, their humans experience loss and grief in much the same way—often equivalent to how they do for other close friends and family (Archer & Winchester, 1994; Walsh, 2023). However, many social structures that support grief for lost loved ones are not in place for those dealing with the loss of a pet. There are no accepted rituals around pet death, such as funerals. People in mourning are often expected to act as if their loss is not a big deal in the face of "but it's only a dog" comments from outsiders. This chapter addresses the complex issues around pet loss and how therapists can help patients going through the end-of-life and mourning processes for their pets.

The Heart of the Human–Animal Bond

For those of us who feel deep connections with our dogs, we know the emotional support they give us is real. Many dog owners consider their dogs to be members of the family or best friends (Geller, 2002; Walsh, 2009, 2023). Research has consistently shown that humans form attachment bonds with their dogs and often consider them their closest confidants and friends (Evans-Wilday et al., 2018; Kerns et al., 2017; Kurdek, 2009; Payne et al., 2016). People also form attachment bonds with their dogs like they do with close friends and family. Those who do not have pets can often discount the human–dog bond's importance, which is an important factor in how grief around the loss of a pet is treated in society. As such, it is worth reviewing existing research that has established psychological attachments between people and their pets.

The Bowlby-Ainsworth attachment theory has four main attributes of an attachment bond (i.e., proximity management, separation distress, secure base, and safe haven; Ainsworth, 1991, 2006; Bowlby, 1979). Proximity management is where people try to stay physically close to the person to whom they are connected. Separation distress is when someone misses the source of their attachment when they are apart. A secure base is when the source of attachment is a reliable and consistent foundation. Finally, a safe haven is when someone can rely on another in times of distress. Although dog lovers clearly enjoy spending time with their dogs and miss them when they are apart, research has shown that dogs play the role of secure base and safe haven for their human companions (Geller, 2002; Golbeck & Colino, 2023).

An in-depth study into pets and families by Geller (2002) found dogs serve as attachment figures, which can strengthen family relationships. By modeling unconditional love, families with dogs are happier and create an environment where the whole family unit operates more lovingly and successfully. Cain (1983) found 70% of pet owners reported their family was happier and had more fun after they got a pet, and more than half of respondents said their families spent more time together after getting their pet. Dogs change the dynamics in a family, as they become a joyful focal point for shared attention and affection. Dogs are reliable, supportive members of the family that bring the unit together.

Carr and Rockett (2017) explored how dogs helped foster families. The researchers followed children in foster homes with dogs and found the relationships the kids formed with dogs fulfilled emotional attachment needs. The benefits extended into the foster families, softening the children's perceptions of foster parents and creating the opportunity to build closer relationships (Carr & Rockett, 2017).

Dogs also play a safe haven role for humans (Ainsworth, 1991, 2006; Bowlby, 1979). This role manifests in how people treat their dogs as confidants and how dogs offer social support. Kurdek (2009) found dog owners were more likely to turn to their dogs as confidants in times of emotional distress than to turn to their parents, siblings, friends, or children. People uncomfortable with self-disclosure were even more likely to confide in their dogs. Evans-Wilday et al. (2018) found similar results; participants were more likely to confide in their dogs about difficult emotional issues than almost anyone else. Dogs played similar roles to partners, and people were more willing to talk to their dogs about difficult issues (e.g., depression, jealousy, anxiety, and fear) than with close friends.

Social support is a critical component of mental and physical health (Taylor, 2011). Traditionally, social support may come from other people, but dogs can serve as social supports and give people the same benefits. Although individuals will vary in the strength of the bonds they form with their pets, it is critical to understand that these attachment bonds are psychologically well-grounded. Emotional conflict around a pet (e.g., anxiety) has been shown to pose the same psychological burden as conflict with human family members (Kogan et al., 2022). Furthermore, the intensity of people's bonds with their dogs influences the intensity of the grief they feel when that bond is broken (Sharkin & Knox, 2003). For those with strong attachments, the death of a dog is the loss of a confidant, safe haven, and beloved companion.

Facing End-of-Life Decisions with Pets

Unfortunately, living with dogs almost always means seeing the end of their lives. Dog owners must navigate illness, declining abilities, and the complex decisions around when to give or withhold treatment. This process can lead to deep feelings of guilt (i.e., feeling bad about choices), shame (i.e., feeling bad about self), and anticipatory grief (i.e., complex emotions that occur before death). Pet deaths resulting from accidents, forced family separations, or compounded by other losses (e.g., a house fire) can be especially traumatic and stressful for families (Walsh, 2009).

Nearly 80% of dogs die from euthanasia (Lewis et al., 2018), a choice their humans must make for them. There is rarely a bright line indicating the correct time to make this decision. Quality of life often declines slowly and has peaks and valleys, similar to how care through terminal illness is complicated and often logistically challenging for people. This period can involve many trips to the vet, frequent administration of medicine, and the requirement to cancel plans for travel or other obligations that would keep the owner away from their dog. These challenges can make it difficult to sort out how much the choice for euthanasia is based on what is best for the dog versus what is best for the people. Financial barriers to expensive treatments sometimes force people to choose euthanasia for their dogs, even when they could be medically saved (Boller et al., 2020). These choices set the stage for complex feelings around decision-making and guilt once a dog has passed.

Laing and Maylea (2018) found anticipatory grief was a particular concern for pet owners in the face of impending euthanasia. Majid and Akande (2022) defined four stages of anticipatory grief: time of diagnosis, transition to hospice care, nearing death, and the moment of death. Although their work focused on human-to-human caregivers, these stages also apply to pet owners. These stages each demand different coping mechanisms, and caregivers' responses vary based on the time they have had to prepare for the death, the quality of caregiving they were able to provide, the roles they played in caretaking, and individual characteristics. Supporting pet owners through anticipatory grief at the end of their pets' lives may help them take the greatest advantage of the time they have left and make their decisions more clearly.

When facing the prospect of losing a dog, their owners should consider a "last best day" (i.e., or weekend or week) if their dog is up to it. Taking time to give the dog a last chance at things they loved or always wanted—a last car ride, a fast-food cheeseburger, a chocolate bar—can add a sense of purpose to those final difficult days (Gardner, 2017). Veterinarians are often willing to provide a few days of serious pain medicine and steroids to give owners extra quality time.

I adopted my golden retriever, Hopper, as a puppy, and she was the smartest, most empathetic dog I have had. When she was eight years old, she developed a limp that turned out to be synovial sarcoma—a cancer in her elbow joint. The only treatment was to amputate her leg. She did well as a three-legged dog for over a year, though my family knew she had arthritis in her remaining elbow that would eventually become an issue. By 18 months after her amputation, Hopper struggled to get up and walk, and a few months after that, she could not even touch her front leg to the ground without being in pain.

We knew it was time to say goodbye to Hopper, even though she was happy, playful, and engaged when she did not have the strength to stand. This realization gave us the opportunity for a great farewell. We took her out for a sunset paddleboard ride, snuck her into our neighbor's pool for a last swim, and bought her an extra-large Hershey bar. She always tried to steal our chocolate, and there was no reason to deny it to her that day. We brought her to the vet to say goodbye and fed her one square of chocolate at a time. She absolutely lit up, with her eyes bright and ears perked. That chocolate blew her mind, and she ate squares until the moment she fell asleep from the sedative before the euthanasia. She died happy, loved, and experiencing one of life's great joys. That evening we spent together—and the joy we were able to bring her—was such a comfort to us as we mourned.

Grieving the Death of a Dog

Grief for pets follows a similar process to that of grief for other loved ones. The typical grieving period lasts 6 months to 1 year, with an average of 10 months (Wrobel & Dye, 2003). The grief begins to abate after around 6 months, with a decline in symptoms such as crying, guilt, and anger. Still, after 1 year, approximately 22% of people have some symptoms of grief (Wrobel & Dye, 2003). Women tend to have stronger grief responses for their pets than men. The grief process of the bereaved must be supported to improve well-being and resilience, especially in the face of unique issues related to guilt and disenfranchised grief.

Guilt is common after a pet's death, especially because of the euthanasia issues discussed previously. One veterinarian interviewed by Packman et al. (2014) said, "95% feel guilty no matter how the death occurred, even after they have given all their possible care for their pet or the animal died because of his old age" (p. 351). It can be incredibly difficult to be the one to determine the exact moment of a dog's death, even if that choice was clearly a kind and compassionate way to prevent unnecessary suffering. This choice is also a less common source of guilt—though not unheard of—with human loss. Therapists should pay particular note to guilt as an element of grief in their clients who have lost pets.

Consider Kathy, who lost her dog, Scout. He was an eight-year-old English Shepherd with soulful eyes; a sweet, confident heart; and a calming aura in any room he entered. In late 2019, Scout started acting differently. He could not lie down without help, seemed to be in pain, and his personality changed. He had developed a hemangiosarcoma—an extremely malignant cancer that can produce massive tumors seemingly overnight. When the vet shared the results and the news that Scout likely would not survive more than a few days, Kathy's grief began, even though she still had Scout with her. She and her husband, Doug, started making plans to maximize their time with Scout. They took Scout to Sonic for a hot dog, but he got sick after eating it. They wanted to invite his friends over to say goodbye, but he was not interested in seeing most of them. As she recounted the story, Kathy shared, "Then he went into the backyard and started looking for a place to die." Just a day after his diagnosis, Scout died.

Though Kathy had never had issues with anxiety, she found herself in her car, pulling over on the side of the road, screaming in frustration, and having a panic attack after someone cut her off in traffic. She was overcome with guilt. Should she have noticed something was wrong sooner? Was a certain medicine he had taken responsible for the cancer? Even when vets and dog-loving friends explained that medicines did not cause this illness and that even if she had noticed something sooner, there was nothing she could have done, Kathy could not get past that feeling of guilt.

Kathy started looking for help. She tried group therapy and then three individual counselors before finding one who did not try to make her let go of her guilt. Releasing the guilt felt like losing her connection to Scout. Therapists working with patients grieving their pet's death must keep in mind that resilience is not the same as solving problems; rather, resilience is the process of listening to and validating clients' feelings and experiences while cultivating client-centered healing.

By far, the most pressing problem for grieving dog owners is the lack of social acknowledgment for the legitimacy of their grief, thereby leading to disenfranchised grief. This type of guilt creates confusion and shame for the bereaved and inhibits healthy grief processes. Adams et al. (1999) found the overarching theme of people's reactions to their pet's death was trying to understand their feelings in the context of what society expects. Adams et al. found people struggled to reconcile their actual feelings of profound grief with a lack of societal structures to acknowledge and support that grief. The social expectation that they quickly get over the death of a pet—or the perception of that expectation—created additional bereavement burdens for people.

Some of Adams et al.'s (1999) participants felt pressured to suppress their grief and regain emotional control as quickly as possible. These participants felt this suppression was necessary so they could return to work and social interactions without appearing too upset over the loss of their dog in the face of social pressures that disapproved of grief over "only" an animal. It may be helpful for therapists to help patients name the pressures they feel from significant others. Social norms and how they impact the patient's experience may be deconstructed during the conversation.

For others in Adams et al.'s (1999) study, proper social and emotional support was critical for processing their grief. The researchers found "when participants were alleviated from some of their confusion and turmoil by a supportive veterinarian, they felt justified in feeling badly that their pet had died and then permitted themselves to grieve" (Adams et al., 1999, p. 36). Although Adams et al. focused on veterinarians as social support, family members, friends, or therapists can all provide a social structure that removes confusion around what feelings are "allowable" so the bereaved can actually feel their grief.

Another complicating factor, centered on the lack of cultural support for grieving dog owners, is the lack of consistent social rituals around grief. Pets will need to be buried or cremated, and these options follow a fairly consistent process but do not serve the same purpose as structured ceremonies. As Lensing (2001) described, the bereaved's sense of loss leads to the psychological need to share their grief and memorialize the dead. Funerals, shiva, and other religious and social ceremonies provide those options, and the lack of these supports for pet owners often leaves them wanting more.

Some pet owners create their own rituals around death. They may put pets' ashes in a place of honor, hold funerals, or write poetry in their honor (Hoffman et al., 2020). These rituals are not new Western inventions, either; pet cemeteries have existed for a long time. Archeologists have found what they believe may be the world's oldest pet cemetery at an Ancient Egyptian site, suggesting that even 2,000 years ago, people formed strong bonds with their pets and honored them with rituals (Grimm, 2021).

Even with these attempts at creating rituals, dog owners often experience disenfranchised grief—grief that is not acknowledged or supported by social mores (Cordaro, 2012; Kogan et al., 2022). For the therapist or counselor, granting permission to grieve is an essential step in helping clients who are struggling with losing their pet. It is also important to recognize the importance of the relationship. Many people equate the loss of a pet to the loss of people with whom they have close human relationships. Validating clients' grief is critical to re-enfranchising it and allowing them to mourn properly (Cordaro, 2012). Re-enfranchising is important because disenfranchised grief after loss of a pet has been tied to inhibited posttraumatic growth, especially when grief is severe (Spain et al., 2019).

A colleague, Dr. Therapist Dave, advises patients to treat the pain they feel at the loss of a dog as something that honors the love and connection they had. This advice validates the relationship and grief, acknowledges the emotional difficulty, and gives purpose to the suffering. Grief treatment with a resilience focus empowers clients to talk about loss. The clinician may encourage this discussion by saying:

> I remember when you described Hopper's last day, you spoke about how painful it was to let her go and how joyful it was to finally see her taste chocolate. Let's continue to discuss your range of emotions. What is sustaining you in your sorrow? How do you continue to honor Hopper's joy?

Beyond the client–therapist relationship, social support is important for a healthy mourning process. Pet owners' social circles and support networks often fail to be empathetic in the face of a dog's death (Packman et al., 2014). Therapists should encourage clients to seek out support and—if not available in patients' social circles—pet loss support groups in person or online can be useful (Sharkin & Knox, 2003). Something as simple as an anonymous, fairly private forum to express grief can be therapeutic for those dealing with disenfranchised grief. Packman et al. (2014) surveyed grieving pet owners and provided space for them to share their feelings freely and anonymously about the loss of their pet. Without prompting, many respondents (13%–14%) commented on the therapeutic value of the survey process, noting it was the first time many had been asked to share their experience.

Conclusions

The death of a beloved dog can carry the same emotional impact as the loss of a friend or family member. People form close attachment bonds with their dogs, and most dog owners consider them family. Unfortunately, the relatively short lives of dogs mean that dog owners often need to deal with decisions around euthanasia and mourning the loss of their pets. Both factors impart unique psychological challenges to the grieving process.

Euthanasia, even when perfectly timed and chosen out of kindness, carries a burden of guilt that owners must bear after their dog's death. Furthermore, the significance of the human–dog bond and the resulting grief are not socially acknowledged as legitimate nor supported by accepted rituals, even though people are impacted as much by the loss of a dog as by the loss of a human. This situation can lead to issues surrounding disenfranchised grief, which can, in turn, inhibit healing, well-being, and resilience. It is critical for therapists helping patients through the grieving process for their pets to acknowledge the importance of their bond, work through related issues of grief, and validate their grief to re-enfranchise it. Outside of therapy, finding social support through friends, support groups, or even online forums can help people get through the grieving process.

Though the cultural and practical issues around pets involve some unique factors, at heart, people with pets have an important, broken bond that impacts them. Ultimately, the key to supporting healing and resilience after the loss of a dog is to provide acknowledgment, permission, and encouragement for people to share their feelings and work through their grief.

References

Adams, C. L., Bonnett, B. N., & Meek, A. H. (1999). Owner response to companion animal death: Development of a theory and practical implications. *The Canadian Veterinary Journal, 40*(1), Article 33.

Ainsworth, M. D. S. (1991). Attachments and other affectional bonds across the life cycle. In C. M. Parkes, J. Stevenson-Hinde, & P. Marris (Eds.), *Attachment across the life cycle* (1st ed., pp. 33–51). Routledge.

Ainsworth, M. D. S. (2006). Attachments and other affectional bonds across the life cycle. In C. M. Parkes, J. Stevenson-Hinde, & P. Marris (Eds.), *Attachment across the life cycle* (2nd ed., pp. 41–59). Routledge. https://doi.org/10.4324/9780203132470-6

Archer, J., & Winchester, G. (1994). Bereavement following death of a pet. *British Journal of Psychology, 85,* 259–271. https://doi.org/10.1111/j.2044-8295.1994.tb02522.x

Boller, M., Nemanic, T. S., Anthonisz, J. D., Awad, M., Selinger, J., Boller, E. M., & Stevenson, M. A. (2020). The effect of pet insurance on pre-surgical euthanasia of dogs with gastric dilatation-volvulus: A novel approach to quantifying economic euthanasia in veterinary emergency medicine. *Frontiers in Veterinary Science, 7,* 1039. https://doi.org/10.3389/fvets.2020.590615

Bowlby, J. (1979). The Bowlby-Ainsworth attachment theory. *Behavioral and Brain Sciences, 2*(4), 637–638. https://doi.org/10.1017/s0140525x00064955

Cain, A. O. (1983). A study of pets in the family system. In A. H. Katcher & A. M. Beck (Eds.), *New perspectives on our lives with companion animals* (pp. 72–81). University of Pennsylvania Press.

Carr, S., & Rockett, B. (2017). Fostering secure attachment: Experiences of animal companions in the foster home. *Attachment & Human Development, 19*(3), 259–277. https://doi.org/10.1080/14616734.2017.1280517

Cordaro, M. (2012). Pet loss and disenfranchised grief: Implications for mental health counseling practice. *Journal of Mental Health Counseling, 34*(4), 283–294. https://doi.org/10.17744/mehc.34.4.41q0248450t98072

Evans-Wilday, A. S., Hall, S. S., Hogue, T. E., & Mills, D. S. (2018). Self-disclosure with dogs: Dog owners' and non-dog owners' willingness to disclose emotional topics. *Anthrozoös, 31*(3), 353–366. https://doi.org/10.1080/08927936.2018.1455467

Gardner, M. (2017). The final chapter. In M. Gardner & D. McVety (Eds.), *Treatment and care of the geriatric veterinary patient* (pp. 337–341). Wiley. https://doi.org/10.1002/9781119187240.ch29

Geller, K. S. (2002). *The power of pets: How animals affect family relationships* [Master's thesis, Virginia Tech]. VTech Works. https://vtechworks.lib.vt.edu/handle/10919/42776

Golbeck, J., & Colino, S. (2023). *The purest bond: Understanding the human-canine connection.* Atria.

Grimm, D. (2021, February 6). Graves of nearly 600 cats and dogs in ancient Egypt may be world's oldest pet cemetery. *SCIENCE Magazine.* https://doi.org/10.1126/science.abh2835

Hoffman, L., Moats, M., & Greening, T. (Eds.). (2020). *Our last walk: Using poetry for grieving and remembering our pets.* University Professors Press.

Kerns, K. A., Koehn, A. J., van Dulmen, M. H., Stuart-Parrigon, K. L., & Coifman, K. G. (2017). Preadolescents' relationships with pet dogs: Relationship continuity and associations with adjustment. *Applied Developmental Science, 21*(1), 67–80. https://doi.org/10.1080/10888691.2016.1160781

Kogan, L. R., Bussolari, C., Currin-McCulloch, J., Packman, W., & Erdman, P. (2022). Disenfranchised guilt—Pet owners' burden. *Animals, 12*(13), Article 1690. https://doi.org/10.3390/ani12131690

Kurdek, L. A. (2009). Pet dogs as attachment figures for adult owners. *Journal of Family Psychology, 23*(4), Article 439. https://doi.org/10.1037/a0014979

Laing, M., & Maylea, C. (2018). "They burn brightly, but only for a short time": The role of social workers in companion animal grief and loss. *Anthrozoös*, *31*(2), 221–232. https://doi.org/10.1080/08927936.2018.1434062

Lensing, V. (2001). Grief support: The role of funeral service. *Journal of Loss & Trauma*, *6*(1), 45–63. https://doi.org/10.1080/108114401753197468

Lewis, T. W., Wiles, B. M., Llewellyn-Zaidi, A. M., Evans, K. M., & O'Neill, D. G. (2018). Longevity and mortality in Kennel Club registered dog breeds in the UK in 2014. *Canine Genetics and Epidemiology*, *5*(1), 1–17. https://doi.org/10.1186/s40575-018-0066-8

Majid, U., & Akande, A. (2022). Managing anticipatory grief in family and partners: A systematic review and qualitative meta-synthesis. *The Family Journal*, *30*(2), 242–249. https://doi.org/10.1177/10664807211000715

Packman, W., Carmack, B. J., Katz, R., Carlos, F., Field, N. P., & Landers, C. (2014). Online survey as empathic bridging for the disenfranchised grief of pet loss. *OMEGA-Journal of Death and Dying*, *69*(4), 333–356. https://doi.org/10.2190/om.69.4.a

Payne, E., DeAraugo, J., Bennett, P., & McGreevy, P. (2016). Exploring the existence and potential underpinnings of dog–human and horse–human attachment bonds. *Behavioural Processes*, *125*, 114–121. https://doi.org/10.1016/j.beproc.2015.10.004

Sharkin, B. S., & Knox, D. (2003). Pet loss: Issues and implications for the psychologist. *Professional Psychology: Research and Practice*, *34*(4), Article 414. https://doi.org/10.1037/0735-7028.34.4.414

Spain, B., O'Dwyer, L., & Moston, S. (2019). Pet loss: Understanding disenfranchised grief, memorial use, and posttraumatic growth. *Anthrozoös*, *32*(4), 555–568. https://doi.org/10.1080/08927936.2019.1621545

Taylor, S. E. (2011). Social support: A review. In *The Oxford handbook of health psychology* (pp. 190–214). Oxford University Press. https://doi.org/10.1093/oxfordhb/9780195342819.013.0009

Walsh, F. (2009). Human-animal bonds II: The role of pets in family systems and family therapy. *Family Process*, *48*(4), 481–499. https://doi.org/10.1111/j.1545-5300.2009.01297.x

Walsh, F. (2023). *Complex and traumatic loss: Fostering healing and resilience.* Guilford.

Wrobel, T. A., & Dye, A. L. (2003). Grieving pet death: Normative, gender, and attachment issues. *OMEGA-Journal of Death and Dying*, *47*(4), 385–393. https://doi.org/10.2190/qyv5-llj1-to43-uof9

12

BEYOND PATHOLOGY

The Role of Diagnosis in Resilience

Jameson Natwick

Jameson Natwick, PhD, LMFT, is an assistant clinical professor in couples and family therapy at Seattle University. His research includes work on changes to self-identity and family identity and the use of hope in psychotherapy. In conjunction with his position at Seattle University, Dr. Natwick is in private practice in Seattle. His pronouns are he/him, and he identifies as a White, cisgender man.

Reflect on the following words: psychopathology and diagnosis. What thoughts, emotions, memories, or meanings come to mind? People have a variety of experiences, emotions, and thoughts regarding these words and must acknowledge these words are not neutral. Diagnosis has been used to oppress marginalized groups (e.g., not considering the lack of resources that may contribute to symptoms of anger or defiance or harmful stereotypes about equity-deserving groups) or to depersonalize someone's experience of mental health (Doyen, 2021; Van Den Tillaart et al., 2009). The current socioeconomic context has made diagnosis a

DOI: 10.4324/9781003373513-12

necessity—and if clinicians are to use diagnostic codes to seek reimbursement and to be able to provide therapy to clients who cannot self-pay, they must use it ethically and to the benefit of clients. The accurate and compassionate use of psychopathology and diagnosis can promote justice, increase access to treatment, facilitate authentic client encounters, and foster resilience by seeing the whole person.

I am a Euro-American, heterosexual, cisgendered man (i.e., pronouns he/him) who is able bodied and middle class. My social location has informed and influenced my nine years in the mental health field. I currently teach master's-level therapists. I have witnessed several trends in psychopathology and diagnosis: (a) a clear divide between nonpathologizing clinicians and diagnosis-focused clinicians (McNally, 2012), (b) clinicians feeling uncomfortable with diagnosis and only billing insurance with "less intense" diagnoses (i.e., adjustment disorders; Jensen-Doss & Hawley, 2011), (c) and the boom of social media that has made mental health diagnosis popular and cool (e.g., TikTok trends of individuals talking about their diagnosis/diagnoses and their symptoms; Gilmore et al., 2022).

The divide between nondiagnosis- and diagnosis-focused clinicians is partly due to the training differences between mental health professionals. Typically, psychologists are trained to have advanced and specialized knowledge in assessments and diagnosis, viewing the diagnosis as the prime focus of treatment. This approach, rooted in the medical paradigm, is more surgical and focuses on a specific issue or symptom, whereas the treatment plan is concentrated on decreasing unwanted symptoms of a diagnosis (Hairston et al., 2019). This training differs from that of marriage and family therapists, where the education process has a systemic, strengths-based approach and focuses treatment on relational healing and connectedness (Karam et al., 2014). Both training programs have strengths and limitations, as students from respective programs may overly align with their training paradigm and not challenge their diagnostic construct.

It is easy to understand why some therapists rebel against the medical paradigm and see the depersonalization of a client as a travesty against the sacred relationship between client and therapist; however, I argue this medical paradigm of psychopathology is necessary for the holistic treatment of a client and is essential for fostering resilience within clients and systems. Psychopathology helps us, as therapists, recognize behaviors, moods, cognition, motor activity, or other observable data that present during the therapeutic process (McNally, 2012). The instinctual response of either–or thinking to try and simplify complex topics needs to be tempered to explore how diagnosis and understanding of psychopathology have a role in fostering resilience. As therapists, we need to embrace the tension between differing paradigms of understanding mental health—the postmodern and medical paradigms. This process is hard, and one I continually learned throughout my professional development.

Psychopathology, often called abnormal psychology in undergraduate courses, is the study of mental disorders and unusual or maladaptive behaviors (Comer & Comer, 2018). The hallmarks of psychopathology are disorder, dysfunction, deviance, and danger, referred to as the four Ds of psychopathology (Comer & Comer, 2018). *The Diagnostic and Statistical Manual of Mental Disorders* (DSM V-TR) is the collection of decades of research, observations, and development in understanding psychopathology; the manual provides a regulatory criterion for all mental disorders recognized in the United States (American Psychiatric Association, 2022).

Advocates for a postmodern mental health perspective often view diagnosis as pathologizing and imposing labels upon clients (Aviv, 2022; Frances, 2013). Licensed mental health counselors trained in positive psychology typically see the medical model as the disease model, too focused on dysfunction and disorder (Kinderman, 2021), and licensed marriage and family therapists trained in narrative therapy or collaborative language systems may rebel against the rigid narratives and language that can stem from such diagnostic terms and processes. Clinicians cannot be so quick to simply throw away all the work and research of the DSM V-TR because they believe diagnosis is pathologizing to clients (McNally, 2012). The DSM-V TR and psychopathology have their foundations in the medical paradigm, which is the explorative model of illness, including mental health (Lake, 2007). This paradigm is focused on observing what is happening in objective reality. What are clinicians witnessing in sessions? What do clients' symptoms, observable data, and self-reports tell clinicians about the person for whom they are providing care? Simply put, the medical paradigm sees the client as more of a subject to be studied than a person to be understood.

Psychopathology and the development of the DSM have been developed primarily with focus on the individual (Clegg, 2012). The DSM provides individual diagnostic codes, though the most recent editions of the DSM V-TR have shifted to include systemic diagnostic codes. These codes are not yet accepted by insurance, and using individual diagnostic codes still has priority (Finlay, 2019); however, when taking a systemic approach, the individual diagnostic codes are not just for individual psychotherapeutic treatment. The diagnosis of an individual will influence the systems of which they are a part, and the therapist needs to attend to how the systems respond and influence the diagnosis (Strong & Busch, 2013).

Individuals are part of systems, part of families, part of communities. An individual's diagnosis of anxiety, bipolar, depression, or whatever diagnosis is present will absolutely influence how the individual engages in relationships and how systems engage with the individual. Therapists who identify as anti-diagnosis therapists may argue that individual diagnosis does not make sense or does not fit how they conceptualize the system. Such a dismissal of psychopathology is dangerous (McNally, 2012). Holistic treatment must account for the whole person of everyone—their biopsychosocial-spiritual identities—and dismissing aspects of a system due to a personal conceptualization or philosophy is malpractice. The interconnection of a system can serve as a source of resilience as the system works to become adaptable to accommodate and support the diagnosis, along with how the diagnosis can positively inform a system (e.g., fostering compassion and tolerance to different lived experiences).

All therapists need to develop culturally attuned skills in a manner that appropriately integrates individual diagnosis into a systemic hypothesis (Olufowote et al., 2019; Romney & Jones, 2020). A well-documented example that exemplifies the necessity for culturally attuned diagnostic skills is how Black students are often perceived as more aggressive and out-of-control or how teachers and other professionals negatively view their behavior (Dee, 2005; McGrady & Reynolds, 2013). Culturally attuned clinical skills are necessary for accurate diagnosis and as a source of resilience for individuals and families to stop harmful and false biases and assumptions connected to culture, race, religion or spirituality, gender, and so on. Each family system will have a unique experience of how the multiple factors of social location will intersect with the diagnosis.

My personal example of diagnosis and its influence on a family is my brother, who has Tourette's syndrome. Tourette's is a disorder from the DSM V-TR characterized by vocal and motor tics (American Psychiatric Association, 2022). Though my brother is the individual experiencing the tics and lives every moment with this disorder, my family has been greatly impacted by the symptoms of his Tourette's disorder. My parents were often focused on my brother with concern for the bullying he experienced and questioned how to accommodate his Tourette's while not giving him an excuse from responsibilities. Furthermore, my sister would become embarrassed and upset when my brother's tics drew unwanted attention in public spaces. I found myself withdrawing from these aspects of my family, not wanting to be involved in such uncomfortable situations. Though this withdrawal was my reaction as a teenager, my experiences with my family and my brother's Tourette's greatly influenced my career choice and who I am. I learned to see the world from a more divergent perspective, exploring how people can be isolated and how to encounter people without focusing on a diagnosis. My brother was my best friend who simply happened to have tics.

Expanding Identity as Resilience

Concerns about stigma, labeling, and pathologizing are not rooted in misleading thought or pure speculation. There is evidence of the wounds a diagnosis can inflict upon an individual or a system (Ben-Zeev et al., 2010). As I have argued, this position is narrow and restrictive. Deepening the meaning of diagnosis and working collaboratively with a client and their family or community to integrate diagnosis into wellness can foster meaningful resilience for all.

In my clinical work, I have always been fascinated by how easily people are able to accept physical diagnosis, take medication, or follow through on treatment. A person who is diagnosed with arthritis will take medication and maybe go to physical therapy; a person who has a laceration will limit movement and change dressings until the cut is healed. Though people are resistant to seeing medical doctors, generally, individuals are even more resistant to seeking proper mental health treatment and diagnosis (Blumenthal & Endicott, 1997; Byrow et al., 2020). As clinicians, when we encounter such individuals or systems resistant to mental health treatment, we *slow down*. We slow down to build resilience; take the time to listen, learn, and understand a client's concerns; and gently encourage the client to expand the way they see mental health treatment in a way that is congruent with their cultural, familial, and personal beliefs and lived experiences.

It is vital for treatment to expand the client's beliefs surrounding diagnosis or mental health so it does not become internalized and consume a client's self-identity or a family's identity. A mental health diagnosis is just a part of a person's identity. If an individual focuses too much on anxiety or depression, for example, their identity may be consumed. More specifically, a client may be so focused on their anxiety that they perceive the world solely through their anxiety. When a mental health diagnosis is central to a person's self-identity and they have negative beliefs or meanings associated with it, the diagnosis becomes a barrier to fostering resilience. Clients often will feel "stuck in a rut" or "lost in a fog" and will be resistant to any suggestions. Often, I have heard in my clinical practice, "We've tried everything," and every area or idea I inquire about is quickly dismissed. The psychological disorder becomes internalized and infused with self-identity.

The internalized experience of a diagnosis limits a person's perception about their self-identity. A person with depression focuses too much on feeling down, combating negative self-talk, and sleeping too much, and all of these factors are part of the way this person sees the world. This person has a limited self-identity (e.g., "I am depressed, and I can't make friends because of my depression"). A robust self-identity is not limited to one or two factors. There should be multiple *ands* as a person describes their identity (e.g., "I am a husband and father and professor and therapist and a lover of Lord of the Rings and a down-hill skier and foodie and avid reader"). Expansive self-identity has more access to explore possibilities of resilience and strengths.

In addition to self-identity, every family has a family identity. When a member of the system has a diagnosis, it can also limit the way the family perceives their family identity. For example, a family with an autistic child can be too focused on accommodating the autistic child when planning vacations, meals, or schedules. Though attending to needs of an individual is important, an over focus on the autistic child can create a system where needs of other individuals are left unattended. The family's identity then becomes limited to the needs of the autistic child. When a self-identity or family identity becomes centered on the diagnosis, too many *ands* are lost and resilience is limited.

As a systemic therapist, I believe in the importance and power of systems. Research has demonstrated the importance of a system embracing and coming together to face challenges (Patterson, 1988; Walsh, 2003, 2016). A mental health diagnosis needs to be encountered as a system. Many times, members of the system without the diagnosis also need to learn to externalize. Statements such as "my partner is depressed, and it keeps us from having sex" are deeply wounding to the individual with depression and to the system. Helping other members of the system to shift perceptions of the diagnosis and come together as a system is necessary for treatment. The burden of a diagnosis is not for one person to carry. When the whole system is transformed, the diagnosis is no longer a burden; rather, the system and individual have developed new skills, insights, and meanings to find resilience within themselves.

Fostering Resilience: Bias, Experience, and Unconscious Meanings

The first step in fostering resilience with diagnosis is to address and understand clients' biases or how their past experiences shape their encounters with diagnosis. Walsh (2016) identified that family belief systems or family meaning-making processes are key to building resilience. Clients come with their personal histories, transgenerational histories, family narratives about mental illness, past experiences with providers, or stigma from social discourses. As clinicians, if we move too quickly to diagnosis without understanding the meanings, history, and narratives around psychopathology, the role of diagnosis will not be a source of resilience; rather, the diagnosis will continue to affirm the dominant, unhelpful narrative of clients.

Assessment matters throughout the therapeutic process. Clinicians need to slow down and hear about past experiences with doctors or therapists, family narratives or histories with mental health, or personal meanings each individual holds about diagnosis. The clinician should consider: What is important in assessing how clients process diagnosis or psychopathology?

Psychopathology and Diagnosis Assessment Checklist:

- Family history of mental health diagnoses:
    - How did the family successfully cope?
    - What strengths/barriers can be identified in family history about diagnoses?
    - Are there unspoken aspects to the client's family history?
- Attitudes and beliefs (positive, negative, and neutral) about diagnosis, individual and systemic.
- Experiences with medical and mental health care:
    - What was beneficial and worked well?
    - What did not go well and was unhelpful?
- Other people's experiences with medical or mental health care:
    - How have positive experiences or messages from friends or communities (e.g., church, school, work) influenced your client?
    - Are there negative experiences or messages from others that are influential upon your client? How so?
- What does diagnosis mean to the client (e.g., getting diagnosed means I will have to take medication)?

Including diagnosis as an overt part of the therapeutic process allows clients to have a deeper understanding of mental health. As clinicians, we can acknowledge stigma or bias and collaborate to understand clients' experiences and reframe rigid beliefs and meanings. When working with a system with an individual with a diagnosis, therapists can open conversations and emotions to help foster compassion and communication within the family system. To expand beliefs and conversations, therapists need to tune into behaviors and statements from the system.

Case Example

I worked with a family where the mother wanted a diagnosis for her ten-year-old son. The mother had suspected something was different about her son since he was four. Pursuing diagnosis and treatment was delayed because her husband (i.e., son's father) was against diagnosis, saying, "It is just a phase. He will grow out of it." Still, behavioral problems of defiance and emotional outbursts increased over six years, and the father became more open to acknowledging a diagnosis, uniting the parents. Many sessions required considerable intention to explore the father's resistance, meanings, and beliefs about mental health and diagnosis. The delay in treatment and diagnosis also created a significant wound for the mother, who felt betrayed by her husband and guilty for not pursuing treatment years prior. Processing these system dynamics was vital for embracing their son's diagnosis and for the healing needed in the marital relationship.

When exploring family history, experiences, and beliefs about mental health with clients, clinicians acknowledge that personal beliefs and meanings about diagnoses will inform their approaches to conversations with clients and how we diagnose clients (Hairston et al., 2019). It is critical to become more aware of blind spots and biases carried into the therapeutic process. As therapists, we do not want to get in the way. Slowing down to explore experiences, meanings, and beliefs about diagnosis can be difficult for clinicians, as we must acknowledge our own biases and meanings that we bring to the therapeutic process. Clinicians should take time to reflect on the self-of-the-therapist using these question prompts:

- What meanings and beliefs about diagnosis do you bring to the therapeutic process?
- How might you influence clients in understanding psychopathology or diagnosis?
- What would it be like to inform a client of a diagnosis that you determined?
- Do you shy away from diagnosis? Do you focus too much on diagnosis?
- What is linked to diagnosis? Medication? Stigma? Othering? Clarity?

These questions can assist in deepening our understanding of our self-of-the-therapist, and such work is crucial. Many theories in existing psychotherapy literature have articulated the therapist's role in the therapeutic process (Metcalf, 2018); however, it is important to consider if the role of the therapist changes when diagnosing or assessing for psychopathology is involved. I have found a balance between two roles for a therapist: expert and observer.

Therapists have invested much time, energy, and resources into their training. It is *good* to be an expert. Part of this training is to diagnose and provide psychoeducation about psychopathology. Dr. Google is dangerous! Many clients will search the internet and come to their own conclusions. I do not need to elaborate on how this instinct is not good. As clinicians, we can and will provide in-depth conversations and accurate information that can assuage projections and assumptions from clients.

For example, one client came in for their intake session and informed me they had "severe generalized anxiety disorder" and needed cognitive-behavioral treatment. This client had already bought a workbook and brought it to session! Though cognitive-behavioral therapy is a fantastic treatment modality, I was uncomfortable with the rigidity of the therapeutic process. For this client, anxiety was a disease to eradicate, much like our medical approach to smallpox. I met the client where they were and explored how they found the information and personal and family beliefs about anxiety and mental health. Over the course of many sessions, the diagnosis of generalized anxiety disorder (GAD) was met, but the client's beliefs about anxiety were transformed from a negative emotion into a natural emotion that is a part of the human experience. The client became more resilient and capable by integrating new meanings about anxiety rather than eliminating anxiety from her experience. The diagnosis of GAD was not a stigmatizing aspect of the client's anxiety, and over the course of treatment, the diagnosis no longer fit the experience and presentation of the client.

The second role of the therapist is that of an observer. The role of the observer mirrors the heart of the medical paradigm. As clinicians, we observe behaviors, patterns, and symptoms that are present during the session; however, the observer role needs to go beyond the medical paradigm. We need to observe the individual and the system where the individual resides. Even though there are times when other system members are not physically present, through the stories the client tells, we can understand the system and its influences on the client. As observers, our perceptions must expand beyond diagnostic behaviors and symptoms; we must also see and identify patterns of resilience demonstrated by the individual and system. Holding this *both/and* approach in observation provides a necessary scope to accurately diagnose and recognize the resilient factors in the system and build upon them.

Diagnosis as Justice

The *ideal* concept of justice is that people are treated fairly, impartially, and reasonably within the systems in which they participate; however, given humanity's tendency towards biases and stereotypes, it is not a reality that fair, impartial, and reasonable treatment is always provided. Many advocates against diagnosis might point out how stigma, bias, or othering occurs, reinforcing harm to individuals and larger systems. Stigma and ostracization do occur; thus, diagnosis can be an unjust process for many individuals. Unfortunately, these situations occur, and individuals with diagnosis (and their families) may have to find resilience to encounter experiences of stigma or othering. When diagnosis and psychopathology are ignored, injustice toward clients can further reinforce stigma and bias.

An accurate diagnosis, attuning to the DSM and a client's culture and lived experience, can allow clients to gain access to treatment, medications, care, and correct treatment plans. A misdiagnosis or the refusal to diagnose can create many barriers for clients. As therapists in the US health system, we need to acknowledge the importance of a correct, appropriate, and just diagnosis. The following clinical example highlights how diagnosis is just:

> Ashley had been seeing a therapist who did not believe in diagnosis, and the focus of treatment was on highlighting strengths and exploring new possibilities. However, Ashley continued to display clear signs of bipolar disorder: depressive and manic episodes, excessive spending, and extreme energy. The subsequent treatment dismissed the diagnosis and psychopathology, so important assessments and psychoeducation on bipolar were completely absent. Due to treatment being absent from this particular clinical attention, Ashley almost lost her house, car,

and other possessions due to excessive spending. Only in this crisis state did Ashley become connected with a clinician who provided a proper diagnosis of bipolar and put a treatment plan in place.

An accurate diagnosis can provide new sources of resilience. From a practical perspective, many disorders require the collaboration of many different providers: (a) a bipolar diagnosis will require treatment with a psychiatrist and therapist, (b) an eating disorder diagnosis will require a nutritionist and therapist, or (c) a selective mutism diagnosis will require a speech therapist and a psychotherapist (Novak et al., 2022; Rugkåsa et al., 2020). The correct diagnosis can help determine who needs to be a part of the treatment team. I have experienced that an accurate diagnosis can open doors for more intensive treatment. Many eating disorder clinics and programs require a formal diagnosis. This requirement mirrors many substance misuse programs and in-patient psychiatric programs.

Furthermore, being able to provide explanations and information about a diagnosis to a person or system to explain why certain behaviors, patterns, or symptoms are present can be empowering. As clinicians, we can inform and collaborate to create new patterns, behaviors, or beliefs about the diagnosis (Walsh, 2016). Excessive spending during a manic episode is no longer someone "going crazy," but rather, reflects an informed understanding of bipolar disorder, which can help foster new strategies to assist the clients and others in relationships with the client. It is possible to make the diagnosis only a part of the individual or system's identity and not the main phenomena of focus.

Fostering Resilience: A Narrative Approach

One way to foster a therapeutic environment where a diagnosis is only a part of an individual or system's identity is by using aspects of narrative therapy. Historically, narrative therapy, created by White and Epston (1990), would be an anti-diagnosis therapeutic modality. Narrative therapy identifies how rigid dominant narratives are barriers to how individuals and families find new possibilities and solutions (White & Epston, 1990). The theory is relevant to this discussion after explaining previously how diagnosis and psychopathology have histories in family beliefs and meanings, stigma, and stereotypes. These factors can all serve as dominant narratives that are problematic and rigid.

For example, Ashley may have experienced negative narratives about herself regarding self-control—specifically, spending; however, introducing an accurate diagnosis into her negative narrative provided an opportunity to integrate the narratives about symptoms and experiences Ashley had following her diagnosis. This integration led to the creation of new, strength-based narratives Ashley had about herself. Narrative therapy, therefore, provides a unique opportunity to have its strength-based approach align with diagnosis and psychopathology. This approach is not done by dismissing the DSM-V TR but by working to reframe the narrative, beliefs, and meanings surrounding diagnosis.

Externalization: Separating the Diagnosis From the Individual/Family

Narrative therapy has the intervention of externalization that would be useful in holding a strengths-based approach and attending to diagnosis (White & Epston, 1990). Externalization works to take internalized problems and separate them from an individual or family system. This process occurs by (a) defining the problem, (b) being aware of the language surrounding the problem, and (c) the clinician using externalizing questions to linguistically shift the adjectives people use to describe themselves into nouns (White & Epston, 1990). For example, instead of asking Ashley about her depression with "How did you become depressed?", clinicians should externalize depression and ask, "What made you vulnerable to depression so that it was able to dominate your life?" The transformation of the therapists' questions can subtly transform clients' narratives about diagnosis, self-identity, and systemic perceptions of diagnosis. This process does not dismiss the reality of symptoms and lived experiences of the client and diagnosis but will allow the experience of diagnosis to take on new meaning.

This externalization process increases the power of the individual and the system. Both entities can start to claim and take power back from the diagnosis and move to have power over the diagnosis. For Ashley, externalizing bipolar disorder facilitated her into a position to have power (e.g., "I have the abilities and strategies to be successful with bipolar disorder") and knowledge (e.g., "I have identified my warning signs for a manic episode, and I know how to cope with my depressive experiences") to determine how she wanted to respond to the diagnosis.

Simply put, the diagnosis does not have the person or the system—the person has a diagnosis, which is just one part of a full and robust identity.

Conclusion

Psychopathology and diagnosis are integral parts of being a therapist. As clinicians in the mental health field, there will inevitably be encounters with varying opinions, thoughts, and perspectives on diagnosis. Though the multiple arguments for and against diagnosis have valuable points, I argue that the holistic view of the individual and the family system allows diagnosis to be part of an inclusive conceptualization for treatment. Exploring how self-identity, meaning, and relational dynamics are influenced by diagnosis (or vice versa) offers opportunities for resilience to emerge and to avoid barriers of stigma and internalization of the diagnosis onto an identity. This exploration of how clients understand diagnosis requires us clinicians to do our own work to understand our biases or unconscious meanings that we bring into the therapeutic process. When diagnosis is used accurately and openly with clients and for all those who are part of treatment, the therapeutic process can transform a list of criteria into a deeper meaning of understanding self and facilitating the holistic care all people deserve.

References

American Psychiatric Association. (2022). *Diagnostic and statistical manual of mental disorders* (5th ed.). https://doi.org/10.1176/appi.books.9780890425787

Aviv, R. (2022). *Strangers to ourselves: Unsettled minds and the stories that make us.* Farrar, Straus and Giroux.

Ben-Zeev, D., Young, M. A., & Corrigan, P. W. (2010). DSM-V and the stigma of mental illness. *Journal of Mental Health, 19*(4), 318–327. https://doi.org/10.3109/09638237.2010.492484

Blumenthal, R., & Endicott, J. (1997). Barriers to seeking treatment for major depression. *Depression & Anxiety, 4*(6), 273–278. https://doi.org/10.1002/(SICI)1520-6394(1996)4:6%3C273::AID-DA3%3E3.0.CO;2-D

Byrow, Y., Pajak, R., Specker, P., & Nickerson, A. (2020). Perceptions of mental health and perceived barriers to mental health help-seeking amongst refugees: A systematic review. *Clinical Psychology Review, 75*, Article 101812. https://doi.org/10.1016/j.cpr.2019.101812

Clegg, J. W. (2012). Teaching about mental health and illness through the history of the DSM. *History of Psychology*, *15*(4), 364–370. https://doi.org/10.1037/a0027249

Comer, R., & Comer, J. (2018). *Abnormal psychology* (10th ed.). Worth Publishers.

Dee, T. S. (2005). A teacher like me: Does race, ethnicity, or gender matter? *American Economic Review*, *95*(2), 158–65. https://doi.org/10.1257/000282805774670446

Doyen, P. (2021). The overdiagnosis of bipolar disorder within marginalized communities: A call to action. *Columbia Social Work Review*, *19*(1), 80–99. https://doi.org/10.52214/cswr.v19i1.7388

Finlay, L. (2019). *Practical ethics in counselling and psychotherapy: A relational approach*. SAGE Publications. https://doi.org/10.4135/9781526481764

Frances, A. (2013). Saving normal: An insider's revolt against out-of-control psychiatric diagnosis, DSM-5, big pharma and the medicalization of ordinary life. *Psychotherapy in Australia*, *19*(3), 14–18. https://search.informit.org/doi/10.3316/informit.464019439257830

Gilmore, R., Beezhold, J., Selwyn, V., Howard, R., Bartolome, I., & Henderson, N. (2022). Is TikTok increasing the number of self-diagnoses of ADHD in young people? *European Psychiatry*, *65*(S1), S571–S571. http://doi.org10.1192/j.eurpsy.2022.1463

Hairston, D. R., Gibbs, T. A., Wong, S. S., & Jordan, A. (2019). Clinician bias in diagnosis and treatment. In M. Medlock, D. Shtasel, N. H. Trinh, & D. Williams (Eds.), *Racism and psychiatry: Contemporary issues and interventions* (pp. 105–137). Humana Press. https://doi.org/10.1007/978-3-319-90197-8_7

Jensen-Doss, A., & Hawley, K. M. (2011). Understanding clinicians' diagnostic practices: Attitudes toward the utility of diagnosis and standardized diagnostic tools. *Administration and Policy in Mental Health and Mental Health Services Research*, *38*, 476–485. https://doi.org/10.1007/s10488-011-0334-3

Karam, E. A., Sprenkle, D. H., & Davis, S. D. (2014). Targeting threats to the therapeutic alliance: A primer for marriage and family therapy training. *Journal of Marital and Family Therapy*, *41*(4), 389–400. https://doi.org/10.1111/jmft.12097

Kinderman, P. (2021). The disease (medical) model vs the positive psychology model: Do we need a revolution in mental health? *Islamic Psychology and Counselling*. https://spring-foundation.com/the-disease-medical-model-vs-the-positive-psychology-model/

Lake, J. (2007). Emerging paradigms in medicine: Implications for the future of psychiatry. *Explore*, *3*(5), 467–477. https://doi.org/10.1016/j.explore.2007.06.003

McGrady, P. B., & Reynolds, J. R. (2013). Racial mismatch in the classroom: Beyond black-white differences. *Sociology of Education, 86*(1), 3–17. https://doi.org/10.1177/0038040712444857

McNally, R. J. (2012). *What is mental illness?* Belknap Press. https://doi.org/10.4159/9780674059481

Metcalf, L. (Ed.). (2018). *Marriage and family therapy: A practice oriented approach* (2nd ed.). Springer. https://doi.org/10.1891/9780826161253

Novak, J. R., Robinson, L. P., & Korn, L. E. (2022). What MFTs should know about nutrition, psychosocial health, and collaborative care with nutrition professionals. *Journal of Marital and Family Therapy, 48*(2), 502–522. https://doi.org/10.1111/jmft.12540

Olufowote, R. A. D., Turns, B., & Eddy, B. (2019). The sibling subsystem: The effects of being raised with an individual with ASD. In R. A. Dansby Olufowote, B. Turns, & B. Eddy (Eds.), *Systemically treating autism: A clinician's guide for empowering families* (pp. 53–59). Routledge Publishing.

Patterson, J. M. (1988). Families experiencing stress: The family adjustment and adaptation response model. *Family Systems Medicine, 5*(2), 202–237. https://doi.org/10.1037/h0089739

Romney, J. S., & Jones, E. R. (2020). A systemic treatment of families with a child diagnosed with ASD using a narrative lens. *American Journal of Family Therapy, 48*(5), 478–494. https://doi.org/10.1080/01926187.2020.1745718

Rugkåsa, J., Tveit, O. G., Berteig, J., Hussain, A., & Ruud, T. (2020). Collaborative care for mental health: A qualitative study of the experiences of patients and health professionals. *BMC Health Services Research, 20,* 1–10. https://doi.org/10.1186/s12913-020-05691-8

Strong, T., & Busch, R. (2013). DSM-5 and evidence-based family therapy? *Australian and New Zealand Journal of Family Therapy, 34*(2). https://doi.org/10.1002/anzf.1009

Van Den Tillaart, S., Kurtz, D., & Cash, P. (2009). Powerlessness, marginalized identity, and silencing of health concerns: Voiced realities of women living with a mental health diagnosis. *International Journal of Mental Health Nursing, 18*(3), 153–163. https://doi.org/10.1111/j.1447-0349.2009.00599.x

Walsh, F. (2003). Family resilience: A framework for clinical practice. *Family Process, 42*(1), 1–18. https://doi.org/10.1111/j.1545-5300.2003.00001.x

Walsh, F. (2016). *Strengthening family resilience* (3rd ed.). Guilford Press.

White, M., & Epston, D. (1990). *Narrative means to therapeutic ends.* W. W. Norton & Company.

13

BEYOND SELF-CARE

Intentional Practices of Resilient Therapists

Rebecca A. Cobb and Christie Eppler

Rebecca (Becky) Cobb, PhD, LMFT, is a cis-female, European-American in her early 40s who identifies as spiritual and not religious. She is a clinical professor for Seattle University's Master of Arts in Couples and Family Therapy program. She received her Master of Science in Child Development and Family Studies, with specialization in Marriage and Family Therapy, from Purdue University and PhD in Marriage and Family Therapy from Florida State University. Dr. Cobb is an American Association for Marriage and Family Therapy (AAMFT)-approved supervisor and is passionate about leadership in the field of couples and family therapy.

Christie Eppler, PhD, LMFT (she/her), is a program director and professor in Couples and Family Therapy at Seattle University. She is a Euro-American, middle class, spiritual, heterosexual, cisgender woman. Her qualitative research areas include systemic resilience, justice, and narrative therapy. Dr. Eppler is an AAMFT-Approved Supervisor and a Licensed Marriage and Family Therapist (LMFT; Washington). She enjoys helping new interns mitigate their anxieties while utilizing systems theories and common factors to conceptualize clients. She is a certified yoga instructor and marathoner who loves hiking with her Golden Retriever, Mossy.

DOI: 10.4324/9781003373513-13

Therapist well-being is commonly addressed in ethical codes of conduct for mental health professionals. For example, the American Psychological Association's (APA, 2002) *Ethical Principles of Psychologists and Code of Conduct* stated, "Psychologists strive to be aware of the possible effect of their own physical and mental health on their ability to help those with whom they work" (Principal A). Likewise, the American Association for Marriage and Family Therapy's (2004) *Core Competencies* advised clinicians to "monitor attitudes, personal well-being, personal issues, and personal problems to ensure they do not impact the therapy process adversely or create vulnerability for misconduct" (5.4.2). Typically, these dynamics are addressed in the literature as they relate to the critical nature of self-care (Corey et al., 2024).

Self-care is a protective factor against burnout and compassion fatigue (Dorociak et al., 2017). For therapists from marginalized populations who experience additional stressors such as racism and discrimination, self-care can also support in resisting the oppressive systems that threaten well-being (Wyatt & Ampadu, 2022). Self-care messaging, however, perpetuates stereotypes, such as what constitutes self-care and who may engage in it. For example, self-care is often marketed with expensive spa treatments and vacations as venues for care. However, self-care can be free, community-based, and steeped in liberation (Wyatt & Ampadu, 2022). It can be mindfulness, community gatherings, rituals to honor grief, or time spent laughing with friends. It is anything that cultivates radical joy or realistic hope. It can also be "aligned with cultural values and practices that draw from ancestral wisdom" (Wyatt & Ampadu, 2022, p. 219).

Therapists with a regular practice of self-care have reported greater well-being and quality of life than those without a routine (Dorociak et al., 2017). Therapists with greater engagement in self-care are also better able to manage personal and professional stressors and are more capable of implementing healthy coping mechanisms in the face of adverse situations. Outcomes of not practicing self-care include burnout, vicarious trauma, secondary traumatic stress, compassion fatigue, reduced standard of care, and diminished quality of care for clients. As a result, self-care for therapists has been identified as an ethical imperative (Corey et al., 2024).

Self-care refers to engagement in practices that promote and maintain personal well-being (Posluns & Gall, 2020). Self-care is multifaceted and may be attended to by focusing on the health and wellness of body (e.g., going to the gym, taking a walk), mind (e.g., reading a book, taking a class), emotions (e.g., journaling about feelings), spirit (e.g., meditating, praying), relationships (e.g., talking on the phone with a friend, cuddling up on the couch with a furry companion), and even work (e.g., catching up on paperwork). Resilience is a related construct that can be tied to any dimension of self-care.

Resilience is the ability to cope with and adapt to adverse life experiences (Walsh, 2016). Inherent in the profession, therapists face adversity daily as clients discuss their life struggles with them. Therapist resilience is a key factor in preventing negative outcomes such as burnout, vicarious trauma, secondary traumatic stress, compassion fatigue, reduced standard of care, and diminished quality of care for clients.

Many people think resilience is a fixed trait or personality characteristic; however, as Watters and Seshadri discussed in Chapter 4, it is not. Resilience is a dynamic process that changes and fluctuates with time and experience (Flynn et al., 2021). Resilience can be developed and maintained by (a) belief systems (e.g., meaning making, positive outlook or hope, transcendence or spirituality), (b) organizational processes (e.g., flexibility, connectedness, social and community resources), and (c) communication processes (e.g., clear information, emotional sharing, problem solving or prevention; Walsh, 2016). It is essential for therapists to develop their resilient beliefs, processes, and practices well before they become licensed and carry these dynamics forward throughout their careers.

Resilience can be fostered and supported by certain self-care practices. For example, self-care practices that include psychosocial components, such as identification of personal and professional strengths and competencies, stress reduction techniques, and connection with supportive friends and family, can help build and maintain resilience (Swartz, 2017), but it goes beyond just these practices. With intentional practice, therapists can foster their resilience to help navigate the difficult demands of clinical work and life in general. The following reviews characteristics of resilient therapists, provides questions for personal reflection, and offers suggestions for intentionally enhancing therapist resilience.

Resilient Therapists

At a personal level, resilient therapists maintain a desire to learn and grow (Hou & Skovholt, 2020), are curious about themselves and others, and monitor emotional well-being. Resilient therapists keep themselves healthy and attend to important aspects of self-care (Clark, 2009), such as having interests and hobbies outside of work. Resilient therapists are also able to recognize their struggles and imperfections (Eppler, 2018) and proactively address personal problems (Skovholt, 2001) and self of the therapist concerns (Clark, 2009). When personal struggles arise, resilient therapists allow themselves the same grace they would afford their clients (Eppler, 2018). This grace may look like rescheduling clients and taking a sick day when not feeling well or practicing self-compassion and forgiveness when forgetting the details of a story that a client told the week before.

Interpersonally, resilient therapists develop and maintain supportive personal relationships (Clark, 2009; Hou & Skovholt, 2020). Within these relationships, resilient therapists maintain clear boundaries (Skovholt, 2001) and avoid assuming unwarranted responsibility for others' well-being (Clark, 2009). When family of origin issues arise, resilient therapists attend to these issues as needed (Clark, 2009). Focus on differentiation of self, a key concept of Bowen's family systems theory, assists resilient therapists in this endeavor by supporting mindful functioning and helping to avoid secondary traumatic stress, vicarious trauma, and burnout (MacKay, 2017). A therapist who has worked on their own differentiation, for example, may initially feel reactive when their family members attempt to get them to "fix" a sibling's disordered eating; however, as an act of resilience to honor their own boundaries while being supportive of others, the therapist may opt to provide resources for therapeutic services elsewhere and offer a listening ear as they feel capable without feeling depleted.

Cultivating relational resilience is particularly important as it relates to workplace settings. For example, therapists in private practice are less likely to experience burnout and are more likely to experience compassion satisfaction than those who work in schools and community agencies, although caseload and number of high-risk clients are important to consider (Lawson & Myers, 2011). Those in organizational settings are more likely to experience burnout (Laverdière et al., 2019) and secondary traumatic stress (Owens-King, 2019). These outcomes are likely due to the experience of greater demands and lower levels of autonomy (Laverdière et al., 2019) and perceived control over work (Rupert et al., 2015) in organizational settings.

Resilient therapists maintain and can contribute to positive workplace environments, regardless of professional setting. They proactively identify and correct problems, manage work stressors (Skovholt, 2001), and address emotionally exhausting situations as they arise (Clark, 2009). In organizational settings, these actions can potentially have an even greater systemic impact that may benefit the workplace environment of others. In addition, resilient therapists seek training opportunities to facilitate professional growth (Clark, 2009).

Interpersonal and professional characteristics intersect as they relate to the intentional development and maintenance of peer relationships. Within this respect, resilient therapists actively engage in professional organizations, network to develop supportive and professionally enriching relationships with colleagues (Clark, 2009; Skovholt, 2001), and maintain connections with these colleagues (Clark, 2009). For example, therapists might intentionally attend networking events at conferences and make a point of exchanging contact information with a certain number of people at each event. Those with whom networking does not come naturally might ask other colleagues to introduce them to others they would like to meet. They might intentionally reconnect with new acquaintances at future events to develop and maintain those relationships, reach out for consultations regarding areas of expertise, or provide referrals.

Interpersonal and professional characteristics intersect again—specifically, as they relate to therapeutic work and professional relationships with clients. Clinically, resilient therapists maintain a sense of meaning and purpose in their work and believe that their work makes a difference and contributes to the welfare of others, even if the impact is small (Clark, 2009). Resilient therapists also avoid taking inappropriate responsibility for clients' well-being and can hold difficult client stories while caring for themselves and their families (Eppler, 2018). These findings are consistent with Walsh's (2016) understanding of belief systems (e.g., meaning and purpose in work), organizational processes (e.g., development and maintenance of peer relationships), and communication processes (e.g., focus on problem solving and prevention) as key factors in resilience.

How clinicians make sense of what is shared in client sessions is another factor that can inhibit or contribute to resilience. Hearing clients' stories of suffering can lead to compassion fatigue and secondary traumatization (Owens-King, 2019). Conversely, there are opportunities for vicarious resilience (Hernandez-Wolfe, 2018; Hernandez-Wolfe et al., 2015). Therapists can enhance their positive outlook, self-care practices, and resourcefulness by listening to client stories about how they solved problems, overcame challenges, and transformed their self-perceptions.

Questions for Reflection

Reflecting on one's resilience affords the opportunity to identify strengths and opportunities for growth. This type of reflection in and of itself allows for the enhancement of resilience. Readers should consider writing down responses to each of the following questions to aid in identifying areas in which future efforts might benefit from focus (Wicks, 2008).

It is common practice for therapists to reflect on self-care practices. Self-care can enhance and enrich resilience. Thus, reflection questions related to self-care are presented first.

Self-Care

- How do you attend to important aspects of self-care—physically, mentally, emotionally, spiritually, relationally, and professionally?
- How does your self-care practice impact your relationships, both personally and professionally?
- How does your self-care practice impact your sense of gratitude for self and others?
- How does your self-care practice impact your own resilience and that of others?
- How might you expand your self-care practices to enhance your own resilience and resilience in your contexts (e.g., work, family)?

The following questions encourage self-reflection on personal, inter-personal, and professional aspects related to therapist resilience. Peer relationships and clinical work are key components of professional resil-ience for therapists that warrant special focus.

Personal

- How do you proactively address personal problems and self-of-the-therapist concerns individually and in a community of support?
- Do you allow yourself the same compassion that you afford clients and others?
- How do you maintain curiosity?
- In what ways have you committed to learning more about yourself, others, and the world?
- What is your practice of identifying your own struggles and imper-fections? How can you use a community of support to help promote this practice?

Interpersonal

- How do you maintain curiosity about others?
- How do you promote the well-being of others?
- How do your relationships with others help you learn about yourself?
- How do you develop and maintain supportive personal relationships?
- How do you avoid assuming unwarranted responsibility for others' well-being?
- What mechanisms do you have in place to maintain clear boundaries with others?
- How do you attend to family of origin issues as they arise?

Professional

- How do you enhance, create, and maintain positive workplace envi-ronments for yourself, colleagues, and clients?
- What is your practice of proactively managing work stressors?
- How do you collaborate with others to address work stressors when appropriate?
- How do you identify and correct workplace conflicts and problems as they arise?

- How do you address emotionally exhausting situations, both personally and relationally, as they arise in professional settings?
- Do the training opportunities you seek facilitate professional growth in desired ways rather than simply checking a box?

Peer Relationships

- Are you a member of professional organizations? If so, do you actively engage in these organizations and any networking opportunities they might provide? What do you get out of your membership in them? What do you wish you got out of them? If you are not currently experiencing your desired outcome, what might you do to change that?
- How do you network to develop professionally enriching relationships with colleagues?
- How do you maintain connections with colleagues?
- How do you rely on the support of colleagues to expand your professional network further?

Clinical

- How have you experienced vicarious resilience (e.g., learning from your clients' solutions and strengths)?
- What is your sense of meaning and purpose in your work for you and those in your kin network?
- Do you believe that your work makes a difference or contributes to the welfare of others? Even a little bit?
- How do you avoid taking inappropriate responsibility for the well-being of your clients?
- Are you able to hold difficult client stories while simultaneously caring for yourself and significant others in your life?

In reviewing responses, it is important to imagine how to intentionally foster resilience as a therapist. Looping back to self-care, after reflecting on lived experience, one should consider the following:

- In what ways might you expand your self-care practice to promote resilience?

Intentionally Enhancing Resilience

The process of maintaining therapist resilience requires intentionality (Clark, 2009). Inherent in the concept of systemic resilience, the process of maintaining resilience also occurs within the context of relationships. The following offers suggestions for therapists to intentionally enhance resilience in community.

For intentional practice, therapists should return to these questions to examine growth and change in resilience over time. To ensure this task is not forgotten or set aside, one should make a calendar note and block off time regularly to check in on it. Therapists might also consider setting aside time to meet with colleagues to discuss these questions and support one another in fostering resilience.

Another opportunity for intentionally addressing resilience is by bringing it up and discussing it in personal therapy. For example, therapists can bring reflection questions that focus on personal and interpersonal resilience factors to discuss. There, they might reflect on prior and current experiences and future opportunities to enhance resilience in their personal lives (e.g., increasing differentiation of self, avoiding taking unnecessary responsibility for others). Therapists might also bring the reflection questions that focus on professional and peer relationships to personal therapy. Reflection questions that focus on clinical work can likewise be brought to supervisors or consulting peers to discuss. There, they might reflect on prior and current experiences and future opportunities to enhance resilience in their professional lives (e.g., managing work stressors, identifying and enhancing networking opportunities, and supportive peer relationships).

A topic of discussion for personal therapy and supervision may regard the high demands of organizational settings. For example, when working in organizational settings, therapists may not be able to decrease high demands but can work to change their mindset about these demands. Therapists might discuss and reflect on their personal expectations regarding work—are they realistic? Therapists can also focus on increasing autonomy in whatever ways possible, which may mean discussing ways to gain autonomy at work with a supervisor. It could also look like examining current work and recognizing ways in which autonomy is already experienced.

Conclusion

In therapeutic work, be it working directly with clients or consulting with peers, therapists' inter- and intrapersonal characteristics intersect with their professional way of being. Resilient therapists develop supportive personal relationships, maintain clear boundaries, and avoid assuming unwarranted responsibility for others' well-being. Also, they emphasize the importance of understanding their own patterns and dynamics to prevent or cope with secondary traumatic stress, vicarious trauma, and burnout. Resilient therapists maintain a sense of meaning and purpose in their work; they learn from supervisors and clients. Clinicians who cultivate resilience in themselves and others avoid taking inappropriate responsibility for clients' well-being and can hold difficult client stories while caring for themselves and their families. Clinicians who cultivate systemic resilience spend time celebrating and grieving with significant others. Reflecting on one's resilience affords the opportunity to identify strengths and opportunities for growth. Whether it be on one's own, within a supportive peer relationship, in personal therapy, or in a supervision setting, personal reflection and intentional practice of behaviors related to therapist resilience beyond typical self-care endeavors supports the development and maintenance of therapists' own resilience and ultimately supports their work as successful therapists.

References

American Association for Marriage and Family Therapy. (2004). *Marriage and family therapy core competencies.* www.aamft.org/Documents/COAMFTE/ Accreditation%20Resources/MFT%20Core%20Competencies%20 (December%202004).pdf

American Psychological Association. (2002). *Ethical principles of psychologists and code of conduct.* www.apa.org/ethics/code

Clark, P. (2009). Resiliency in the practicing marriage and family therapist. *Journal of Marital and Family Therapy, 35*(2), 231–247. https://doi. org/10.1111/j.1752-0606.2009.00108.x

Corey, G., Corey, M. S., & Corey, C. (2024). *Issues and ethics in the helping professions.* Cengage Learning.

Dorociak, K. E., Rupert, P. A., & Zahniser, E. (2017). Work life, well-being, and self-care across the professional lifespan of psychologists. *Professional*

Psychology: Research and Practice, 48(6), 429–437. http://doi.org/10.1037/pro0000160

Eppler, C. (2018). *The resilient family therapist.* American Association for Marriage and Family Therapy.

Flynn, P. J., Bliese, P. D., Korsgaard, M. A., & Cannon, C. (2021). Tracking the process of resilience: How emotional stability and experience influence exhaustion and commitment trajectories. *Group and Organization Management, 46*(4), 692–736. http://doi.org/10.1177/1059601121102767

Hernandez-Wolfe, P. (2018). Vicarious resilience: A comprehensive review. *Revista de Estudios Sociales, 66,* 9–17. https://doi.org/10.7440/res66.2018.02

Hernandez-Wolfe, P., Killian, K., Engstrom, D., & Gangsei, D. (2015). Vicarious resilience, vicarious trauma, and awareness of equity in trauma work. *Journal of Humanistic Psychology, 55*(2), 153–172. https://doi.org/10.1177/0022167814534322

Hou, J. M., & Skovholt, T. M. (2020). Characteristics of highly resilient therapists. *Journal of Counseling Psychology, 67*(3), 386–400. http://doi.org/10.1037/cou0000401

Laverdière, O., Ogrodniczuk, J., & Kealy, D. (2019). Clinicians' empathy and professional quality of life. *Journal of Nervous and Mental Disease, 207,* 49–52. http://doi.org/10.1097/NMD.0000000000000927

Lawson, G., & Myers, J. E. (2011). Wellness, professional quality of life, and career sustaining behaviors: What keeps us well? *Journal of Counseling & Development, 89,* 163–171. http://doi.org/10.1002/j.1556-6678.2011.tb00074.x

MacKay, L. M. (2017). Differentiation of self: Enhancing therapist resilience when working with relational trauma. *Australian and New Zealand Journal of Family Therapy, 38*(4), 637–656. https://doi.org/10.1002/anzf.1276

Owens-King, A. P. (2019). Secondary traumatic stress and self-care inextricably linked. *Journal of Human Behavior in the Social Environment, 29*(1), 37–47. https://doi.org/10.1080/10911359.2018.1472703

Posluns, K., & Gall, T. L. (2020). Dear mental health practitioners, take care of yourselves: A literature review on self-care. *International Journal for the Advancement of Counseling, 42*(1), 1–20. https://doi.org/10.1007/s10447-019-09382-w

Rupert, P. A., Miller, A. O., & Dorociak, K. E. (2015). Preventing burnout: What does the research tell us? *Professional Psychology: Research and Practice, 46*(3), 168–174. https://doi.org/10.1037/a0039297

Skovholt, T. M. (2001). *The resilient practitioner: Burnout prevention and self-care strategies for counselors, therapists, teachers, and health professionals.* Allyn and Bacon.

Swartz, M. K. (2017). A strength-based approach to care. *Journal of Pediatric Health Care, 31*(1), 1. http://doi.org/10.1016/j.pedhc.2016.10.008

Walsh, F. (2016). Family resilience: A development systems framework. *European Journal of Developmental Psychology, 13*(3), 1–12. http://doi.org/10.1080/17405629.2016.1154035

Wicks, R. J. (2008). *The resilient clinician.* Oxford. https://doi.org/10.1093/oso/9780195316971.001.0001

Wyatt, J. P., & Ampadu, G. G. (2022). Reclaiming self-care: Self-care as a social justice tool for Black wellness. *Community Mental Health Journal, 58*(2), 213–221. https://doi.org/10.1007/s10597-021-00884-9

14

A PERSONAL REFLECTION ON PROMOTING RESILIENCE IN THE SYSTEMIC TREATMENT OF ADDICTION

Jasmine L. Pickens

Jasmine Pickens, MS, AMFT (she/her/hers), is the director of psychological services at an inpatient hospital and adjunct professor at Seattle University. She is a doctoral candidate at Alliant International University. Jasmine enjoys spending time with her two-year-old daughter and pets and in the outdoors with her family. She identifies as a cisgender, heterosexual, Black woman.

Recovery is a difficult journey but not impossible. Oftentimes, clients have multiple tools for coping and healing buried within themselves, but they require a clinician's professional guidance to uncover their strengths. As an instructor in a clinical training program, my first step in teaching about addiction treatment is defining what addiction is and is not. When we cover the biological basis for addiction, students often wonder, "How can addiction be considered a disease?" They may feel shocked or even insulted when the word *disease* is used to describe someone addicted, possibly including their own loved ones.

DOI: 10.4324/9781003373513-14

Next, I ask, "can we imagine how hard the experience was for the client without judging what led to their addiction or how they have coped through substance use?" In this discussion, students often develop empathy. It helps them to conceptualize the biological and social factors that contribute to the development of addiction behaviors and realize that recovery is possible. The insight that recovery *is* a choice, whereas addiction is not, often pushes students to reframe their understanding of addiction. Treatment and recovery from any disease require accountability and responsibility, which I think of as sources of resilience. The fact that addiction is a disease does not take away from the emotional pain family and friends experience when a person suffers from it, but it may shift clients and their family's perspectives about what is the problem (e.g., understanding that using or abusing drugs may not be the source of problem; unresolved trauma or suffering could be the underlying issue).

Training and supervision can support those working with challenging populations. I became a marriage and family therapist in my early 20s. During this time, I experienced significant self-discovery, growth, and pain. My graduate and postgraduate clinical experiences taught me to provide honest and powerful care to my clients. But first, I needed to heal from and find strength in my own traumas and shortcomings. To do so, I began reliving parts of my past I never expected to see again. The closer I got to healing or recognizing my resilience, the stronger I became professionally and emotionally. A significant encounter was when I acknowledged my personal bias regarding the treatment of addiction. This created opportunities for me to practice finding the balance between offering support and asking for accountability for myself and when working with clients who struggle with addiction.

As a child, I grew up without my biological mother because of her substance abuse. In kindergarten, I attended a court hearing where my biological mother told the judge she had no interest in being a mother or raising children. She frequently stepped in and out of my life during my childhood and adolescence, viewing motherhood as an afterthought. Although I faced abuse from those who cared for me daily, it never quite compared to the trauma I suffered from a mother who chose drugs over me. During my first year of graduate school, my biological mother berated me for not wishing her a happy Mother's Day and even said, "How could you be a therapist when your own family ain't shit."

In years of therapy, I made great progress in understanding my trauma. I reframed narratives about my family, particularly the stories I held about my addicted biological mother. My first job as an outpatient therapist led me to notice that anger and judgment resurfaced when I worked with individuals who were addicted. Despite my coursework and intellect, I often asked myself, "Why can't she just quit?" After trying to suppress these feelings for several months, I finally realized such a perspective was related to my own addicted family problems.

Reframing Addiction

Myriad laws, school policies, family traditions, and media campaigns have taught people to fear addiction and to vilify people with an addiction. Less has been said about what addiction is and the process of recovery (Erickson, 2018). Understanding addiction is the first step to providing dynamic care. The American Society of Addiction Medicine (2011) defined addiction as:

> A primary, chronic disease of brain reward, motivation, memory, and related circuitry. Dysfunction in these circuits leads to characteristic biological, psychological, social, and spiritual manifestations. This is reflected in an individual pathologically pursuing reward and/or relief by substance use and other behaviors. Addiction is characterized by inability to consistently abstain, impairment in behavioral control, craving, diminished recognition of significant problems with one's behaviors and interpersonal relationships, and a dysfunctional emotional response.
>
> (p. 1)

Addiction can also be defined as an increasing desire for something with a decreasing ability to satisfy that desire (Juhnke & Hagedorn, 2019).

In my practice, I often asked myself: Would accepting addiction as a disease allow me to forgive someone who was not remorseful or deserving? If I accepted addiction as a condition and not a moral deficit, would I be another person making excuses for those not "trying hard enough?" When I worked with clients who struggled to cultivate resilience because of addiction and drug misuse, I noticed their decisions were never just about having fun with drugs. It was never as simple as the phrase popularized in the late 80s of "just saying no" (Ronald Reagan Presidential Foundation, 2023). Often, drug use was a way of escaping reality and coping with systemic inequalities and generational trauma.

I studied the biological and social factors contributing to addiction to promote resilience in myself and my clients. In the early days of addiction research, substance use was viewed solely from a moral perspective by not only practitioners but clinicians as well (Erickson, 2018). The American Medical Association classified alcoholism and dependence/misuse/abuse of other illicit substances as diseases in 1956 and 1987, respectively. Although decades of research have defined addiction as a disease, substantial opposition to this concept has persisted. Even with the increase in research, some clinicians continue to lack an understanding of what a disease is and fear the client will no longer be accountable if addiction is considered a disease instead of a character flaw (Erickson, 2018).

Undoubtedly, addiction impacts the family system differently than heart disease, diabetes, or high cholesterol. Erickson (2018) advocated that individuals must be responsible for their behaviors while under the influence and for seeking recovery; however, individuals are not responsible for the cause of their disease. Addiction is not a choice, but recovery is. The same dichotomy applies to every disease and ailment. Often, people cannot change their diagnosis, but they can improve their healing and resilience. It became clear to me that I could love my mother from a distance, forgive her for her mistakes, and empathize with her pain. I could care for her without denying her role and responsibility in my suffering.

Identifying the risk factors associated with addiction can help clinicians understand what is needed for their clients' recovery. Childhood abuse, other family members' substance use, and parent–child relationships are common risk factors for substance use (Whitesell et al., 2013). From an early age, my mother experienced abandonment, rape, and physical assault. She felt less than, and whenever she reached out for love, she was met with abuse. She never really knew when a habit became an addiction or how she started using drugs. Although she cannot recall abandoning her children in court 20 years ago, she has shared her regrets about not being an active mother. Although she has gained more insight into her past experiences, addiction remains at the forefront of her story.

When someone has an addiction, it is easy for their loved ones to see only their deficiencies. Recognizing the strengths of those struggling with addiction can help them succeed in recovery. Yet, in my experience, years of expressed or pent-up hurt and anger can block seeing positives or interpreting behaviors in a generous light. According to Rudzinski et al. (2017), resourcefulness is the most common strength among drug users. Although substance abuse and its consequences have adverse effects on a person's family, many people who are addicted are successful in navigating their communities and social networks to find drugs, hustling to make ends meet to support themselves and their use, and finding ways to minimize risk when they use. Acknowledging the clients' strengths, even if currently maladaptive, may help them reframe their negative views of themselves and instill hope in their resilience and ability needed for recovery. By using clients' resourcefulness in healthier ways, as clinicians, we can help them find success on a day-to-day basis. When an individual enters addiction treatment, they may feel hopeless and only hear from everyone around them how badly they have hurt others and how badly they are hurting themselves. They rarely hear they already have what it takes to be successful. That is where a realistic and resilient-based therapist can help. A former client comes to mind when I think of promoting resilience in substance use treatment. The following case is an amalgam of several clients who supported me in my professional growth of becoming a strength-based therapist when working with clients who are addicted. This case also highlights the importance of cultivating resilience in addiction work.

Clinical Case Example

Name: Leigh

Age: 18

Housing: Lived with mother, stepfather, and younger brother (age 8). Leigh lived with her biological father every other weekend, on holidays, and over portions of the summer.

Education: In her last semester of high school.

Previous diagnosis: ADHD at the age of 6, per her mother.

Leigh, an 18-year-old biracial woman, was referred to the practice for marijuana use and was brought in by her mother, Dorna. Dorna stated within the last year, she had noticed a major decline in Leigh's motivation, poor academic performance, mood instability, and dramatic weight loss. During an argument regarding Leigh's grades, her phone was confiscated. Dorna found Leigh had sent approximately $350 via a cash app to an unfamiliar name within the last month. When questioned, Leigh admitted she had sent money to a "friend of a friend" to buy marijuana. Dorna searched her daughter's room and found marijuana and other drug paraphernalia.

Dorna also shared within the last year, Leigh had lost close to 25 pounds, and she believed it was because of drugs. Dorna wanted her daughter to go to rehab immediately and expressed frustration and disappointment with her substance use. Leigh refused to attend rehab, engage in group therapy, or attend meetings because she did not believe she had a drug problem. However, Leigh shared she would be willing to work with a therapist to prove to her mother she was fine. During an individual session, Leigh stated she typically smoked two–three times on weekdays and three–four times over the weekend. She first began experimenting with drugs at the age of 14 and had smoked marijuana daily since the age of 16, when she began working.

Leigh was employed at the time of her referral and reported spending close to $400 per month on marijuana. She described marijuana as her medicine and stated it was the only thing that kept her calm. Leigh did not believe it was possible to be addicted to marijuana and expressed anger with her mom's description of it as a drug. Leigh was unable to identify the last time she went a day without smoking but shared if she chose to quit, she could do so at any time. She admitted to mild irritability if she was unable to smoke in the morning on her drive to school or in the evening after work. She denied tobacco or other drug use. Leigh also reported being a social drinker and said she typically drank every weekend with friends. During my first session alone with Leigh, she was guarded and defensive over any words related to drug treatment, addiction, or dependency. She shared she did not want help and was hyper focused on explaining the benefits of marijuana and how any good outweighed any bad. I immediately agreed and shared there is positive research regarding the topic. Leigh was initially shocked and mentioned this perspective was one to which she usually received negative reactions when sharing the information with her family. I explained I was not there to judge her use or to lecture her on substance use as a teenager or young adult and knew that would not lead to any movement in session. I exclaimed it was clear she already felt pressured and defeated by her family, and my goal instead was to make this time useful for her. I attempted to start our time by just supporting her reality and advocating for her journey.

During my time with Leigh, she was able to become vulnerable with me and shared times in her life when she often felt worthless and unsupported (e.g., with her mother and father before their divorce, feeling like an outcast with her mother, stepfather, and younger brother). She then shared she often began using marijuana as a band-aid for her feelings of isolation, and although she was initially in denial of her use, she feared the consequences of continued use and how it could potentially ruin the school year and her future postsecondary plans. I worked with her to identify moments of strength, asking: When had she pulled herself up? This time was initially challenging to identify, and we worked to reframe what success and strength meant to her.

Leigh shared about a time in elementary school when she said, "I was tired of feeling dumb." When she was first diagnosed with ADHD, she felt like a burden to her family and at school. Leigh said she felt like she had not been enough for years, but with support, she was able to find a passion for reading. For the first time, something clicked for her, and she used this realization to begin to excel in school and to escape during her parents' separation and her mother's remarriage.

I assigned Leigh homework to list other wins in her life, and she was able to see she had experienced more triumphs than failures. This exercise pushed the client toward a journey of recovery, and she could take charge of her recovery with the power of resiliency innate within her. The transition from guarded to acceptance could not have occurred without highlighting what was already present.

Strategies to Build Resilience

The following are a few suggestions and ideas that have worked in my clinical practice when cultivating resilience among substance users. First, ask: "What does resilience during or after addition look like for you?" Many times, clients believe they are not resilient because they have used drugs to confront other life problems. Through dialogue and psychoeducation, clients can learn resilience is an innate trait for all. When they look back on their own lives, they can see how they were able to bounce back even when they felt defeated. Clients reexamine their relationship with drugs—how drugs helped them cope and when the drugs became as big, if not bigger than, the original problems. When one can identify moments of strength in their darkest times, they can likely see that power within themselves when on the path of recovery.

Next, be the client's biggest cheerleader. The word *cheerleader* initially made me cringe because it seemed corny. However, we as clinicians must think about our clients' unfulfilled needs. Clients have often been villainized for their disorders due to stigma and ignorance. Despite great strides made in recent years to destigmatize seeking mental health, people with addictions are still misunderstood and often feared (Bradbury, 2020). Although society has come to understand depression, bipolar disorder, or schizophrenia better, people still have ingrained misunderstandings about those who have addictive behaviors. Increasingly, society does not view someone struggling with depression as a bad person (they may be sad or seen as disconnected); however, many people may automatically assume that a client with an addiction has failed or not tried hard enough to get clean and sober. Models of resilience indicate that everyone needs significant, supportive people in their lives (Walsh, 2021). Clients who misuse or abuse drugs and alcohol need someone rooting for them—and a therapist may be the first person in a long time who does not make them feel worthless. Instilling hope is such a simple but powerful intervention within the field. The therapist's role is to cheerlead—honoring the strengths as clients begin to recognize their own assets while (re)building relationships outside of sessions built on mutual caring and trust.

It is hard for clients to see success when they are suffering from addiction, especially when there is backlash from their family and potential legal consequences due to their addiction. When working with this population, it is vital to identify times when they were successful in concrete ways. The list should range from the most minute wins to more major successes. The goal is simply to name what works in a variety of contexts. When clients can literally visualize their wins—on a piece of paper and out of their mind—they can start to believe in their power and how it can encourage them on their road to recovery. They can identify times when they wanted to use but did not. They can create a list of alternative behaviors that give them a similar sensation to the release they felt from using substances. They can remind themselves of their hopes, dreams, and visions. And they have a tangible way to share these expectations with significant others.

Conclusion

Recovery is a challenging journey, but it is possible with professional guidance. As a marriage and family therapist, I have learned to heal from my own traumas and shortcomings to provide honest and powerful care to clients. By reliving parts of my past, I became stronger professionally and emotionally. I also learned my personal bias regarding addiction treatment and how to find the balance between support and accountability. To build resilience in addiction treatment, clinicians should empathize with clients by acknowledging that their disease was not a choice and help them to recognize their need for accountability and responsibility in recovery. By asking clients about their resilience, they can learn to bounce back even in their darkest times. Being a cheerleader for clients can help them see success and encourage them on their recovery journey. Identifying moments of success, from minor wins to major victories, can help clients see their power and encourage them on their path to recovery. As clinicians, we can help our clients see they truly are the most important members of the treatment team, and they have the power to rewrite their story.

References

American Society of Addiction Medicine. (2011, August 15). *Public policy statement: Definition of addiction.* www.asam.org/docs/default-source/public-policy-statements/1definition_of_addiction_long_4-11.pdf?sfvrsn=a8f64512_4

Bradbury, A. (2020). Mental health stigma: The impact of age and gender on attitudes. *Community Mental Health Journal, 56*(5), 933–938. https://doi.org/10.1007/s10597-020-00559.

Erickson, C. K. (2018). *The science of addiction* (2nd ed.). W.W. Norton & Company.

Juhnke, G. A., & Hagedorn, W. B. (2019). *Counseling addicted families* (2nd ed.). Routledge. https://doi.org/10.4324/9781315771076

Ronald Reagan Presidential Foundation. (2023). *Nancy Reagan: Her causes* [Review of Nancy Reagan: Her causes]. Ronald Reagan Presidential Foundation & Institute; Reagan Foundation. www.reaganfoundation.org/ronald-reagan/nancy-reagan/her-causes/

Rudzinski, K., McDonough, P., Gartner, R., & Strike, C. (2017). Is there room for resilience? A scoping review and critique of substance use literature and its utilization of the concept of resilience. *Substance Abuse Treatment, Prevention, and Policy, 12*, Article 41. https://doi.org/10.1186/s13011-017-0125-2

Walsh, F. (2021). Family resilience: A dynamic systemic framework. In M. Ungar (Ed.), *Multisystemic resilience* (pp. 255–270). Oxford University Press.

Whitesell, M., Bachand, A., Peel, J., & Brown, M. (2013). Familial, social, and individual factors contributing to risk for adolescent substance use. *Journal of Addiction*, 1–9. https://doi.org/10.1155/2013/579310

15

CREATE MODEL OF CULTURALLY ATTUNED, RESILIENCE-BASED SUPERVISION

LaDonna M. Smith

LaDonna Smith, LMFT, is a clinical coordinator and instructor at Seattle University's Master of Arts in Couples and Family Therapy Program. LaDonna is an American Association for Marriage and Family Therapy (AAMFT)-approved supervisor who enjoys helping interns and new clinical professionals gain the knowledge and skills they need to thrive. As a doctoral candidate, she focuses her research on the experiences of racialized trauma in Black communities. LaDonna identifies as a Black woman with a foundation in Christian faith. LaDonna values creating spaces that foster community, support, wellness, compassion, and growth.

This chapter introduces the CREATE model, a justice and resilience-focused model of clinical supervision. CREATE—Curiosity, Responsibility, Equity, Awareness of Self, Teamwork, and Empathy—helps clinical supervisors facilitate resilient and culturally attuned supervision. This approach aims to enhance collaboration, awareness of identities, and awareness of the inevitable hierarchy and power in the supervision

DOI: 10.4324/9781003373513-15

space. A systemic resilience supervision approach can prepare future clinicians to recognize their strengths and overcome challenges using those strengths.

When cultivating just and resilient supervision spaces, it is important to consider how intersectional social location and related dynamics may influence supervisees' clinical development (Hardy & Bobes, 2016). Mental health providers and their supervisors navigate myriad roles through the lens of their intersecting identities. I am a Black, able-bodied, Christian woman. My identities inform the ways in which I show up as a licensed marriage and family therapist, American Association of Marriage and Family Therapy (AAMFT)-approved supervisor, professor, and doctoral student. I belong to groups that have power (e.g., able-bodied, Christian, and nonindigenous) and groups that have limited or no power within dominant cultural norms (e.g., being Black and female). Power exists in any area of my life where I have access to more resources, where my thoughts may be more valued because of my association with the group, or where my abilities may be ascribed respect. Conversely, my areas of powerlessness are those where I lack access to resources, where I am treated as less, where my voice is considered insignificant, and where I am treated differently (e.g., being paid less than male colleagues).

There has also been a tendency among many within cultural, institutional, and academic spaces to believe my voice and contribution are less valued than those of my colleagues who hold greater power. It is an interesting dichotomy for supervisors of color to attempt to create safe, equitable, and resilient environments while not having the power of White clinicians. Supervisors of color can explore this dichotomy to identify ways in which they would like to take action based on their awareness of inequities, disparities, and marginalization to promote supervisee development and resilience.

The CREATE model can be used by supervisors from across social locations. Supervisors who belong to dominant groups in US society (e.g., those who are not people of color, those who were born in the United States, or those who are from the upper social class) must recognize and maintain awareness of individuals' disparities and marginalization. Furthermore, these supervisors should use their privileges to advocate for justice in and out of the supervision room. To CREATE a resilient and socially just supervision space, one should (a) develop a reflective practice, (b) engage in advocacy, (c) speak with colleagues from nondominant groups about their experiences, (d) ask instead of assuming ways to help, and I stay aware of social justice issues as they emerge, both in public and private spheres.

Reflecting on my own challenges as a clinician has helped me better identify what may be affecting my supervisees' clinical work and how to manage difficult situations to promote resilience. I used these experiences to develop the CREATE model: Curiosity, Responsibility, Equity, Awareness of self, Teamwork, and Empathy. CREATE highlights the factors that help supervisors foster resilience, including self-compassion, awareness of self, dedication, integrity, engagement in reflective practice, a strong supervisory relationship, innovation, valuing of others, and the ability to identify strengths (Hou & Skovholt, 2020). These constructs are integrated into CREATE. An additional factor I have found that supports resilience in the supervisory relationship is the ability to be confident and have trust in oneself while still seeking support from others who are more experienced.

CREATEing Resilient, Strength-Based Systemic Supervision

A strong therapeutic alliance between a clinician and client is the best predictor of change (Sprenkle et al., 2009). Building strong supervisory relationships is essential to CREATE. As with the relationship between a therapist and a client, a supervisor's relationship with a trainee is fundamental—relationships matter, and scholars have found supportive relationships foster resilience (Walsh, 2016). Lee and Nelson (2014) described a supervisor as "a coach, a teacher, an administrator, a mentor, a gatekeeper, an evaluator" (pp. 27–28). Supervisees and supervisors are held accountable by ethical and legal standards, and they must attend to power dynamics embedded within each facet of clinical work. Common metaphors for supervisors emphasize hierarchy and power over collaboration, thereby reinforcing the colonization of clinical spaces. The CREATE model is relational and collaborative and promotes decolonization. The model prioritizes maintaining high standards while cultivating resilience through collaboration to then navigating any clinical experiences that arise within the supervisory relationship and for clients.

Clinical supervisors must cultivate their own resilience along with their supervisees' and supervisees' clients' resilience. Supervisors can actively engage in CREATEing by reflecting the following tenets:

- **C**uriosity through relationship building and encouraging the use of supervisee voice.
- **R**esponsibility through accountability within the relationship of both the supervisee and supervisor to uphold ethical and legal standards of the field.
- **E**quity by providing resources and ensuring the supervisee's voice is heard across systems.
- **A**wareness of Self by encouraging reflective practice of oneself as the supervisor and encouraging supervisees to engage in continuous reflective practice.
- **T**eamwork by collaborating with supervisees on their development and collaborating with other stakeholders involved with supervisees' development to support supervisees for the overall success of the students' internship and clinical development.
- **E**mpathy by normalizing and validating developmental processes and experiences.

In the CREATE model, different aspects are emphasized throughout the entire supervision relationship to create a holistic and resilient approach to supervision (e.g., Responsibility is addressed in early, middle, and later stages of supervision). CREATE elements can be emphasized at particular stages (e.g., in the initial supervision sessions, being curious about the supervisees' backgrounds).

I applied the CREATE model to the following fictional supervision example. Details of this deidentified case come from an amalgam of my professional clinical experiences. I was Tessa's individual site supervisor and met with her weekly for one year. Tessa was a Euro-American Christian woman in her late 50s who began her marriage and family therapy internship. Tessa primarily worked with adult individuals and couples who identified as people of color within a community mental health agency.

Curiosity

Systemic resilience involves Curiosity, which may look like an eagerness to learn about a supervisee's background, goals, and ideas. During our supervision sessions, I checked in with Tessa regarding how her week was going, not just her case questions. In this way, I engaged in curiosity about Tessa's whole self. Further, I participated in Curiosity by assisting Tessa in identifying the implications of her clients' whole selves through her assessment of them during the case conceptualization process (e.g., identifying culture, internalized oppressions, strengths, protective factors, and support systems). I often asked Tessa to share her case conceptualization with me and to explain why she chose the interventions she did. As an example, Tessa once told me how she chose solution-focused therapy for a family coping with grief. I then asked her what influenced her decision to use solution-focused therapy, rather than assuming why she chose this theory. Asking Tessa to practice Curiosity about why she chose the therapeutic approach allowed her to identify why it was or was not an appropriate tactic to use with these clients. In doing so, Tessa researched evidence-based theoretical models that would meet the clients' needs. This process helped Tessa cultivate several resilience traits and processes, such as increasing competence, mastering theory use, and collaborating with a supervisor who guided instead of mandated.

Continuing to explore Curiosity as a factor that fosters resilience and justice-oriented spaces, I need to reflect on supervisor and supervisee identities. Curiosity, as it pertains to the exploration of identities within the supervision space, occurs by exploring supervisor and supervisee ADDRESSING factors. Hays (1996) developed the ADDRESSING model, which defined the complexities and intersections of individuals' multiple identities: "age, disability (developmental), disability (acquired), religion/spiritual identity, ethnicity, socioeconomic status, sexual orientation, indigenous heritage, nationality, and gender" (p. 332). The interactions between these identities inform the way in which an individual views themselves and the world at large and considers the aspects of their identities that hold power, compared to the aspects that do not. As a supervisor, I value acting as a model by revealing, as appropriate, my own identities that pertain to the areas where I hold power and powerlessness. This collaboration promotes the balance of power within the supervisor–trainee relationship (Dollarhide et al., 2021). To engage in creating a foundation of self-awareness and reflective practice, Tessa and I engaged in exploring our ADDRESSING factors at the onset of the supervisory relationship, prior to any clients being assigned.

As Tessa and I explored our ADDRESSING factors, I asked Tessa to share her perceptions of being in a position of power (e.g., White, Christian) and being in a position of less power (e.g., female, student/supervisee). Tessa was able to identify the impact of her ethnicity on her role as a therapist in training. Specifically, Tessa identified the ways in which her ethnicity could influence her interactions as she leads therapeutic processes with clients. Tessa committed to increasing her own Curiosity; as such, she set a goal to become more mindful of how to be antiracist and more collaborative in her clinical work.

Responsibility

Responsibility in supervision promotes resilience. Clinical supervisors and supervisees are responsible for the manner in which they present themselves clinically, such as by adhering to all relevant professional, ethical, and legal standards. As supervisors and supervisees collaborate on client care, this Responsibility is shared. Among Tessa's responsibilities were ensuring knowledge of therapeutic models, attesting to holding ethical and legal standards, adhering to her school's and internship site's policies, and participating in forming strong therapeutic alliances, among other professional practices. As Tessa's supervisor, I was responsible for training her, orienting her to the internship site, reviewing her clinical documentation, reviewing client session videos, and ensuring compliance with all ethical and legal standards.

Each supervisory relationship should begin with setting goals for supervisee development, with specific times in which goal progress is assessed. This goal setting also promotes Equality and Teamwork by inviting Tessa's agency and letting her know she will be heard and respected throughout the supervision process. By creating supervision goals, supervisors can help supervisees take responsibility for their own growth with the supervisor's support. I asked Tessa to identify one or two professional competence items where she would like to see improvement in the next two or three months.

As the next step, I assisted Tessa in creating two specific, measurable, attainable, realistic, and timely (SMART) goals. I ensured a resilient focus by asking that the goals focus on building on strengths or using positive language (e.g., "I will increase . . ." instead of "I will no longer . . ."). Tessa identified a focus on building a strong therapeutic alliance. She wrote that she would align with AAMFT's (2004) standard to "establish and maintain appropriate and productive therapeutic alliances with the clients" (AAMFT, 2004, p. 2). In her own language, Tessa wrote, "I will enhance my therapeutic alliances with clients, as evidenced by a 10% increase in client retention." Tessa's objectives included engaging in creating one collaborative treatment plan with each client and seeking feedback from clients through session rating scales once per month. Through these resilient SMART goals and objectives, Tessa was able to monitor her Responsibility, and I was able to observe Tessa's strengths and continued areas of growth.

Equity

Systemic resilience in supervision is promoted through creating equitable environments. To balance the hierarchical structure innate to supervision, fostering Equity early in the supervision process is crucial. Equity involves acknowledging power when working with supervisees. I hold a Master of Arts degree, am independently licensed, and am currently completing the requirements to earn my doctorate degree. Power is attributed to each of these credentials. To promote resilience, I must use this power wisely (e.g., by sharing wisdom and setting ethical boundaries) while building collaborative environments by using strength-based language and inviting supervisees to express themselves (e.g., by empowering them to form their own case conceptualizations and inviting them to share concerns).

Using Curiosity to foster justice and resilience, Tessa and I discussed how she could provide me with feedback on supervision and our dynamics. It was important for me to ask Tessa the best and worst ways she receives feedback. The focus of supervision is often on providing feedback to supervisees, but it is equally important to receive feedback from supervisees (Lee & Nelson, 2014). After Tessa shared her perceptions, I repeated what I heard and asked if I understood everything correctly. I then engaged in Curiosity by asking any questions, explaining that I would reflect on the feedback the supervisee provided, and noting that supervision would begin the following week. This supervision would provide support options, and I would explore what I could and could not comply with based on my Responsibility to ensure ethical client care.

During a supervision session, Tessa told me she sometimes feels that policies and procedures hinder client care. Tessa and I agreed we would discuss options at the next supervision session after I had had a chance to reflect on this sentiment. In the next supervision session, I explained the reasoning behind the policies and procedures to Tessa. Tessa felt better equipped to explain policy to her clients after having a better understanding of policy. Tessa's resilience and Curiosity increased as a result.

Equity must also be considered when managing supervisees' potential unethical behavior. When unethical behaviors are present, it is important to assess the barriers to resolving unethical behaviors through Curiosity and hearing supervisees' thoughts regarding what influences their decision-making. For example, Tessa attended a mandated reporting training and learned it was not her responsibility to report incidences of child abuse and neglect if there was awareness by the perpetrator, who then made changes accordingly. However, in our state, child abuse and neglect in this situation are still reportable. To ensure that Tessa was acting with Responsibility, I asked Tessa to consider applicable ethical and legal standards to discuss in our next meeting. In our next meeting, we discussed and confirmed Tessa's mandated reporter requirements, some of which were non-negotiable. Though I set a boundary around reporting, I also empowered Tessa's resilience by inviting her into the process. Creating Equity through Teamwork allows supervisors to work within their ethical codes while continuing collaborative dialogue.

Awareness of Self

In supervision, increasing awareness supports systemic resilience. As supervisors, we CREATE Awareness of Self by modeling continuous self-awareness and providing opportunities for supervisees to do the same. To cultivate Awareness of Self, Tessa and I discussed our faith backgrounds and how our beliefs could intersect with the therapy process. When Tessa wanted to work with clients from a different faith tradition from her own, I modeled the process of examining how my faith informed my view of relationships and how I could work successfully with clients who did not share my beliefs. I also described examining my perspectives on what a relationship "should'" encompass while honoring how my clients defined their own relationships.

To enhance Tessa's Awareness of Self, we watched Tessa's client session video. I asked her to consider if her worldview unduly influenced the questions she posed and, if so, how Tessa could shift the questions to align with the client's values and beliefs. When supervisees share their case conceptualizations, supervisors can assist in cultivating supervisees' Awareness of Self by (a) asking them to assess how their ADDRESSING factors may be influencing their clinical work, (b) prompting them to identify cultural factors that may impact clients who present difficulties, (c) increasing their awareness of clients' protective factors, and (d) fostering awareness of their personal strengths and those of the clients they serve to use those strengths as resources to navigate presenting concerns. For example, I asked Tessa the following questions:

- How do ADDRESSING factors influence your view of the client's presenting problem?
- What cultural factors may be influencing the client's internalized oppressions?
- What are the client's protective factors that can assist them in overcoming their presenting difficulty?
- How can you encourage the client to use their protective factors for support?
- Does the client have a diversified support system?
- Using strengths-based language, what is a strength that you have noticed within yourself as you have navigated this complex client care situation?

Tessa's Awareness and responses to these questions allowed her to engage in resilience by identifying additional solutions and interventions for the presenting problem her clients reported.

Teamwork

Collaboration and Teamwork promote systemic resilience in supervision. CREATEing Teamwork involves collaboration throughout the supervisees' development. It is important to honor the inner wisdom supervisees possess from their lived experiences and educational backgrounds. When Tessa asked me a question about a case, I encouraged her to share her hypothesis and plan with me. Following Tessa's explanation, I then offered feedback, noting her areas of strength and her areas of growth. It was important to provide specific strength-based language and explain why certain strengths were present or could be used; for example, I told Tessa:

> Your self-awareness was evident as you identified the areas where you felt your personal experiences influenced your reactions. Additionally, I noticed that you used creativity when you adapted the intervention to be understood by a 5 year old. As an area of growth, I encourage you to utilize your strength of time management in sessions with this family by providing a warning before the session is over to provide ample time for session closure.

This example does not mean power will disappear or the hierarchical structure will disappear if Tessa uses her voice first and I provide feedback second. Still, it is important to find ways to use Teamwork balance power, identify strengths, and promote collaboration as much as possible (Lee & Nelson, 2014). In our conversation, Tessa identified her additional strengths as resilience, courage, leadership, and organization.

Empathy

Empathy is a component of systemic resilience in the CREATE model. CREATEing opportunities for Empathy is vitally important and should be established at the onset of supervision and throughout all sessions. I have seen how the beginning of an internship can be a great stressor as student interns balance completing school requirements, seeing clients for the first time, adjusting to practice policies, navigating changes within their work–life balance, and more. The Empathy and attunement that a supervisor CREATEs with their supervisee is essential to promoting resilience.

Empathizing with supervisees validates and normalizes that many beginning clinicians experience different emotions during their transitions. To empathize with supervisees, supervisors should ask them about their personal and professional feelings regarding the transition, inquire if anything has been challenging, make empathetic statements, and share experiences as new clinicians. As with many first-quarter interns, Tessa found clinical documentation to be overwhelming. My role was to normalize and validate Tessa's experiences and help identify potential solutions for strengthening her skill set (e.g., using templates and practicing concurrent documentation). By honoring Tessa's feelings and assisting her in finding a solution to a difficult situation using Empathy, I fostered her resilience.

It is important to discuss strengths and areas for improvement to foster resilient and empathic supervision. By using strengths, clinicians can overcome barriers (e.g., negotiating when clients provide less-than-ideal feedback). Tessa's client rated their therapeutic relationship poorly on a session rating scale and later contacted Tessa via email to request a new clinician. Tessa came to the supervision session discouraged by the client's reports. I normalized Tessa's experience and reminded her each client has a right to access the clinician best for them, which does not always mean we are the right fit. Following this discussion, I asked Tessa what she learned about herself and about the therapeutic process from this experience. Tessa was able to maintain her awareness of herself, identify opportunities for repair between her and her client, and exhibit Empathy for herself and her client.

As a helping professional, mistakes will occur, and areas for growth must be noted to develop competence. Researchers have linked resilience and strengths-based conversations with surviving a difficult or challenging experience (Walsh, 2016). During difficult conversations, supervisors can use the CREATE model to foster resilience. How supervisors handle mistakes contributes to whether supervisees are forthcoming with their mistakes or feel unable to share them (Lee & Nelson, 2014). A discussion about how mistakes will be handled at the beginning of the supervision relationship can facilitate supervisees sharing their mistakes more openly. A supervisor may say, "Mistakes are bound to happen as you grow and learn; in fact, I expect mistakes to occur. I want you to know that we can work with mistakes through dialogue and collaboration." This approach allows Teamwork to be the foundation of the supervisor–supervisee relationship.

CREATE: A Circular Model

CREATE is a nonlinear model that helps build a supervisory alliance to promote justice and growth throughout supervision. The model's constructs often overlap or work independently (e.g., use curiosity and empathy simultaneously or focus more specifically on building teamwork in a select session). Early on in a supervision relationship, a supervisor may focus on one stage (e.g., curiosity), whereas, after working together for some time, a supervisor may attend to another stage (e.g., being more explicit about a supervisee's responsibilities)—although there is no formula for these interactions. When Tessa presented with an ethical concern, I used all elements of the CREATE model to help build Tessa's resilience and ethical decision-making skills. I asked the following questions:

- Curiosity: How can I be curious about what occurred to foster resilience before coming to conclusions? What are the barriers that might inhibit resilience, and how can these barriers be overcome? How might Tessa be able to increase her capacity for curiosity and reflection?
- Responsibility: To what extent does Tessa feel accountable for resolving this difficulty? What are the ethical and legal responsibilities? How can I foster resilience by increasing Tessa's sense of responsibility?
- Equity: How can I empower Tessa even when she has made mistakes? How can I create a culture of collaboration while setting ethical limits?
- Awareness: How can I help promote Tessa's resilience by helping her become more aware of blind spots? How can I model awareness and growth in a challenging situation?
- Teamwork: How can Tessa and I work together to support client care (e.g., review client session video, provide recommendations for interventions) to overcome the current challenge and prevent it from happening again?
- Empathy: How can I ensure that Tessa is heard? How can I validate emotions without excusing unethical behaviors?

The CREATE model is recursive, and clinical supervisors can focus on the needs of their supervisees at various developmental stages. Though these suggestions may be adapted for specific situations, I encourage supervisors to use their own creativity to implement the CREATE model.

Conclusion

Through supervision reflective of the CREATE model, beginning clinicians have an opportunity to become aware of who they are, their responsibilities to the field, and their ability to implement CREATE approaches in their work with supervisees and clients alike. As part of her internship, Tessa practiced the CREATE framework by maintaining Curiosity with clients, taking shared Responsibility for the client's growth, valuing clients' opinions through practices reflective of Equity, maintaining Awareness of Self when working with clients, taking the perspective of Teamwork rather than being an expert about clients' lives, and having a dynamic sense of Empathy for clients. As a therapist, Tessa emphasized the importance of balancing her power within the therapeutic relationship with clients (e.g., collaborative treatment planning, goal setting, and ways clients can provide feedback to the therapist). During Tessa's supervision, I often asked her to discuss her perceptions of clients' strengths and resilience factors. In doing so, Tessa was able to identify the ways in which her clients could use their strengths to cope with difficult situations, along with factors that promote resilience.

Resilience can be nurtured by supervisors and supervisees who CREATE Curiosity, Responsibility, Equity, Awareness of Self, Teamwork, and Empathy. A supervisory environment that encourages resilience may help decolonize the profession (i.e., by helping supervisees navigate disparities, oppressions, and marginalization). To CREATE is to find meaning in challenging situations, to establish an environment for resilience to be a possibility, to position justice as a priority, and to grow as a therapist and supervisor. Although becoming a therapist is challenging, resilience-focused supervision mediates these hardships.

Reflection Questions

The following reflection questions may enhance your use of the CRE-ATE model:

- Based on your ADDRESSING factors, how do your intersecting identities impact the way in which you identify your supervisees' strengths?
- What can you do to increase your awareness of your supervisees' strengths to shift away from solely focusing on supervisees' areas of growth?
- Thinking back to when you received supervision, what made you feel safe or unsafe in your relationship with your supervisor? How might the areas of your perceived safety or lack of safety influence your supervision style and your ability to foster resilience within your work with your supervisees?
- How will you work with trainees at the onset of supervision to establish a strong supervisor and supervisee relationship?
- Considering the CREATE framework, what specific ways can you integrate each factor within your work with supervisees to further foster resilience?
- How might you consider the CREATE framework when working with identities that differ from your own?

References

American Association for Marriage and Family Therapy. (2004). *Marriage and family therapy core competencies.* www.aamft.org/Documents/COAMFTE/Accreditation%20Resources/MFT%20Core%20Competencies%20(December%202004).pdf

Dollarhide, C. T., Hale, S. C., & Stone, S. S. (2021). A new model for social justice supervision. *Journal of Counseling & Development*, 99(1), 104–113. https://doi.org/10.1002/jcad.12358

Hardy, K. V., & Bobes, T. (Eds.). (2016). *Culturally sensitive supervision and training: Diverse perspectives and practical applications.* Routledge/Taylor & Francis Group.

Hays, P. (1996). Addressing the complexities of culture and gender in counseling. *Journal of Counseling & Development*, 74(4), 332–338. https://doi.org/10.1002/j.1556-6676.1996.tb01876.x

Hou, J., & Skovholt, T. M. (2020). Characteristics of highly resilient thera-pists. *Journal of Counseling Psychology*, 67(3), 386–400. https://doi.org/10.1037/cou0000401

Lee, R. E., & Nelson, T. S. (2014). *The contemporary relational supervisor*. Routledge. https://doi.org/10.4324/9780203739525

Sprenkle, D. H., Davis, S. D., & Lebow, J. (2009). *Common factors in couple and family therapy (electronic resource): The overlooked foundation for effective practice*. Guilford Press.

Walsh, F. (2016). *Strengthening family resilience* (3rd ed.). Guilford Press.

INDEX

Note: Numbers in **bold** indicate tables on the corresponding page.

For Product Safety Concerns and Information please contact our EU
representative GPSR@taylorandfrancis.com
Taylor & Francis Verlag GmbH, Kaufingerstraße 24, 80331 München, Germany